THE
TECHNIQUE OF STUDY

*A textbook for use with upper secondary and
lower division college students*

BY

CLAUDE C. CRAWFORD, Ph.D.
Professor of Education, University of Southern California

HOUGHTON MIFFLIN COMPANY
BOSTON · NEW YORK · CHICAGO · DALLAS · SAN FRANCISCO
The Riverside Press Cambridge

The Riverside Press

CAMBRIDGE · MASSACHUSETTS

PRINTED IN THE U.S.A.

PREFACE

THE writer's idea of a methods book is that it should be made up largely of material which actually answers the question *how*. Material of the *why* type should be treated as next in importance, though it should be definitely related to the former type of material. It is for the above reason that every paragraph heading in this book is stated in the form of a rule or a suggested action. The volume contains a considerable amount of material which tells *why* rather than *how*, but such material has been organized in the form of support for the *how* material rather than as a section by itself.

The present volume is a result of a long period of research and practical work in the classroom which may be summarized briefly as follows: (1) The writer became interested in the how-to-study problem in 1919, and in 1920 offered his first course in it. (2) In 1921 he began the systematic collection of material for such a course, working under the direction of Dr. W. W. Charters. (3) Experimental and statistical work was done in the same field for the Ph.D. thesis at the University of Chicago. (4) Courses in study and teaching how to study were taught by the writer in the Carnegie Institute of Technology, the University of Idaho, and the University of Southern California. (5) The material was first organized in book form in the summer of

1925, and was used as a basis for lectures at the
University of Idaho in the year 1925–26.   This material was published by the author, in the summer
of 1926, under the title *Methods of Study*, and was
used as a textbook in a number of colleges during the
following year.   (6) Additional material was assembled during the year 1926–27, and this has been
embodied in the present volume, the earlier work
having been completely rewritten and materially
improved.

The technique of assembling the material was
that of "collecting unrecorded specifics," which has
been sponsored by Dr. Charters.   The principal
steps have been as follows: (1) A complete list of
difficulties confronting students was first made.
(2) Methods of overcoming these difficulties were
collected by interviewing college professors, and by
having students submit their methods in writing.
About threescore professors were interviewed, and
several hundred students made detailed reports as to
their methods of work.   (3) These specific ways of
overcoming specific difficulties were classified into
major divisions, in outline form, so that all the ways
of overcoming each difficulty could be examined and
compared at once.   (4) The various methods were
evaluated in the light of scientific research, wherever
this was possible, and in other cases simply by the
application of the author's own judgment and the
judgments of persons who submitted the methods.
While the book does not pretend to absolute scientific accuracy or finality, being rather a tentative

list of methods which are yet to be tested and evaluated by the application of rigid scientific procedures, the author nevertheless feels that the resulting organization is of such a nature as will prove very useful and very helpful as a textbook for use with upper secondary and lower division college students.

The writer is indebted to Dr. W. W. Charters for the procedure employed in collecting the material, to Dr. C. H. Judd for his guidance in the statistical and experimental studies, and to Dr. J. F. Messenger for the opportunity to try the material with classes at the University of Idaho. The list of those who contributed time in interviews or who coöperated in other important ways to promote the project would be too long to present here. The writer is indebted also to those who have used the previous book as a text in their classes and thus made possible this new and rewritten volume.

Without the sympathy, encouragement, and self-sacrifice of a perfect wife, Ina Zachary Crawford, the work would never have been begun or finished.

C. C. CRAWFORD

CONTENTS

THE
TECHNIQUE OF STUDY

CHAPTER I
SELECTING COURSES

THE content or subject-matter which you study is vitally important in determining the value of your education. If you select courses and subjects wisely, the result will be training and experience which will prove of great worth, but if you misapply your effort by studying what does not meet your needs, your labor will be all for nothing. Selecting courses for study is a much more serious problem than the average student seems to realize, if we may judge by the apparent lightness of heart with which he makes his decision. It may be that the lack of thought that he gives to the subject is due, with the ordinary student, to his lack of knowledge as to how to attack the problem. If so, possibly the following points may be of help:

1. **Plan your educational career as a whole instead of developing it piecemeal.** The education of the average student is very much like Topsy, in *Uncle Tom's Cabin*, in that it just "grows up." Students take certain courses by chance in the high school, then in college they take more courses in the subjects they liked, and thus they explore their

way through the curriculum one step at a time, with little thought of the major objectives of their education as a whole. It is not to be expected that an education that is pieced together in this fashion will be complete, proportionate, or in harmony with the needs of the individual. How much better it would be for him to decide on his life objective and then build an educational career purposely to achieve it!

2. Select each course for a few specific objectives. A carpenter does not nail planks on the house merely because they are good planks, but rather because each serves a definite and specific purpose in building that particular house. Neither should the student take any course, however good it may be, except for a definite purpose. There is much loose thinking prevalent with regard to the curriculum. Many people still boldly declare that it makes little difference what is studied provided it is difficult and unpleasant enough to give the student genuine exercise in surmounting obstacles. Also a large number of well-informed persons still think that the study of any subject brings about a sort of general mental development which makes it easier to cope with any situation, even though that situation be radically different in nature from the subject studied. Yet both of these fallacies have been thoroughly exposed by psychological investigations, which have shown that direct teaching is more economical than indirect or transferred training. If you propose to study analytical geometry, or qualitative chemistry, or Elizabethan literature, the first thing to ask is, "What in particular do I expect to accomplish by studying this subject?"

3. Thoroughly analyze the list of courses offered. The college catalogue has been referred to as the "Freshman's Bible." At least it deserves to be read diligently by every student, whether freshman or upper-classman. Attempting to plan a course or an educational career without intensive and systematic examination of the offerings available is as unwise as trying to order a meal at a restaurant without consulting the menu. The latter performance is not impossible, of course, since you can ask for roast beef or sirloin steak on the strength of your previous experience at restaurants. In like manner you can order your courses from memory, but it limits you to the few fields with which you have chanced to come in contact. A better thing to do is to study all available courses listed in the schedule, and then to talk to experienced persons and so learn still more about the nature and advantages of each course.

4. Discount prejudiced advice. One of the most difficult things for a student to obtain is genuinely disinterested and unprejudiced advice as to what to study. If he goes to a professor of mathematics, he is told to take mathematics, or if he consults a foreign-language teacher, he is directed into that line of study, and so on indefinitely. If he goes to a friend who is not teaching any subject at all, he is likely to be advised to take what the friend took or to dodge the subjects which he disliked. There is really a serious need for some system for advising students in regard to their choice of courses, but so far it has been most difficult to put such plans into operation because of the difficulty of securing unprejudiced advisers. A good thing to do when one is counseled to take a given course or subject is to find out the specialty of the person who is advising and to discount the advice accordingly. In the business world we have come to expect that a salesman will prefer to sell his own goods rather than those of his competitors, and it seems that in the field of education we shall be obliged to recognize the same principle.

5. Respect your own individuality. There is as much room for individuality in your choice of courses and subjects as there is in your choice of clothing. What is good for other people may not be good for you. The mere fact that a friend whom you greatly admire knows a certain subject need not signify that you should put that subject on your list. You must dare to be ignorant of some things because, however hard you try, it will not be possible to escape having to meet sooner or later the situation where some of your associates will know something you do not know. You cannot imitate everybody you meet or associate with, and you cannot take all the advice proffered you on the subject of what to study. After all has been said and done, you will have to take things into your own hands to a certain extent, and choose those subjects for study which will offer a chance for expressing your own individuality.

6. **Select courses according to your capacity.** Most students know whether they are bright or dull. Their previous experience in school work has resulted in success or failure, and they have had the opportunity to compare their ability with the abilities of their fellow students. In addition to these bases for the estimation of individual capacity, they can take advantage of the intelligence tests which are given in most schools, the results of which are used more or less for guidance in the choice of courses and subjects. Such information as they reveal should be utilized to the maximum. Two very serious errors may be thus avoided. The first is the error of wasting valuable years trying to attain a goal which is beyond your reach; the second is setting the goal too low and thereby failing to go as high as your ability would warrant. It should be borne in mind here that physical and social capacity are to be considered in addition to intellectual capacity. Certain physical disabilities, such as speech defects or low physical vitality, are insuperable barriers to success in some callings, while they have little or no relation to success in certain others.

7. **Select courses with regard to the total amount of time that you expect to continue in school.** Your course should be quite different, if you expect to leave school at the end of the year, from what it should be if you intend to remain for the four-year period. Some subjects are of little value except

as foundations or preparations for others that are to come later, and if you are reasonably sure the others are not to come, then the foundation would stand for nothing. The writer passes every day, a spot where some unfortunate person prepared a foundation for a large apartment house and then was unable to complete the structure. For months this example of unrealized hopes has remained unchanged, and now the land is worth less than it was before the foundation was made. This incident is no more tragic than hundreds that occur annually in the lives of students who lay foundations for mental mansions when they are to have only time enough in school to complete modest mental cottages. If you know you are not going to be able to complete the course, take what will be of the greatest value to you and let the degree or graduation requirements wait.

8. Compare the relative values of courses. The fact that a course has value is not always a sufficient reason why you should study it. It should have more value for you than any other subject which you could take in its place. Shoestrings have value, but that does not justify your purchasing a hundred pairs. There are many things in the curriculum that are worth while, but not relatively worth while. Since there is so much more material available to be learned than you can possibly hope to learn in a lifetime of study, each particular item must be judged in comparison with every other item, and the decision based on relative values.

9. Select courses for their probable rather than their possible value. Students are sometimes required or urged to take certain courses, and are shown how it might happen that they would be of value, when the odds against such an outcome are so great as to make it extremely unlikely that those benefits would be gained. For example, all high-school students in some schools are urged to study geometry on the ground that if they take engineering courses in college they will need it. A little calculation will readily show that such an argument is entirely unsound, since only about one half of the high-school students graduate, and only about one half of those go to college, while considerably less than one half of those who do go to college take up engineering. Again, students sometimes study Spanish because of its serviceableness in South American commercial connections, without giving any thought to whether more than a small percentage of students will ever have any such use for the language. It is extremely important, therefore, that you draw a careful distinction between probable and possible values, and also that you get some rather definite information about the degree of probability.

10. Select courses which emphasize the present rather than the past or the future. For ages education has been looking backward and glorifying the achievements of men who are gone. Students have been more intimately acquainted with Julius Cæsar than with the President of the United States, and have been able to tell more about the government of ancient Athens than about that of their own country to-day.   Nor is this statement intended as a criticism of history in the curriculum, for that has its own vital purpose; but even history should emphasize the present and relate past events to it.   Emphasis on the past in education, however, is little worse than emphasis on the future.   Education which looks only to the future is almost certain to be futile; it is simply cold-storage education.   What you study to-day, with the idea of retaining it until you are out of school and engaged in your civic or occupational pursuits, is simply cold-storage information, and it is likely to degenerate or disintegrate considerably before the time comes for you to use it.   We all know that a pond of water not in circulation soon becomes stagnant; the same is true of knowledge idle in storage.   The surest way to make your education really vital and worth while is to take those courses and subjects which you can put to use now in solving the pressing problems of the present.   If you once make your adjustments with the present wisely and well, you can grow as time passes, and, when the mythical and all-important future arrives, it will simply be an outgrowth and modification of the present.   To be more specific, you should choose a fairly large number of courses which deal with current problems, whether social, scientific, or industrial.

11. **Study some one thing thoroughly.**   It has been said that the well-educated man should know

something about everything and everything about something. Our intention here is to stress the importance of the second part of this statement. In selecting courses it is well to apply the principle of depth by going into some one thing with sufficient thoroughness to master it. This is an age of experts, when each man is an expert in his own line and exchanges his high-grade services in that one line for the high-grade services of others in other lines. Consequently, each person must know enough in his own line to have something which others need and are willing to pay for. The great danger in this doctrine, however, is that of carrying it to extremes. If you become an expert in only one thing and do not learn something about everything else, you do not know how to choose or to follow the advice of the experts in the other lines. As a solution of the issue between intensive and extensive study the writer would suggest a policy of separating the educational program into two parts. One of these parts would follow the "something-about-everything" policy, and the time for the other part of the program would be devoted to the "everything-about-something" plan.

12. **Sample many fields of knowledge.** In a sense it pays to be a dabbler, or to dip lightly into each of many fields instead of going to the bottom of one and ignoring the rest. The value of succeeding courses in a given subject or field is subject to the law of diminishing returns. You obtain greater educational returns from your first semester of

geology, physics, or psychology than from your second, because in the first term it is so extremely new and so different from what you have ever had before.   Just as the third banana you eat has less value than the first as a means of satisfying your hunger, so the third course in history, or mathematics, or English gives less than the first in the way of educational returns.   A good rule to follow in your choice of courses, outside of the field of your specialty, is to come into contact with as many different fields of knowledge as you can, contenting yourself with about one semester in each.   For example, in science take a semester each in physics, chemistry, botany, zoölogy, geology, and astronomy in preference to three years' work in any one of those branches.   The same principle should apply within the field of your specialty.   Thus, if you are studying medicine, sample all branches of the medical field in preference to "digging in" in one to the total exclusion of the others.   One of the common dangers in vocational training by the apprenticeship method is that it does not allow sufficient dabbling.   The employer tends to put the apprentice to operating one machine, and to keep him at it for his entire seven years, without giving him a chance to shift about in the plant and learn the manufacturing process as a whole.

13. Select courses that provide variety in the day's work.   A rotation of subjects and courses allows you to use your capacities more nearly up to their maximum than does a steady grind along

one single line. Even if you tried to spend all your time on mathematics, you could not, because of the sheer fatigue it would involve for those particular nerve centers that are most used in mathematical studies. Human nature needs what some one has called a "counter-irritant" to prevent lopsidedness and eccentricity. As a general rule, except possibly in more advanced study, it is well to have many irons in the fire at once, or to carry subjects in several different fields all the time instead of taking all work in one field for one semester and then all in another for the next semester. Not only does variety in your program add interest and reduce fatigue, but it facilitates forming associations and cross-connections between the different subjects. You are more likely to associate your chemistry and your cooking if you study them simultaneously than if you study them one after the other.

14. Get general survey courses before taking highly specialized ones. In recent years increased recognition has been given by educators to general survey courses as a preliminary to more specialized courses in particular fields. For example, in the high school the course in general science has quite commonly been accepted as the best work in science for the first year; this may be followed by any one of several special sciences, such as chemistry, physics, or botany. Colleges are adopting a similar practice in many cases by giving general "survey" or "orien-tation" courses in the freshman year to provide a perspective of the various fields of study, in order that the choice of later courses may be based on fair knowledge of what is to be expected. If you pick a specialty without knowing anything about the other specialties which you pass by, you have little assurance that the one you choose is really what you want or need. A general survey course helps to overcome this difficulty.

15. Organize your education as a whole on the spiral plan. The spiral principle involves covering the field once in a somewhat general way, then coming back over it the next year and covering it more thoroughly, then following this by another and even more thorough round the third year — and so on throughout the whole time at school. In each "spiraling" you get a more enriched experience with the field, and you have the advantage of always studying the field as a unit or a coherent whole. One of the weaknesses of much of our education is that it consists of isolated fragments which do not compose any unified whole. In recent years the work in mathematics has been reorganized on the spiral plan, so that a student may get the elements of arithmetic, algebra, geometry, trigonometry, and so forth, in a course in General Mathematics in the seventh grade and follow it by other complete rounds of these fields in the eighth, ninth, tenth, eleventh, and twelfth grades, and in college, each time coming into contact with more and more advanced and difficult problems and operations. The repetition involved in such a plan is thought to serve as an excellent review and to fix the essentials in mind. It has another advantage in that if you have to leave school before completion of the course, you do not find yourself well informed about some things and totally ignorant of others.

16. **Select some general or fundamental subjects which will help you to synthesize your training.** A good brick wall requires mortar as well as bricks, or something to give unity and solidity. So also it is necessary that the various bits of your knowledge and training be cemented together into some kind of coherent system of thought and action, or else you can hardly consider yourself as having obtained a real education. The chemist can analyze the human body into its various chemical elements and be able to tell how much of each it contains, but he cannot put these separate elements together by mechanical means and produce a living human being. Neither can mere mechanical accumulation of facts and skills produce an educated man. It is necessary at some time in the process to deal with life as a whole, or knowledge as a whole, or the universe as a whole, and to see it all in its most general and universal aspects if such a result is to be achieved. For this purpose such subjects as philosophy are more likely to bring results than the more minutely specialized courses in the vocations.

17. **Choose the subjects of which you know the least.** When all other factors are equal, you should take a course of which you already know little or nothing in preference to one on which you are reasonably well informed, because it offers you

greater opportunities for growth. When Charles Lamb on one occasion expressed his dislike for a certain man and was reminded that he did not even know the man, he replied that that was the reason he did not like him. If you dislike to venture into a subject or a field which is entirely new, a little knowledge in regard to it might do much to remove your prejudices.

18. **Select courses according to the school's equipment and facilities.** When other considerations and factors are equal, the ability of the school to provide good educational opportunities in the various branches should strongly influence your choice of courses. If the school or college has a well-equipped laboratory for chemistry but not for physics, or has a first-rate engineering school and only a fourth-rate medical school, you should weigh well the lines that offer the best facilities. While it is true that such factors as these should not be the only deciding influences, still you had better be a success as an engineer than a failure as a physician, and the facilities of the school will have much to do with the way you evolve.

19. **Choose the courses that are taught by the best teachers.** Other things being equal, choose the courses given by the outstanding members of the faculty, the men who seem to have unusual vision and mental power. The information which you obtain from a course is not the only good you get from it; the inspiration is equally important. Musicians usually tell *under whom* they studied

rather than *what* they learned; and it is the high importance of this personal element that sometimes makes graduate students cross the continent to study under a certain man. There are, of course, other things that must be considered besides the man, but certainly he is not to be neglected when you make your choice.

20. **Select courses that are well calculated to promote health.** Health is listed in practically all the recent statements of the aims and objectives of education. We are all inclined to do lip service to it, even though as a general rule our hearts are far from it. The older ideals of mortification of the flesh have given way to the new doctrine of the glorification and exaltation of physical fitness as one of the primary ends of education. There are three major ways in which you can provide for health training by means of your choice of courses. The first is by including a certain amount of work of the physical-education type, which seeks primarily to establish habits of taking regular exercise and recreation. A second is by taking courses which provide scientific knowledge upon which sound health is based, such as biology, chemistry, nutrition, and psychology. A third is by taking courses which will strengthen your desire to be physically strong and healthy, such as literature and the social sciences.

21. **Select courses that will contribute to home membership.** The educated person must be prepared for the duties and responsibilities of parent-

hood. He must know something about the family as an institution, about the nature and responsibilities of married life, about the biology and psychology of sex, about the care and training of children, about the art of living harmoniously and happily in intimate daily association with others day after day, and about innumerable similar things if he is to be able to perform happily and efficiently his duties as a member of the family. Certainly some definite and purposeful preparation for these things is as necessary and as justifiable in a course of study as training in the technique of cattle-breeding or of accounting. The writer's personal opinion is that in order to perform these duties effectively each person should have at least an elementary course in each of the subjects, biology, psychology, and sociology. Additional training in the study of heredity, eugenics, embryology, economics, education, hygiene, and other such branches, would also contribute toward attaining this objective.

22. Include some kinds of vocational studies. To be a good citizen, you must be a productive worker in addition to having a cultivated mind. In other words, you must be good for something. You cannot be a good citizen without a job, and the quality of your citizenship depends in part upon your vocational efficiency. There are those who consider labor degrading, and who tend to look down upon vocational education as not being real education. They prefer to stress the "cultural" or "liberal" aspects of learning, and to keep away from the "mean and sordid things of practical life." It is our intention here not to belittle culture or refinement, but rather to warn against completely neglecting the practical. You do not spend all of your waking hours in earning a living, but you spend more of them on that than on any other single activity and so need at least a little training for meeting the responsibility. If those who are interested in culture and refinement and the promotion of the fine arts and leisure occupations would devote more effort to vocational training, the resultant increase in efficiency of production would soon provide a considerable margin of time and money above the necessities of life which could be turned to a genuine enjoyment of these finer things. The fine arts thrive best where there is leisure, and leisure is possible only where there is a considerable margin of production above the absolute necessities of life.

23. Select courses which will contribute to citizenship. In addition to individual and family responsibilities, each person has definite duties which he owes to society as a whole The educated man not only must have a feeling of good will toward his fellow men, but must be able to translate that feeling of good will into intelligent and constructive service. Mere sentimental patriotism does not make a good citizen; patriotism must have intelligent guidance. In order to be prepared for your civic responsibilities, you should take courses which help you to understand the problems which society is facing, such as crime, poverty, war, dishonesty in high places, disease, the destruction of natural resources, industrial disorders, etc. Without an understanding of the real issues involved in these problems, you are not prepared to vote or hold office or to serve on a committee to formulate group action, or in any other way to exercise constructive leadership in public affiairs. The social sciences are, of course, the most directly related to the achievement of these ends of all the courses in the curriculum.

24. Select courses that will promote character. High standards of conduct in your own personal life and in your relations with your fellow men constitute one of the greatest essentials of your education. A man cannot simply by an act of will acquire a highly ethical character, but he can put himself into an environment which is favorable to its development. There are two types of courses which contribute to this objective. The first, such as literature, is the kind that inspires you to want to do the right thing; and the second is the kind which increases your ability to know what is the right thing and to make correct ethical judgments. In this latter class are such subjects as ethics, psychology, and the social sciences in general.

25. Select courses which will contribute to the enjoyment of leisure time. The fact that our waking hours are not all spent in gainful activities naturally suggests that education should prepare us for harmless and wholesome enjoyment of our leisure hours. One of the common objections to shorter hours for labor is that it means an increase in the amount of leisure which workmen are not sufficiently trained to make use of. It has been found, in some instances at least, that longer hours for leisure meant for the laborer more time to spend in drunkenness and vice, and that if he was to be kept out of these degrading activities he must be kept on the job until he grew too tired for anything except sleep. For this gloomy picture education can provide a remedy by developing new avenues for the enjoyment of leisure. Probably literature and the fine arts are the subjects which have most to contribute toward this goal.

26. Select courses which teach the fundamental processes, or study arts. Schools cannot complete your education. At best they can only teach you a few things and then show you how to learn others as you need them. Since this is the case, you should be fully as alert for new methods of study as for new facts. Facts may be compared with useful goods, and methods of study with the tools or machinery by which the goods are made. If you only get facts, your education remains stationary and as the world moves on you are left behind, but if you acquire the technique for mastering new facts, you have the necessary prerequisites for growth and adaptation to a progressive civilization. Some of the simpler study arts are reading, writing, and arithmetic. A somewhat more advanced type may be illustrated by the use of the library, outlining, organizing material for a paper, etc. At a still more advanced stage in the schools you have an opportunity to take special courses which are devoted almost wholly to highly technical study arts. Among these may be mentioned such courses as methods of historical research, statistical methods, experimental methods, theory of social research, methods of testing the strength of material,. etc. Such courses serve a very real need in the curriculum, and should be given a place in your program of studies. It is fully as important to know how to study as it is to remember what you have already studied.

QUESTIONS AND EXERCISES

1. With which of the points in the chapter do you agree and which ones strike you as being of doubtful wisdom?
2. Which of the points do you feel that you have actually applied in the selection of your present list of studies?
3. Analyze your present courses in the light of this chapter and decide which courses you are really justified in taking and what errors you have made in your selection.
4. Draw up a plan for your entire educational career from the present time forward.

MATCHING TEST

Directions: Write beside each number the number of the paragraph in the chapter which discusses it.

.... 1. Philosophy.
.... 2. Intelligence.
.... 3. Specialization.
.... 4. Personality of teacher.
.... 5. The fine arts.
.... 6. Studying the "menu."
.... 7. Ignorance.
.... 8. General mathematics courses.

.... 9. Physical fitness.
.... 10. Disinterested guidance.
.... 11. Patchwork selection of courses.
.... 12. Patriotism.
.... 13. Learning the technique of learning.
.... 14. The family.
.... 15. Likelihood of use.
.... 16. Dropping out of school.
.... 17. Diversification.
.... 18. Morality.
.... 19. Cross-connections.
.... 20. Bread and butter education.
.... 21. Orientation courses.
.... 22. Cold storage education.
.... 23. Comparison of worth of courses.
.... 24. Laboratories.
.... 25. Definite purposes.
.... 26. Personal peculiarities.

TRUE–FALSE TEST

Directions: Indicate which statement is true and which is false, using plus (+) for true and zero (o) for false.

.... 1. In choosing courses one should be a dabbler.
.... 2. Philosophy synthesizes knowledge more than the practical arts.
.... 3. School should complete your education.
.... 4. Morality is mainly a matter of good intentions.
.... 5. Vocational studies should be chosen only as a last resort.
.... 6. Training for home membership should be primarily a girl's subject.
.... 7. The teacher is a very small factor that should affect choice of courses.
...... 8. General science should precede physics or chemistry.
.... 9. Civic education should consist of training that will be needed when one is grown.
.... 10. A course that is really good is good for all students alike.
.... 11. Every student should choose courses as if he expected to graduate.
.... 12. The need of mathematics in engineering justifies it as a high school requirement for boys.

.... 13. The best guide for choosing courses is your experience in previous courses.

.... 14. Sequence of courses should be such as to prevent one's covering the same ground twice.

.... 15. The more courses you take in a subject the more you get from each.

.... 16. An education should include a thorough knowledge of some one thing.

.... 17. It is unwise to insist on a special purpose for each course.

.... 18. The advice which teachers give about what to study is usually unbiased.

.... 19. If people had leisure they would have no trouble in enjoying it.

.... 20. Literature study is practically neutral as to its contribution to health.

.... 21. It is better to have courses in several fields than several courses in one field at once.

.... 22. Patriotism is the chief element in citizenship.

.... 23. Choice of courses should be independent of such little things as the school's supply of equipment.

.... 24. If a course has value you are justified in studying it.

.... 25. Bright students should take the same courses as dull students.

.... 26. It is best to choose courses as you go instead of planning all at once.

SHORT-ANSWER TEST

Directions: Answer each question or complete each statement by inserting a word, phrase, or brief answer.

1. In getting advice about courses the great difficulty is to be sure it is ....

2. What is the relation of vocational training to leisure and the arts? ....

3. In addition to right attitudes and habits, character training must train for ....

4. Which objective of education is best illustrated by learning how to find what you want in the library? ....

5. Training for home membership should be classed with the .... rather than with the vocational studies.

6. What kind of courses should one take who expects to quit school at the end of the year? ....

7. Repetition involved in the spiral plan provides for desirable
....
8. To reduce fatigue you should choose courses that provide
....
9. In order to get balance and proportion in courses when should you select them? ....
10. You should specialize in one thing enough that you are ....
11. Specialized courses should be preceded by ....
12. Selection of courses should be made on the basis of relative
....
13. The best way to find out what courses to take is to ....
14. What you study is sometimes of less importance than ....
15. The desirability of courses is influenced by the available.......
16. For ages the viewpoint of education has been toward ....
17. A good education enables you to see life as a ....
18. A doctrine opposed to education for specific purposes is that of ....
19. The policy of scattering one's courses over several fields is justified by the law of ....
20. Choice of courses should be based on .... rather than .... of use.
21. The most valuable course you get in a given field is usually the
....
22. The major objective of the fine arts is ....
23. For a bright student to take an easy course wastes ....
24. A uniform course for all students fails to provide enough ......
25. What is the main feature of good citizenship? ....
26. The first essential of a good education is that it must produce
....

READINGS

1. Bobbitt, Franklin: *Curriculum Investigations*. University of Chicago Press, 1926.

Reports several scientific studies showing what knowledge is most valuable to have.

2. Bobbitt, Franklin: *The Curriculum*. Houghton Mifflin Co., Boston, 1918.

The book is an excellent treatment of what the curriculum should include.

3. Briggs, Thomas H.: *Curriculum Problems*. The Macmillan Co., New York, 1926.

Presents the underlying principles and problems involved in selecting subject-matter for schools.

4. Charters, W. W.: *Curriculum Construction.* The Macmillan Co., New York, 1923.

    Presents the scientific basis for selection of the material to be studied and reports research work that has been done on the various subjects.

5. Columbia Associates in Philosophy: *An Introduction to Reflective Thinking.* Houghton Mifflin Co., Boston, 1923.

    Chapter X deals with methods of choosing a career.

6. Doermann, Henry J.: *The Orientation of College Freshmen.* The Williams and Wilkins Co., Baltimore, 1926.

    Several chapters are devoted to methods of guidance and advising students.

7. Douglass, A. A.: *Secondary Education.* Houghton Mifflin Co., Boston, 1927.

    Chapters X–XI, "Educational and Vocational Guidance." Chapters XII–XXII, "The Curriculum."

8. Foster, W. T.: *Should Students Study?* Harper.

    Chapter VIII, "Should Specialists Specialize?" Chapter IX, "Ultimately Practical Studies."

9. Inglis, Alexander: *Principles of Secondary Education.* Houghton Mifflin Co., Boston, 1918.

    Contains chapters on the place and value of each of the subjects in the curriculum.

10. McMurry, F. M.: *How to Study and Teaching How to Study.* Houghton Mifflin Co., Boston, 1909.

    Chapter II, "Provision for Specific Purposes."

11. Parker, Samuel Chester: *Methods of Teaching in High Schools.* Ginn & Co., Boston, 1915.

    Chapter IV, "Selection and Arrangement of Subject-Matter."

12. Sandwick, Richard L.: *How to Study and What to Study.* D. C. Heath & Co., Boston, 1915.

    Part II, "What to Study," gives an analysis of the reasons for studying the different subjects.

13. Touton, F. C., and Struthers, Alice B.: *Junior-High School Procedures.* Ginn & Co., Boston, 1926.

    Chapter II, "Guidance Program." Chapters IX–XVI deal with the aims and values of the various subjects.

14. Waples, Douglas: *Procedures in High School Teaching.* The Macmillan Co., New York, 1924.

    Chapter XI, "Subject-Matter and the Course of Study."

CHAPTER II

TAKING NOTES

WHETHER note-taking is good or evil is still being debated in certain quarters, but it goes on just the same. The human impulse to write things down instead of trusting them to memory is so universal that every year millions of dollars are spent merely for note-taking equipment. The practice is by no means limited to school students, since the business world has developed it far beyond the crude and rudimentary forms usually followed by students. In view of the enormous amount of time and effort that is spent in the taking and using of notes, it is hoped that the following suggestions on how to do it more effectively may render a service.

1. **Start a definite system of notes early in your career as a student.** The need for planning your note-taking system instead of just letting it develop by trial-and-error methods is well shown by the reactions of mature students who have followed the latter course. A class composed of about two hundred seniors in the Carnegie Institute of Technology, in 1920 appointed a committee to investigate the question of note-taking systems and to make recommendations. The unpublished report of this committee contained several interesting statements, which are here quoted:

Every man in the class favored the idea of teaching

freshmen how to take notes. . . . Seventy-five per cent of the senior class have changed their system of taking notes since they entered Tech.   Many of them have changed several times.   It is well also to note that all of them have come down to practically the same system.   It seems to us that if after four years of trial all these men arrive at the same conclusion as to the best way of keeping notes, then this system should be carefully worked over and presented to the incoming freshmen.

The writer is inclined to agree with the report of this committee.

2. Use a loose-leaf notebook.   All notes for all courses and all years should be organized into one uniform system.   For doing this a loose-leaf form is absolutely essential; otherwise later material on a given topic cannot be placed with that which came in earlier.   A loose-leaf system saves paper, since you can use every sheet instead of wasting the unused sheets.   It permits notes on all courses to be carried in one binder.   It allows revision of one page without spoiling the whole book, and also without unnecessary copying.   It facilitates reclassification of notes by subjects, so that all material on a given subject can be brought together by physical manipulation of sheets.   In fact, it is the only method which will serve for assembling a large amount of material.

3. Use a large-size notebook.   A pocket-size notebook has several alluring features, but, sooner or later, it leads to trouble and it is almost always abandoned.   The plan is condemned by the test of experience.   It forces you to take brief and sketchy notes to avoid filling up the notebook during the first week. It forces you to put material on several sheets which would have more meaning if it could all be presented to the eye at once. The short lines and lack of room in which to work hinder rapid note-taking. On the other hand, the large notebook serves somewhat the same purpose as a writing-desk. It is a convenient place in which to file themes or other papers before they are due, and a good place in which to keep them after they are returned. It also lends itself more readily to type-writing. Finally, the large size is that upon which the business world has agreed as a standard, and it is the size which you will ultimately be obliged to adopt if you ever have a filing system for your papers. The writer's recommendation is for a letter size, or 8½ × 11 inches. A very good plan is to supply yourself for the entire year with plain type-writer paper, which costs about $1 for 500 sheets, punched beforehand for your notebook.

4. **Plan a filing system along with your note-taking system.** It is not enough to take good notes. It is necessary to plan for the later use of them. If notes are worth taking, they will be worth using later, and so should be readily accessible and easy to identify, but a collection of notes taken without thought for the future can hardly be so arranged or classified as to be of later service. When your collection is small, it may be easy to find what you want by hunting through your notebook, but after the mass has grown for a few years a system of classi-

fication, indexing, and orderly arrangement will be essential. The difficulty of putting order into a mass of miscellaneous notes suggests the importance of keeping them organized as they are collected. The writer's suggestion for a filing system involves the use of manila folders, each labeled according to the subject, and all filed in a box or drawer. Each sheet of notes must be clearly identified.

5. Adopt a fairly small unit. A fundamental question in starting a note-taking system is how much to put on a page, and when to stop and to start a new page. Some people use small cards, one point on a card. Others use larger cards and put several points on a card. Another plan, and one which is usually better for the average student, is to use large paper and to put on one sheet the notes on an entire chapter or lecture, always taking care to start each new chapter or lecture on a new sheet, whether the first sheet is full or not. While this plan involves a slight waste of paper, it is the only satisfactory one. Starting one chapter where the last leaves off involves keeping the sheets together just as if they were fastened together, and so the prime idea of the loose-leaf system is sacrificed. The best plan, then, seems to be always to start a new chapter or lecture on a clean sheet, and never, under any circumstances, to put on the same sheet the notes on two chapters.

6. Give each sheet of notes a clear heading to show its source and its subject. The idea underlying the plan of loose-leaf notes is that since the various sheets will later be separated one from another it is necessary to have each sheet so that it can be identified. A common error is to label a sheet "Chapter II," but to omit reference to the author or book because that information was contained in Chapter I. This would not be serious if you could be sure that the notes would always be kept together, but you can seldom feel sure that they will be. Notes on a book should carry, at the top of each sheet, the name of the author, the title of the book, the chapter title and number, and the number of the page. Notes on an article should give on each sheet, the author, title, journal, volume, page, and year. Notes on lectures should carry identification as to instructor, course name, lecture subject, and date. The author's or lecturer's name should normally be on the first line.

7. Assign to each note a number or letter to represent its status in the outline. Some sort of notation symbols is necessary if your notes are to have their greatest value. A common one is the following:

I.
   A.
      1.
         a.
            (1)
               (a)

There is no special virtue in the particular symbols used, except that some symbols are better adapted to typewriter keyboards, but it is essential that the same scheme be followed throughout a given outline.

8. Indent subdivisions. The chief virtue of indenting subdivisions is that the plan enables you to get a visual impression of the outline. Two common errors in indentation are made in notes. One is a failure to indent sufficiently to give this clear visual impression, and the other is indenting so far that most of the notes are written on very short lines at the right of the page, the greater part of the page being thus left blank.

9. Indent overrun lines slightly more than the beginnings of the first lines. The value of indenting the notation symbols for the various points is often lost through the common practice of starting overrun lines at the extreme left side of the page, thus, in a sense, covering up the outline, or at least giving it less prominence. This error is illustrated by the following:

Wrong:

    (1) This is a sample of overrun lines which have not been properly indented and so tend to interfere with the ready visualization of the outline.

Right:

    (1) This is a sample of overrun lines which are indented properly and so leave the notation symbol standing out prominently.

10. Leave reasonably wide margins. Good form in notes requires a fairly large margin at the top and at the left, and lesser margins at the right and at the bottom. The left margin is especially important for its use later in inserting revisions of the outline, and the top margin is essential for the later addition of index numbers, topical headings, or supplementary identifications required by the scheme of indexing and filing that is used.

11. **Avoid writing notes in long paragraphs.** Notes should be in outline form rather than in running paragraphs. A paragraph of notes containing, say one hundred words, represents one of two note-taking errors. Either it contains several points which could have been stated separately, or else it contains in very verbose form one idea which should have been condensed to fewer words. If you find that you ordinarily need more than two lines for stating your point, it would be well to ask yourself which of these errors you are making.

12. **Ordinarily finish a unit on the back of the sheet.** The question of whether to use the back of a sheet to finish up a given chapter, or article, or lecture, or to put the remainder on a second sheet, is somewhat debatable, but the issue seems to be that of balancing the desirability of having all the material in one unit against the undesirability of having it on opposite sides of the page. As a general rule the present writer finds it preferable to finish on the back, but you should be careful not to transfer this habit to themes or other forms of work which do not involve the loose-leaf idea.

13. **Mark and underline books.** It is better to take notes in the book itself than to take no notes at all, and sometimes it is better to do so than to

record notes in a separate notebook. Marking a book gives it a touch of your own individuality or personality, and makes it more dear to you. It directs your attention to the main points as you read. It aids you later in reviewing. Sometimes marking a book increases its value for a later reader. Marking the book also has the advantage of requiring considerably less time than taking notes in a notebook. There should be limitations, however, to this practice. It usually spoils the book for other readers. Moreover, you cannot carry the notes around, of course, without taking the whole bulky book. Nor can you classify and file notes recorded in books, nor assemble materials from several books. Also your marking of a book makes you somewhat a slave to your first impressions, and hinders rereading from a different point of view. At best such a practice must be classified as a method of studying rather than as a system of note-taking. It is better than no note-taking, but it is only a halfway measure.

14. **Take notes in quotation form only for special purposes.** Copying selected passages exactly is a plan of note-taking which some scholars employ rather extensively. They do it in order to be able to give credit to the author whose material has been used, and also as a means of preserving the expressive or unusually appropriate phraseology of the original author. The plan is sometimes defended on the ground that if you misunderstand the question when you copy it you can still correct your idea

later, whereas an abstract of it in your own words would allow no chance for later correction.

There are certain disadvantages, however, in quotations as a form of notes. Ordinarily you do not expect to use the material in writing books, and so the idea of giving credit is of little importance to you. Another disadvantage is that the copying takes up considerable time. Usually, also, your copying is too inaccurate to be depended upon, unless you check and double-check for small changes you have made. Quotations apart from their context are often distinctly misleading and unfair to the person quoted. They are likely, too, to be less meaningful to you than brief statements of the main points in your own words would be. Finally, copying quotations robs you of the educative experience of boiling the ideas down to brief form. Condensing ideas into your own words is a more thoughtful process than is mere copy work.

15. State points briefly and concisely. Good notes are brief and to the point, yet at the same time clear and meaningful. Just how much brevity to strive for, however, is not always easy to determine. The disadvantages of making full and detailed notes are numerous. It requires much time. Less material can be outlined under this plan. Attempting so much writing may hinder listening to lectures. The mechanical copying involved hinders brain work. Then, also, with extensive note-taking organization is sacrificed; at review time it is hard to find the essential in the mass. Most of the evils ascribed to note-taking are, in fact, the results of writing down too elaborate or too detailed notes. The things which may justifiably be written in more detailed form are as follows: (1) the unfamiliar; (2) the difficult; (3) key facts; (4) that which will be used often; (5) that which will be used after long periods of time; (6) that which is not available elsewhere; (7) quotations or other materials which are useless unless perfectly complete and accurate. Other materials should be condensed as much as possible without sacrificing their meaning. A good plan is to write the notes so fully that another person would have no trouble in getting the meaning now, and then you can be sure that you will understand them yourself later on.

16. **Study and practice the technique of condensing thought.** Since boiling ideas down to a few words is one of the best means of actually mastering them, it is well to give considerable thought to the technique of the process. The following points may be of service in this connection: (1) Read or listen until you really understand the point before you write it down; (2) classify points into groups, and with each one eliminate unnecessary repetition of words; (3) state the point instead of merely naming it, since statements convey more thought per word than topics; (4) omit unnecessary words, even though without them the notes are not grammatical; (5) use abbreviations for ordinary long words, such as ed. for education, psy. for psychology, civ. for civilization, and so forth; (6) look for the

author's summary or topic sentence, which is often much condensed; (7) put in key words or reminders as illustrations that will help you to remember the points. One writer says, "Condensing is not a matter of rule or formula, but rather a condition of mind, and is primarily an evaluation of ideas."

Greenough[1] says, in discussing note-taking:

Listen or read attentively to distinguish between essentials and non-essentials. Essentials are the facts or theories of the matter in hand. Non-essentials are introductory or transitional or illustrative passages, with all that goes to make for interest. It is plain that the first of these should be noted down, and that the second should generally be rejected. Illustrations, which the beginner is inclined to write out in full, can usually be recalled by a mere reference.

For essentials and non-essentials, then, the practice is simple. But between these two lies a class of matter which will be more or less valuable to the note-taker according to his familiarity with the subject, or to his ability to comprehend it at once. This class is explanatory matter, which students will use in different proportions. Good note-taking requires, nevertheless, that as much of this be preserved as will show the sequence and make all essentials clear.

17. Get the points down in their true outline or logical relationship. Organized notes are preferable to mere lists or jottings, and getting the outline is a highly thoughtful mental process. The following suggestions should be in order concerning methods of discovering the outline:

[1] Greenough, N. C.: *Manual of Instructions and Exercises for English A*, section 27, page 45. Published for Harvard students in 1916.

(1) Adapt the outlining procedure to the nature of the book being outlined. Each book has an individuality of its own, and will justify a little preliminary planning of the campaign.

(2) Get the larger outline of the book as a whole before outlining individual chapters.

(3) Sometimes it is better to study out the whole outline before doing any actual writing at all.

(4) In other cases it is better to write down the points in unorganized form in order to get them before yourself, and then organize them later, even in an order different from that of the author.

(5) Sometimes you can make the outline as you read the chapter, and at other times you will have to read the chapter once and then come back to study for the outline.

(6) Hunt for the author's own statement of the outline. Frequently he states in one paragraph the main divisions of the topic which he proposes to cover, or which he has covered.

(7) Weigh, judge, and evaluate the importance of the different points.

(8) Guard against parenthetical or inserted material which departs from the main line of the discussion.

(9) Make full use of transition words or phrases, such as "In the second place," "on the other hand," etc. These are comparable to signposts on the highway to prepare you for a change in the direction of the road.

(10) Make use of such mechanical aids to out-

lining as bold-faced type, italics, etc., which have been embodied in the book.

(11) Do not trust to rules and formulas entirely, but put your best thought into the study. Genuine understanding of the material is probably the surest avenue to discovery of the outline.

18. Practice to increase your speed of note-taking. As a general rule, as determined by unpublished data in the writer's possession, outlining takes about twice as long as ordinary reading. The rate of speed can be greatly increased, however, with practice. The reading portion of the outlining process is obviously open to improvement, as is mentioned in the chapter on textbooks, but the note-taking portion can be speeded up also. The handwriting element can be increased, as all college students can testify, since it is distinctly under voluntary control. The use of a fountain pen instead of a plain pen adds considerably to speed, as does also the use of a large size of paper with a long writing line.

19. Take notes in the best form possible, and revise them later if necessary. Whether to plan to rewrite notes or not, as a regular practice, is a much debated question among students. The factors in favor of rewriting them are as follows: Rewriting improves neatness, improves the outline, and insures reviewing the notes. Reorganizing your notes is a splendid method of studying them. The rewriting can be done on the typewriter and carbon copies can be made. Additions to the original notes can be made.

The disadvantages of the plan are also worthy of note: The fact that you are going to rewrite may discourage your doing your best at the time of the lecture. Moreover, rewriting is often unnecessary, and in that case is mere copy work. Then, the will is weak, and you are likely to neglect to do the work until it is too late. Another consideration is that the same amount of time devoted to learning might be more profitable; still another, that writing puts stress on neatness and fancy work instead of on thought. The writer's suggestion would be to take the notes the first time in the best possible form, and then, later on, to spend such additional time as seems justifiable in improving them, but in no case to do less than your best with the intention of rewriting later. Your best, both at the time and later, is usually none too good.

20. Do not employ shorthand. High-school students are sometimes advised to learn shorthand as a preparation for college note-taking. This recommendation is usually made, however, by persons who do not themselves use shorthand. Those who do use it advise against it for note-taking, for a number of reasons. To begin with, learning shorthand is expensive; also, in using it you are tempted to write down a great deal without selecting important points. Again, the use of it wastes your time later because unless the notes are transcribed you cannot read them. Other objections to it are the difficulty of finding the main points in the mass of material when you review; the fact of its use is likely to mean that outlining will be discarded and organization sacrificed; and that the "taking of a lecture" may become mere word-getting rather than thoughtful listening. The practical verdict is clearly against shorthand; few students who know it actually practice it in taking notes on lectures.

21. Typewrite your notes only in special cases. The main reasons why typewriting your notes would seem to be plausible are that it affords practice in typewriting, that it gives you a good review of your notes, that it makes possible carbon copies, and that the typewritten form of notes has greater serviceability than the handwritten form. Against these considerations we find certain strong counter arguments. The effort required to learn typewriting is great — often more than the knowledge is worth. The typing is a mechanical rather than a thoughtful process, and therefore of little value as a review. It is time-consuming without being highly educative. Unless you are a good typist the form and quality of the typewritten product are hardly superior to those produced by penmanship. Few notes will be used sufficiently to justify the effort required to type them. Also the sound of the typewriter may be a serious annoyance to others. The writer's recommendation would be to think at least twice before adopting a regular plan of typing all notes. Certain notes may well be typed when there is an unusually good reason for doing so, but certainly not all notes need be.

22. Learn the special technique of taking notes on books. The problems involved in taking notes on books are different, in some ways, from those you will meet in taking notes on lectures. The book will wait an indefinite length of time, and therein lies a real danger. This unlimited time makes it possible for you to write as full and detailed notes as you wish; accordingly you are not forced to condense your notes as in the lecture. Lecture notes are generally too brief and sketchy, it is true, but reading notes are too elaborate and detailed. This fault in reading notes is sometimes so extreme as to defeat the very purpose for which the notes were taken. A good rule is not to write a point until you understand it clearly, and to be sure of its place in the outline before you record it. There is practically no need of taking rough notes and copying later. And there is much less justification for having unorganized notes on books than, as is sometimes necessary, having them on lectures.

23. Learn the special tricks of taking notes on lectures. Note-taking on lectures is peculiar in that it requires your doing two things at once. If you give too much attention to the note-taking, your listening suffers, and *vice versa*. While you are writing some things down, others are being overlooked. Relationships between different points are hard to discover, because the lecture will not wait for you as will the book. Some things which experience has shown to be of help in taking notes on lectures are as follows:

(1) Study the topic beforehand so that you can follow the thought more easily.

(2) Be ready to write when the lecture begins, instead of opening up your notebook during the opening statements and so missing them.

(3) If you miss something, leave a blank space and go ahead, instead of worrying over the loss and so missing the next topic.

(4) Take down more detail than you need at the time in order to insure against forgetting.

(5) When securing the outline is too difficult, take the points down in list form and classify them later.

(6) Take the points down in your own words.

24. Beware of becoming a notebook slave. Much has been said and written about becoming such a slave to notes that you spoil your memory. The danger may be more imaginary than real, however, especially if notes are properly used. As a matter of fact, notes *should* become a substitute for memory to a certain extent. Many things which are valuable for reference, are not worth memorizing. There is plenty of knowledge in the world to fill both your head and your notebook. Many things which you remember would never be recalled if you did not have them written down where you would notice them at the appropriate time. It is more desirable to look up some items than to give incorrect snap judgments on them. Any good thing, however, can be abused, and notes are misused, just as are all other human inventions. A few precautions which may prevent notebook slavery are as follows:

(1) Have a strong intention to remember what you write down, and it will stay with you longer.

(2) Thoroughly understand and master the ideas before you write them down.

(3) Make your note-taking thoughtful instead of mechanical.

(4) Review all notes at least once after writing them before you file them away.

(5) Exercise judgment about what you write down, and trust *some* things to memory.

25. Beware of the mental stagnation that comes from relying only on previous notes. There is danger that a good note-taker may accumulate such a large amount of material in his files that he will become satisfied to depend entirely on it instead of continuing to study and acquire fresh material. In other words, a good collection of notes may produce mental stagnation. Merely realizing this danger, however, should help you to avoid it. You should resolve to be a good student and keep learning something new all the time. Try to get notes from more than one source and thus avoid developing a "single-track" mind. If you save all your old notes and keep adding to them, you will always have a wealth of different suggestions which will help you to preserve your originality and keep your intellectual life fresh and growing.

QUESTIONS AND EXERCISES

1. Check up your note-taking practice by the rules in this chapter and see which rules you are actually following.

2. Classify the material of the chapter under the following heads: (*a*) Form of notes; (*b*) Quality of notes; (*c*) Taking notes; (*d*) Using notes.

3. Work out a note-taking system that meets your particular needs and present it for criticism and constructive suggestions.

MATCHING TEST

Directions: Write beside each number the number of the paragraph in the chapter which discusses it.

.... 1. Organization.
.... 2. Crystallized notions.
.... 3. Showing subordination.
.... 4. How to boil material down.
.... 5. Use of typewriter.
.... 6. Length of individual points.
.... 7. Rewriting notes afterwards.
.... 8. Brevity.
.... 9. Card systems.
.... 10. Copying author's exact words.
.... 11. Amount of margins.
.... 12. Reading notes.
.... 13. Spoiling your memory.
.... 14. Using one side of the paper.
.... 15. Value of shorthand.
.... 16. Size of page for notebook.
.... 17. How to take notes rapidly.
.... 18. Lecture notes.
.... 19. Taking notes in books.
.... 20. Reference to source.
.... 21. Notation symbols.
.... 22. Kind of binder for notes.
.... 23. Prominence.
.... 24. Training freshmen in note-taking.
.... 25. Systematic preservation of notes.

TRUE–FALSE TEST

Directions: Indicate which statement is true and which is false, using plus (+) for true and zero (0) for false.

.... 1. Every subdivision should be indented.
.... 2. The back of the sheet should never be used for notes.
.... 3. Notes should be taken in final form the first time as a general rule.

.... 4. Typing of notes is usually wasteful.

.... 5. The rate of note-taking can be readily increased.

. ... 6. Pocket notebooks are the most satisfactory size for most purposes.

.... 7. Long paragraphs of notes represent the ideal type.

.... 8. Any one who expects to go to college should study shorthand in high school.

.... 9. Quotations are usually undesirable as a type of notes.

.... 10. Brief notes require more brain work than full ones.

.... 11. Every point in your notes should be preceded by a number or letter to represent its status in the outline.

.... 12. There should be more margin at the top than at the bottom.

.... 13. Notes have their greatest value if recorded in the text.

.... 14. One who possesses a good supply of notes is almost certain to stop mental growth because of depending on them.

.... 15. Notes should never be a substitute for memory.

.... 16. The Carnegie Tech senior class favored teaching freshmen how to take notes.

.... 17. Outlining is largely a mechanical process.

.... 18. There is more excuse for copying lecture notes than reading notes.

.... 19. Overrun lines should begin at the regular margin.

.... 20. Reading notes should be taken in rough form and copied later.

.... 21. Notes should usually be taken with only one point on a small card.

.... 22. If notes are worth taking they are worth saving.

.... 23. Classification aids condensation of thought.

.... 24. Each sheet of notes should carry the full bibliographical reference to its source.

.... 25. A permanently bound notebook is usually preferable.

SHORT–ANSWER TEST

Directions: Answer each question or complete each statement by inserting a word, phrase, or brief answer.

1. What is the most common fault of lecture notes?..........

2. Why is an outline preferable to a list of points?...........

3. How serious is the danger of becoming a slave to notes? ....

4. What is the most common weakness of reading notes? ....

5. What was the chief recommendation of the senior class committee? ....

6. How full or detailed should notes be? ....

7. What is the best size of notebook? ....

8. How does the rate of outlining compare with that of reading? ....

9. What is the main disadvantage of copying notes on the typewriter? ....

10. What kinds of identification should be written at the top of a sheet of notes? ....

11. In outlining books how often should you start a new page for your notes? ....

12. What is the main essential of a set of notation symbols? ....

13. What should be done with notes after finishing the course? .....

14. If a chapter makes a page and a half of notes, where should the half-page be put? ....

15. What is the method for showing that one point is a subdivision of another? ....

16. Where should the widest margin be left? ....

17. To what extent do persons who know shorthand use it in note-taking? ....

18. How does taking notes in a notebook compare with marking your book? ....

19. What kind of notebook is best? ....

20. Of what value is copying notes as a method of studying them? ....

21. How many lines should the average point in your notes require? ....

22. To what extent should notes be in the exact words of the author? ....

23. How much should the second line for a given point be indented? ....

24. What does boiling ideas down to brief form contribute to learning? ....

25. To what extent do notes result in mental stagnation? ....

READINGS

1. Adams, John: *Making the Most of One's Mind.* Geo. H. Doran Co., New York, 1915.

Chapter VIII, "Listening and Note-Making."

2. Clippinger, Walter G.: *Student Relationships.* Thomas Nelson & Sons, New York, 1926.

Chapter V, "Taking Notes."

3. Dearborn, G. V. N.: *How to Learn Easily*.   Little, Brown & Co., Boston, 1918.

   Chapter II, "Observation and the Taking of Notes."

4. Dow, W. W.: *Principles of a Note-System for Historical Studies.* The Century Co., New York, 1924.

5. Headley, Leal A.: *How to Study in College*.   Henry Holt & Co., New York, 1926.

   Chapter XII, "How to Make Notes."

6. Kitson, H. D.: *How to Use your Mind*.   J. B. Lippincott Co., Philadelphia, 1916.

   Chapter II, "Note-Taking."

7. Lyman, R. L.: *The Mind at Work*.   Scott, Foresman & Co., Chicago, 1924.

   Chapter II, Section I, "Taking Notes on References."

8. Maxfield, E. K.: *Suggestions for Note-Taking*.   Delaware College, Newark, 1910.

9. Robinson, A. T.: *Note-Taking*.   D. C. Heath & Co., Boston, 1905.

10. Robinson, A. T.: *Notes and Outlines*.   D. C. Heath & Co., Boston, 1922.

11. Seward, S. S.: *Note-Taking*.   Allyn & Bacon, Chicago, 1910.

    Contains excellent material on condensing, organizing, and special problems in note-taking.

CHAPTER III

LISTENING TO LECTURES

BEFORE books and printing came into vogue practically all instruction was carried on by word of mouth. A "lecture" originally meant a "reading" from some precious manuscript, the reader proceeding slowly so that the listeners could copy the words, and making such comments as seemed necessary to clarify or emphasize what he read. The lecture method of teaching in schools and colleges to-day has changed considerably from this early form, but the essential purpose still remains — to pass on to the audience a body of ideas or information which they are to retain. Much complaint has been voiced against the lecture method on various grounds, but lecturing continues, both in school and out, and shows little evidence of stopping. It would seem that, instead of crying out against the method, a good plan would be to discover how to make a more effective use of it. It is for that reason that the following paragraphs have been written.

1. Adapt your listening procedure to the purpose of the particular lecture. Each lecture has its particular aim or purpose which is usually definitely announced or implied in the introductory statements of the speaker. Some lectures are intended to inform, others to explain; some are given to convince, others to entertain. One lecture may attempt to

present the solution of a problem and the next may attempt only to raise a problem in the mind of the hearers. Some lectures are addressed to the emotions, others to the intellect. Some try to give definite directions or guidance for definite practical situations; others try only to raise theoretical issues of a sort far removed from practical considerations. The kind of listening procedure suited to one lecture may be the direct opposite of that suited to another. It is essential, therefore, to find out what the objective is and then to adapt your procedure to it.

2. Adopt a study attitude toward most school lectures. As a general rule, lectures in high-school or college classes are on serious topics, and are for something more than mere entertainment. In such cases you must listen studiously rather than passively, just as you must attack a textbook studiously rather than passively. Assume a personal responsibility for getting out of the lecture all there is in it, instead of sitting and waiting for the lecturer to make you aware of his thoughts. It is no more fair to put the whole burden of responsibility on the speaker than to expect a book to read and interpret itself to you without effort on your part.

3. Listen to some lectures as you would to music or literature. Some lectures are for artistic rather than intellectual purposes, and require a fine-arts type of procedure on the part of the listener. Some are addressed to the emotions, and fail unless they cause the proper emotional reactions. A lecturer on the life of a great character in history may have as his chief aim to make you love and admire that character; in this case your method of listening should be to relax and take a leisure-type rather than a work-type attitude toward the lecture. In other words, there are some lectures which are to be heard in much the same way as poems and novels are to be read — for enjoyment rather than for information.

4. **Adapt your procedure to the particular style or method of the lecturer.** The individual differences between lecturers are as great as those between students, and what applies to listening to one lecturer does not necessarily apply to listening to others. One man may lecture from a carefully made outline, and another from no outline whatever. One may summarize his lecture at the beginning, another at the end, and a third make no summary at all. One may lecture rapidly, and another slowly. One may state the point and then explain it, while another may discuss it until it is clear to his hearers, and then state it briefly at the close of the discussion. In fact so many individual peculiarities of style and method of lecturing are represented by lecturers as a body that early in each course it will be well to spend some time and thought getting acquainted with each man's way. Then, having learned what to expect, you will find it easier to work out a plan of listening and note-taking that will fit the methods of the different lecturers.

5. **Keep active during the lecture.** Lecturing has been criticized as a school procedure on the ground

that it allows little opportunity for mental activity on the part of the students. It is an old and well-known truth that we learn only through our own activity, and that the teacher's activity is not a satisfactory substitute for the pupil's. It is not at all necessary, however, that a lecture involve idleness on your part, if you only realize this principle and apply it. There is opportunity for the highest type of mental activity while listening to a lecture. You can be active by taking notes, or by thinking of illustrations, applications, or adaptations of the material to new situations or conditions. If you simply treat each statement as a true-false test, deciding whether to accept it as true or not, you can secure a high degree of mental activity. Probably the surest way to attain and keep a high level of mental activity is to take careful and systematic notes as the lecture proceeds. The mental elements involved in this process are of a high type, and the outward concrete and muscular elements are so objective that they help to keep the inner reactions on a high level.

6. **Listen critically, thoughtfully, and understandingly.** If your procedure during a lecture is simply mechanical, you have failed to do your part. Even a dictaphone can record a lecture. You should test each statement as you hear it, asking whether it advances the thought, and just what its contribution really is. If you do not understand a point, either ask for explanation at the time or else mark that point for further investigation — that is, do

something that registers genuine mental activity on
your part.   Adopt a reasonably critical attitude
toward what you hear, but not necessarily a contrary attitude.   If you hear dogmatic or extreme
statements, make your estimate of the extent to
which they are true, and even go so far as to take
note of your reactions as well as of the statements
which aroused them.   Even if you do not have the
freedom or the courage to challenge the speaker
openly, you can at least challenge him in your own
mind or in your notebook.

7. Supplement the lecture from your own experience. The lecturer knows more about his topic
than he has time to tell, and simply gives a few
selected thoughts from his more extensive supply.
You naturally fail to get the full force of the few
statements he makes, and then you forget a large
part of what you do understand.   The result is
that a tremendous reduction takes place when the
speaker's ideas are communicated to you.   It becomes necessary, then, to introduce some kind of a
corrective from your side.   The corrective may be
illustrated by the radio amplifier.   A full-tone note
is reduced to inaudible ether waves when it is broad-
cast, but the receiving station picks it up and supplements it by power supplied locally, so that it
attains as great volume as it had when first made.
Your success as a listener to a lecture is in large
measure dependent upon your "amplifier"; that is,
upon your ability to enrich the speaker's words by
associations out of your own experience.   Unless

you do this, the lecture is likely to mean to you only a dictation of barren and meaningless outlines. As the lecture proceeds, you should try to think of cases illustrating or contradicting the point stated, or of the limitations of the statement, or of where you have seen or heard similar statements — anything that actually constitutes an enrichment of the lecture material by association of your own ideas with it.

8. Get ready for a lecture by studying the subject beforehand. It takes a certain amount of knowledge to be able to acquire more knowledge, and if you are to get the most out of a lecture you must have already a few ideas on the subject. There are several things you can do by way of preparation for listening intelligently to a lecture.

(1) Review your notes from previous lectures, so that you will have the setting or the background of the present lecture.

(2) Read a chapter or an article bearing on the subject in order to get a general survey of the field to be covered.

(3) Call up your own experiences or personal background of ideas bearing on the subject.

(4) Make a list of what you consider the major topics that should be included in the subject.

Your success in getting the message out of a lecture depends upon how much apperceptive background you have for intelligent interpretation of what is said.

9. Correlate lecture material with material from

other sources.   In the short time available for lectures in any given course it is impossible for the instructor to give a complete treatment of the field. At best he can give only a sketch or outline of the main divisions.   This fact suggests two kinds of correlation between lectures and reading.   The first is that of reading as extensively as possible before the lecture in order to be able to follow the lecturer understandingly.   The second is that of following up the lecture by additional reading in order to enrich and supplement the ideas that were presented.   There are two kinds of lectures and of reading matter.   The first kind is so condensed that it must be amplified and elaborated in order to be understood.   The other is so diffuse and contains so many cases or illustrations, or so much material that was added for the sake of interest, that it has to be boiled down to its essentials before it can be seen in clear perspective.   It is a good idea to decide which of these types is represented by the lectures you hear, and then to supplement the lectures by the opposite type of reading material. Frequently a lecture covers exactly the same material as that covered by the textbook, and some students, consequently, are satisfied with one and neglect the other, but very probably a careful study of both in their mutual relationships would bring out points which it would be impossible to get from only one of them.   Aside from differences in the condensation of the material, the mere difference between oral and visual presentation to the senses makes it worth while to attempt to get something about a topic from each of these two types of sources.

10. Take notes on the lecture. There has been much debate as to the value of taking notes on lectures, but a few facts are available which demonstrate well its value. The writer's experiments on this question [1] have revealed the following facts:

(1) The value of note-taking is slightly higher than that of listening, as measured immediately after the lecture.

(2) It is decidedly higher when measured after a period of days or weeks, when there has been time for forgetting and the necessity for reviewing has arisen.

(3) The value of the notes lies both in the taking and in the reviewing.

(4) The chances of a point's being remembered at quiz time are about even if it was recorded in the notes, but only one in seven if it was not.

The above statements are in accord with the results obtained from one hundred and sixty-two students whose notes were closely analyzed.

11. Get the speaker's outline. To take notes on a lecture is not enough; it is necessary also to get the lecturer's outline. Knowing a great piece of literature involves knowing not only what is in it, but something of the order or relation of its various parts. Your lecture notes should serve a double

[1] Crawford, C. C.: "The Correlation between College Lecture Notes and Quiz Papers"; in *Journal of Educational Research*, November, 1925; and "Some Experimental Studies of the Results of College Note-Taking," in *Journal of Educational Research*, December, 1925.

purpose: first, to provide a record, or to preserve ideas for later study; and second, to express your reaction to the organization or construction of the lecture. There is more to a lecture than an outline, however, and care should be taken to avoid taking down the mere outline without the rich and meaningful associations that belong with it. To get outline without substance is probably a worse error than to get substance without outline.

12. **Get a summary of the entire lecture in a few words.** A brief statement of the main things in the lecture affords one of the finest means of grasping the real message of the lecture, and should always be striven for. Frequently the lecturer himself gives such a summary, either at the beginning or at the end of his discourse; it is a simple task, then, to write it down. Sometimes, however, you must make the summary yourself, either at the end of the lecture or later in your room as you review the notes. Whether the summary is obtained ready-made or not, you have not really mastered the lecture until you can state the gist of the message in a very few words.

13. **Give special attention to the speaker's introductory statements.** The outstanding characteristic of an introduction is, of course, that it introduces something. An introduction is not merely a time-filler; it has a purpose and a definite function to perform. Just as the first sentence in a paragraph or the first paragraph in a chapter is the most important, so the opening statements by the lec-

turer are usually the most significant.   From them
you should get the subject of the lecture, its relation to other lectures in the series, what special
reasons there are for giving this particular lecture at
this particular point, what special purpose there is
for it, what main points it is to cover, and similar
matters that provide perspective or orientation in
the field.   Well begun is half done, and this is
particularly true of listening to a lecture.

14. Get not only the speaker's ideas, but also
the key words by which he expresses them concisely.   Bulky objects need handles, and so do
bulky ideas.   Most lecturers provide such handles
for their ideas in the form of terse statements or
catchwords especially selected to express the whole
idea in compressed form.   If you get such happy
expressions recorded in your notes, and really
understand what they mean, you are fortunate
indeed.   So thoroughly do some students appreciate
the value of these key words or terse statements
that they even sacrifice genuine understanding of
the lecture in the effort to get them down in their
notes.   The writer, for instance, has seen his students begin to write at a furious pace as he expressed
a point in what appeared to be especially good form,
when it was perfectly evident that as they wrote,
the meaning of the statement could not possibly
have yet been clear to them.   Of course their hope
was that the ensuing discussion would explain the
statement and that the note would thus acquire a
meaning not present at the time of writing, but,

it should be said, extra care should be taken to avoid carrying away a handle which is not attached to any object, and to avoid carrying away words that are not attached to any real ideas.

15. **Get both the details and the main points.** It is possible to fail to see the woods for looking at the trees, and to miss the real message of a lecture by paying too much attention to minor details. On the other hand, it is also possible that the real meaning and value of the lecture may be lost if the supporting details are neglected. The ideal should be to get the details, but to associate them so intimately with the major points which they are intended to support that they may be trusted to come up when needed without being written in the notes and without special effort being made to remember them. The person who has generalizations without specific cases or illustrations to support them is as unfortunate as the one who has many independent cases, but cannot sum them up under a few major generalizations.

16. **Follow the rambling lecture and organize it later.** Some of the most effective and interesting lecturers do not attempt to follow a systematic outline, but prefer to speak as they get the inspiration. The advantage of this plan is that it is very much like the natural thought process, in that the ideas do not come into the mind neatly classified and systematically arranged, but rather in a helter-skelter fashion according to the intricate association patterns of the thinker. A lecture that proceeds in

this fashion may be more interesting and more productive of genuine thinking on the part of the listener, even if it is not so effective as a means of reducing the topic to order and system. Your plan as a student in listening to the rambling type of lecture should be to follow all of its ramblings and make a record of the ideas presented, whatever their order, and then later to finish up the process by carefully arranging these points into some order or system. Lack of order or system may be tolerated in the *thought process*, but the *results* of the thinking should finally be systematized.

17. Reproduce the lecturer's diagrams and blackboard sketches in your notes. Just as the effectiveness of the lecture is increased by the use of visual presentations, so your understanding and later retention of it will be improved by a record of these visual representations of ideas. Be sure, however, to record the key or explanation of the meaning of each drawing, else there is little left after the first memory fades. A few lines and circles, properly labeled and clearly understood, can be of infinite service in preserving a clear sense of the relationships between ideas that have been presented.

18. Make the most of humorous or concrete illustrations. Lecturers tell their funny stories or make their facetious remarks for a purpose, as a general rule. The recital of an amusing incident not only serves to provide physical and mental relaxation from the strain of a serious lecture, but also serves as an aid in understanding and retaining the lecture.   Public speakers have learned that one good way to have their audiences remember the points they make is to associate those points intimately with good stories.   While it is hardly necessary to tell students to laugh at a joke, it may not be amiss to suggest that they make a point of associating the real point with the joke so that the real purpose of the joke will be achieved.   The very concreteness of brief, crisp stories makes them easy to remember, but this advantage is often its own undoing, because that quality has a strong tendency to draw the attention away from the principles which they were intended to illustrate.

19. **Learn the speaker's vocabulary, but translate it into your own.**   Getting a lecture down in your own words is essential to a genuine understanding and grasp of it.   Unless you can translate technical terms or big words into terms of your own, you do not really know what has been said; and yet it is also well to get those technical terms or big words as permanent possessions or servants of your own. A new word in your vocabulary is comparable to a new tool in your kit or to a new soldier in an army, and is not to be lightly ignored.   The new words that are used in a lecture should be recorded, even if they seem unnatural, since they will ultimately prove very useful when their meaning and significance have been grasped.   A good way to achieve the mastery of such words is to start using them, at first along with your personal translation of them, and later on their own responsibility.

20. Continue your study of the lecture after the class period. Just as reading a book once will not make you master of its contents, so hearing a lecture once will not produce a mastery of that lecture. It will be necessary to follow up the hearing by additional study. There are several ways to continue the study after the lecture. One is to review the subject mentally and add points that you omitted from your notes. Another is to rearrange or improve your notes. A third is to rewrite the notes entirely. A fourth is to read them over thoughtfully. A fifth is to look up additional material to explain or clarify points which you do not understand. There is much to be said in favor of meditation over your notes on a lecture, simply letting your mind wander over the points and bring up such associations as seem natural and appropriate. Then, finally, there is the method of more thorough memorization of the main points of the lecture by study of the outline. If you wish to master the lecture entirely, it is well to visualize the outline and then memorize the main divisions of it, associating details with them as you do so.

21. Record notes on sources of material bearing on the lecture. It has been said that next in value to knowing a subject is knowing where to go for information about it. As a lecture proceeds, frequent suggestions as to further reading are made, and also frequent allusions to the writings of authorities. Embodying these in your lecture notes gives added value, both to references and to notes, since each is a natural supplement to the other. The good student will use his lecture notes, not as the final and ultimate source of all knowledge on the subject, but rather as a guide or syllabus for further pursuit of the topic.

22. Interpret the lecture partly by the help of the speaker's inflections. We are more willing to listen to a good speaker, as a rule, than we are to read his book. That is because the book is just "cold print" and as such lacks the color and life which the speaker's voice imparts to the very same words. Noting the rise and fall of pitch, the variations in loudness, the placing of emphasis, will help the listener to get the speaker's meaning. The inflections of his voice, particularly, bear a close relationship to the thought he is expressing. For example, the greeting "How do you do" may be so inflected as to express a dozen or more different meanings. It has even been found that inflection of the voice is closely correlated with intelligence.[1] The speaker, of course, puts his best mental effort into the delivery of the lecture, and your part is to listen, not only to his words, but to the tones in which they are expressed, in order to catch the subtle meanings which words alone cannot express.

23. Watch the speaker. Some instructors have been known to forbid note-taking in their classes because it interferes with watching the speaker.

[1] Michael, William, and Crawford, C. C.: "An Experiment in Judging Intelligence by the Voice"; in *Journal of Educational Psychology*, vol. XVIII (1927), pp. 107–14.

The two activities are mutually opposed, but each is extremely important. It is necessary for the listener to watch the speaker, whether the matter is considered from the side of the speaker or from that of the listener. The speaker cannot know when he has made his ideas clear unless the faces of his hearers tell him. The best illustration of this fact is the difficulty experienced by persons who lecture with lantern slides in a dark room, where the audience is in obscurity. On the other hand, watching the speaker helps the listener as much as it helps the speaker. You get more meaning from the words if you see his gestures and his facial expression. Frequently, also, the message lies more in the speaker's personality than in the words he utters, and for this reason it is imperative that some compromise be made between note-taking and watching the speaker that will prevent a complete loss of the values of either method. Of course there are other things than note-taking that interfere with watching the speaker, such as poor lighting, distance, and obstructions to vision, such as the heads of other students or columns or pillars. A resourceful person can usually be depended on, however, to overcome, as far as is possible, most of these obstacles.

24. Enter into the lecture with a coöperative attitude. Nothing is quite so difficult as to lecture to an unsympathetic or unresponsive audience. If the listeners are indifferent or antagonistic, the speaker is depressed accordingly and gives a less

vigorous, less enthusiastic, or less interesting lecture than if they had been otherwise. One way to get a better speech from a dull speaker is to smile when he makes a good statement, nod your head when you agree with what he says, and in numerous little ways show him that you are interested and that you are expecting something from him. A bit of applause or some other evidence that an address is producing an effect can work wonders in improving its quality. Even if nothing is accomplished in the way of changing the speaker's method and offering, a spirit of coöperation is worth while simply for its effect on yourself. If you act as if interested, you are more likely to become interested. The outward evidences of coöperation actually make you more receptive to new ideas; and, furthermore, a coöperative attitude on your part often improves your grade or mark in the course.

25. **Interrupt the lecturer when you have a vital question to ask or a special reaction.** A certain amount of informality or of conversational atmosphere in a class lecture helps to make the lecture interesting and meaningful. As a general rule an instructor is willing to hear questions at any time during the course of a lecture, if they are sincere and genuinely related to the topic under discussion. Some teachers prefer to leave all discussion to the end and then allow time for an open forum or for questions from the students; but it is frequently the case that a question which would have been of great interest and significance at the time it arose

during the lecture has little point or importance at the close, when it is out of its natural setting. Questions or discussion at intervals during the lecture not only add interest, but also enable the lecturer to find out how well his ideas are being grasped, and thus to adapt the lecture more closely to his hearers' needs.

26. Help to keep the lecturer's mind alert and active while he lectures. Students often complain that the lecturer merely says words without thinking about them, and that his lecture is mechanical and formalized because of many previous repetitions to students in other classes. Surely it is as important for a lecturer to be awake, alert, and mentally active as for the student. If your instructor does not put himself sufficiently into his lectures, you can remedy the situation by injecting an idea or question of your own that will shake him loose from his formalized, memorized, or routine procedure and force him to think about what he is saying. If students would assume more responsibility for keeping the professor awake, the professor would have less difficulty in keeping the students awake.

27. Be prepared for tests on what you get from lectures. Instructors do not lecture simply to tickle your ears; they lecture for a purpose, and they check up to see how well that purpose has been achieved. You should assume that whatever you get in the form of lectures will be called for in some kind of test or check-up later. Some instructors check up on their lectures by examining the lecture notes to discover how well the students have understood and recorded the points.   Others give tests to see how much they can remember.   Still others like to set problems for their hearers which apply the ideas given in lectures, in order to see how well they can use these ideas.   As a general rule the lectures are the greatest of the factors that determine the nature of final examinations, since the test questions are prepared from such definite sources as are available to the instructor, and these sources are primarily his lecture outlines and the textbooks.   Students would do well to assume that the substance of the examination questions will be taken in large measure from the instructor's lectures.

QUESTIONS AND EXERCISES

1. Outline the chapter under three heads: (*a*) What to do before the lecture; (*b*) what to do during the lecture; (*c*) what to do after the lecture.
2. Which methods are actual things to do and which are more general guiding principles or policies?
3. What is the most helpful single thing you can tell a student to help him profit from lectures?   Why?

MATCHING TEST

Directions: Write beside each number the number of the paragraph in the chapter which discusses it.

....   1. Note-taking versus listening.
....   2. Individuality of the lecturer.
....   3. Relation of lectures to textbook.
....   4. Gist of the lecture.
....   5. Previous preparation.
....   6. Apperceptive background.
....   7. Work-type procedure.
....   8. Passive attitude.
....   9. Technical terms.

.... 10. Gestures.
.... 11. Delivery.
.... 12. Stories.
.... 13. Generalizing.
.... 14. Bibliographical notes.
.... 15. Follow up.
.... 16. Retention.
.... 17. Questioning attitude.
.... 18. Types of lectures.
.... 19. Terse statements.
.... 20. Organization.
.... 21. Visual aids.
.... 22. Responsiveness of audience.
.... 23. Opening remarks.
.... 24. Self-activity.
.... 25. Unsystematic lectures.
.... 26. Going to sleep.
.... 27. Asking the speaker questions.

TRUE–FALSE TEST

Directions: Indicate which statement is true and which is false, using plus (+) for true and zero (o) for false.

.... 1. The value of lecture notes increases with time.
.... 2. Some lectures are not supposed to be studied.
.... 3. Outlining a lecture helps to understand it.
.... 4. Students should help keep the lecturer awake.
.... 5. You should never interrupt a lecturer.
.... 6. The speaker's first remarks are usually of little importance because he is merely warming up.
.... 7. Reading and listening yield different results, even though the content be the same.
.... 8. For the audience to watch the speaker aids the speaker.
.... 9. A lecturer's meaning is dependent only on the vocabulary used.
.... 10. To understand a lecture you must translate it into your own words.
.... 11. A lecturer's statements should be accepted at their face value.
.... 12. Lecture notes should never be taken in the lecturer's own words.
.... 13. Jokes and stories tend to take attention away from the point.

.... 14. The summary of a lecture is usually too condensed to be of much value.

.... 15. Listeners should avoid expressions of their reactions while the lecture is in progress.

.... 16. A lecture usually has a definite purpose.

.... 17. To study about a lecture subject beforehand detracts from its interest.

.... 18. Hearing a lecture is of small value unless followed by later study.

.... 19. You should expect to be examined on lecture material.

.... 20. Lectures in school are usually for entertainment.

.... 21. It is impossible to get a lecture organized if the lecturer rambles.

.... 22. Lectures are meaningless except as amplified by the listener.

.... 23. There is necessarily very little activity on the listener's part during a lecture.

.... 24. One should seek for main points and ignore details.

.... 25. Lecture notes and bibliographical references should be kept separate and distinct.

.... 26. What applies to listening to one lecturer applies to all.

.... 27. Drawings on the blackboard should be copied in the notes.

SHORT–ANSWER TEST

Directions: Answer each question or complete each statement by inserting a word, phrase, or brief answer.

1. A lecturer's blackboard sketches should be reproduced in ......

2. Reading and listening are mutually ....

3. A good way to prepare for listening to a lecture is to ....

4. A large number of details are of little value unless they are ....

5. If you do not understand a lecture, who is at fault? ....

6. What good is accomplished by asking questions during a lecture? ....

7. Some lectures are for .... purposes rather than intellectual.

8. In listening to a poorly organized lecture you should note the points down and ....

9. After a lecture period you should ....

10. What should be your attitude toward nodding agreement with the speaker? ....

11. You have not mastered a lecture until you can ....

12. Upon what does the meaning of a lecture you hear depend?
    ....
13. The outline of a lecture is unimportant unless you have also
    ....
14. In addition to notes on what is heard you should record notes
    on ....
15. The most important minute in a lecture is ....
16. Lecturers tell funny stories in order to get their hearers to ......
17. Why are examinations based largely on lectures?........
18. What effect does your asking the lecturer a question have on
    him?........
19. The main essential of listening to a lecture is to keep mentally
    ....
20. Lectures are of two main types, intellectual and ....
21. New words you hear in a lecture should be ....
22. At the outset of a series of lectures it is well to get acquainted
    with the lecturer's ....
23. What good is accomplished by watching the speaker? ....
24. If you record the lecturer's own words you should take care to
    ....
25. Spoken words have a different meaning from printed words by
    reason of ....
26. School lectures are not to be listened to but rather ....
27. How do experimental data show note-taking to compare with
    listening?........

READINGS

Adams, John: *Making the Most of One's Mind*.   Geo. H. Doran Co.,
New York, 1915.
    Chapter VIII, "Listening and Note-Making."

Tryon, Rolla M.: *The Teaching of History in Junior and Senior High
Schools*, Ginn & Co., Boston, 1921.
    Chapter III, "Special Methods of Procedure: Lecture."

CHAPTER IV

USING TEXTBOOKS

PROBABLY the greatest single source of information open to the majority of students in school is the textbook. The most common classroom activity is some kind of elaboration of textbook material, and it is doubtless true that more hours of a student's time are spent in studying textbooks than in any other form of study. While the nature of textbooks in different subjects varies greatly, a few general principles which apply fairly well to most types of textbooks have been assembled and are presented in the following paragraphs.

1. **Own your own textbook.** Trying to economize by going without needed tools is one of the most vicious kinds of false economy, and textbooks, certainly, are to be classed among the most important tools of the student. The total cost of a year in school is so great, especially when loss of wages or salary is added to the direct outlay, that the small sum required for textbooks is trivial. Furthermore, the cost of textbooks is extremely small as compared with student expenditures for entertainment, social affairs, and refreshments. In view of these facts the advantages of individual ownership of books are very great indeed. Owning your book means that you are free to mark and underline it as you study and to make notes in the margins to increase its

value to you.   You can associate your ideas directly
with the printed passages, and then retain the book
as your permanent record.   There will be greater
freedom to operate your study schedule if you do
not have to adjust yourself to the convenience of a
partner. In order to save money by borrowing textbooks from the library instead of buying them, your
time would have to be worth less than ten cents an
hour, and if it is worth so little you ought not to
be a student at all.   In fact you really study more
when you have your own book than otherwise.

   2. Take your book to class and use it.   The old
plan of closed books in class is being gradually out-
grown; the class period is used now for teaching
rather than for testing.   If that period is really
devoted to imparting new ideas or to discovering
new meanings in old ideas, the textbook may be
very serviceable as a basis upon which to work.   If
there are things you do not understand, take the
text to class and get them explained. If a new assignment is being made, open the book and get the
new work clearly connected with the pages or parts
upon which it is to be based.   When new material
is presented that was not in the text, associate it
with what you had read, or even add it to your text
account by means of marginal notations.   When
certain things are mentioned by the instructor as
being of unusual importance, indicate directly in the
book what he says.   When debates occur during the
class period, refer to your book for facts, and if
necessary quote your authority by page and line.

Of course it is not advisable that you prepare your lessons entirely in class, but rather that you use the class period for further extending your knowledge. If this plan is followed, longer lessons can be given and a more thorough mastery of them achieved. In fact many teachers now give examinations from the text, and direct the students to use the books freely in making their answers.

3. **Keep your textbook after the course is finished.** If a course is worth taking, the knowledge gained through it should be worth retaining. You cannot retain it all, however, by your unaided memory, and as a rule your notes do not cover it all. The text is usually the best single device for preserving, in readily accessible form, the knowledge you have gained. The resale value of textbooks is very small, especially in proportion to the total cost of a year in school, and the advantages of being free to mark, underline, and make notes in your book are so great that it would be a good thing if every student would definitely plan, at the beginning of the course, to preserve his textbook for all time, as the best possible single source to which he could refer in later years for information on the subject.

4. **Get acquainted with the author.** To many students the textbooks they use are strangely impersonal. If asked what book they are studying in psychology, they reply that it is a large green book, and can give little further information. It would seem that every student should know at least the name of the author of each textbook that he is study-

ing, and also, perhaps, what position he holds.
The title-page usually states his rank and position,
and in some cases the other books that he has written.   The preface also offers an opportunity to get
more closely acquainted with him, since in it he
takes you somewhat into his confidence, telling you
why he wrote the book, and perhaps dwelling to
some extent on his philosophy of life or on the educational doctrines to which he subscribes.   Your textbook writer will influence your thought and action
approximately as much as your teacher, and you
owe it to him as well as to yourself to get acquainted
with him.

   5. **Do not accept as the truth everything that appears in textbooks.**   The textbooks are not always
written by the leading scholars or outstanding
authorities in the various fields.   It is unfortunately
true that in many cases the best scholars, scientists,
and research workers have been so much interested
in their investigations that they have had no time
to reduce their findings to textbook form.   Furthermore, when some of them have attempted to write
textbooks they have been unable to get down to the
proper level of simplicity and freedom from techni-
cality for high-school and college students, with the
result that their books are unsatisfactory as texts.
The outcome of this has been a tendency for textbooks to be written in many cases by laymen without adequate scientific background, rather than by
experts.   For example, some of the public-school
history textbooks which have secured state-wide

adoptions have been written by persons who did not even have a bachelor's degree. These are extreme cases, it is true, but there are enough textbooks on the market and in use in the schools, written by second-rate scholars or by first-rate scholars working outside of their field of speciality, to make it necessary for the student constantly to exercise his critical faculty and refuse to accept unsupported opinion as absolute fact.

6. **Study with a view to finding the sequence and the organization of the main points.** A textbook is as a rule already very much condensed or concentrated, and in a sense it is simply a compressed outline of the subject. Nevertheless, various facts or ideas which it contains vary greatly in importance, and you must carefully weigh, judge, and select before you can determine what are truly the main points. When these have been decided on, further study is required in order for you to discover how they relate to one another, and to arrange them in your own mind in the correct sequence and organization.

7. **Revise and supplement the text.** Add to the author's account the things which he was forced to leave out. Make up illustrations of your own suited to the principles stated. Call up mental images of concrete cases which are related to the textbook content. Rearrange parts of the book or chapter according to your own system of thinking about them. Make up your mind as to what you would leave out if you were rewriting the book, and what

you would put in. Even though your revision is inferior to the author's, the fact that it is yours makes it better *for you*, and the critical analysis and mental activity involved in making the book over according to your plan constitute a high type of study procedure.

8. Study subject units rather than page units. Textbook study as it is often carried out resembles Bible reading, in that it lacks unity, or completeness of topic. If the last of the customary nine pages is reached before a given subject has been finished, the study stops there, and the unfinished part is combined with the next lesson, whether it is related to it or not. This is as inexcusable as the policy of a certain family whose religious devotions required the reading of exactly seven Bible verses every night, even though the seventh verse happened to end in the middle of a sentence. Each textbook assignment should be unified and complete, and your work in studying it should likewise be organized into subject units instead of proceeding arbitrarily by page units.

9. Organize your reviews around the textbook. As a general rule, the textbook offers the most systematic treatment or outline of the subject available for a given course, and should therefore be the best single instrument for securing order and system in your thinking on the subject. If the main chapter headings of the text are used as pegs upon which to hang your knowledge of the whole course, they may serve to unify and coördinate knowledge secured from lectures, discussions, and collateral reading. If the textbook is thus made the central element in the review, and the other knowledge closely associated with it, it should prove extremely valuable as a permanent record for all knowledge gained in the course.

10. Supplement intensive textbook study with extensive reading. Your intellectual menu should not be made up entirely of concentrated mental food. Textbooks may, and do, serve a splendid purpose in providing substantial food for thought, but they should be supplemented by collateral reading. Intensive study of twelve pages may give you a sense of perspective and a knowledge of the elements involved in the subject, but the application of a more free-and-easy reading procedure to twenty-five or fifty pages of collateral material may add color and life, or you might say spice and flavoring, to the more substantial things secured from the textbook. The rewards of extensive study are fully as great as those of intensive study, but since they are of a different nature the two procedures should be combined if the maximum benefit is to be secured. The references for further reading which are usually provided at the ends of chapters are among the most valuable aids available for directing your extensive or supplementary reading.

11. Take advantage of the various special parts of the book. The various chapters of a textbook might be compared to the rooms in a house, and the special features to the furniture. A student who has not learned to use these special parts is comparable to the untrained savage who sits on the floor because he has not discovered the advantages of a chair.   There are large numbers of such students. Some of the special features referred to may be mentioned here.   One is the footnotes.   Another is the glossary, which pronounces names and defines unusual words.   A third is the appendix, which supplies the actual data or materials which are discussed in a more abbreviated way in the various chapters.   A fourth is the index, which enables you to follow up easily a given topic in many parts of the book.   A fifth is the table of contents, which probably contributes more to your sense of perspective than any other single part.   A sixth is the preface, wherein you make the author's acquaintance.   A seventh is the introduction, which gives you the relation of this book to the major field or series of books to which it belongs.   An eighth is the lists of readings and suggestions for further study which are given at the ends of the various chapters.   These things are all included in the book at considerable expense because of their genuine worth and service, and the student who has not acquired the habit of using them is simply robbing himself of his opportunities.   Particularly is this true of the student who fails to use the questions and exercises at the ends of the chapters, since these are ordinarily among the most effective aids to study to be found anywhere.

12. **Make full use of maps, charts, pictures, and**

tables. In spite of our realization that concrete or visual presentation of facts is very helpful, we all have a common tendency to neglect such aids when we meet with them in our textbooks. This is largely due to the fact that the printer must insert such materials into the page of the text where they will fit conveniently, and where they will provide balance or symmetry, instead of at the immediate or exact point in the page at which they would logically come before the reader's attention. The result is that the printed matter often carries us beyond the pictures and designs without giving us a chance to observe them, or else it starts another line of thought before we turn the page that carries them. It is quite common for students in estimating the length of lessons to subtract the pages occupied by pictures, maps, or tables, as if these did not count, when in reality an adequate study of this material would consume more time and repay it to a greater degree than would an equivalent amount of space occupied by the text.

13. **Utilize the typographical aids to clarify the thought.** Paragraph indentations, center headings, bold-faced type, italics, numbered series, etc., are used to clarify thought rather than simply to carry out the dictates of literary style. The author of a number of books reports that one of his most difficult problems is how to get his readers to pay attention to these things. He says they have a common tendency to leap a bold-faced heading without even looking at it and begin at once on the meat of the

topic. The writer conducted a small-scale experiment once which revealed the same tendency. He mimeographed two identical lists of statements, one in outline form and one in list form, and allowed his students a limited time for learning them. The test revealed that the students who studied the lists that were presented in outline form were unable to supply as many of the main divisions of the outline as were those who studied the same points when they were not so boldly displayed. In other words, those who had the lists in outline form had neglected to observe the main divisions of the outline, and had memorized instead the details listed under these main heads. There seems to be a queer trait of human nature which causes us to ignore these most valuable aids; for that reason our attention should be especially called to their importance.

14. Employ intensive methods on difficult parts. Automobiles must be low-geared as well as high-geared because of occasional hills, and similarly students have to resort at times to mental low-geared methods in order to master difficult parts of textbooks. There are several devices which serve this latter purpose. One is consulting the dictionary when unfamiliar words cause a hitch. Another is reading the passage aloud in order to get its meaning by the aid of auditory impressions. Paraphrasing, or restating in your own words, frequently solves the difficulty. If you own the book, it is a good plan to mark a passage or word which is not clear and come back to it later if it does not explain itself in the light of succeeding paragraphs. In some cases it is wasteful to ponder long over a difficult passage, because a little farther on the point is elaborated in detail. For this reason it is usually wise to go over the entire lesson and then come back to the difficult parts when you can bring to bear on them the other knowledge that you acquired farther along.

15. Make some kind of application of the material. Apply what you read to some kinds of life situations. Solve some kinds of practical problems in the light of principles laid down in the text. The text proper is obliged by its lack of space to omit most of the possible applications of its subject and to leave the student to make up applications of his own. It is a good plan to call up in connection with each textbook principle some kind of situation that embodies it, and so test the soundness or genuineness of the principle with reference to the actual case. Simply forming mental associations between what you read and your own past experiences is a step in the right direction. What you read will be of small value to you unless you relate it or apply it to something else in your life or to some knowledge which you already possessed.

16. Vary the procedure, instead of merely reading the lesson over and over. Re-reading a chapter in the text is subject to the law of diminishing returns. Each re-reading adds less new knowledge than the preceding one did. One reading may be very valuable, a second may add something, but a third may be practically useless. Instead of reading your lesson over twice, it is better, as a rule, to read it once and then apply to it some other study technique, in order to get a qualitatively different mental experience with it. For example, you might read the material once and then come back and make an outline. Or you might read and outline as you go, coming back to study the outline. Or you might underline as you go, and outline when you go over the text again. Another plan is to read once, and then, instead of reading again, hunt for answers to questions. Similar to this plan is reading and then solving problems. Whatever plan you adopt, change your method when you go over the material for the second time, since mere repetition of the same method of study, over and over, adds little new knowledge.

17. Mark and underline the textbook. If you own your own textbook, as all good students should, it is well to make it a permanent reference book for your own personal use. A good plan is to mark the parts that have special significance for you, and write in ideas of your own which are associated with special passages in the text. Simply underlining the main points in each paragraph greatly improves the book for your later study, review, or reference use, in addition to giving it a personal significance as a reflection of your own individuality. There is much to be said for recording in the text your doubts, questions, and critical comments, your cross-references to material in other books or other chapters, and possibly some of the points expressed in lectures or class discussions.

18. Outline the text as a method of studying it. Outlining the text is not only recommended by leading authorities on psychology and education, but is also actually practiced by a large number of students. Bennett [1] says: "Outlines are perhaps the best method of making your organization clear and definite, and impressing it on your mind." Parker [2] advocates outlining for the following purposes: (*a*) As a mechanical aid to thinking; (*b*) as a basis for clear thinking preparatory to expression; (*c*) as a means of securing reflective analysis and clear understanding of an assignment that is read; (*d*) as an aid to reciting on the assignment. Woodworth [3] includes as one item, in the exercises at the ends of each chapter in his psychology text, the assignment, "Outline the chapter." A considerable body of data has been made available regarding the extent of the practice of outlining on the part of college students. Mrs. Charters [4] found that a large number reported that they outlined as a method of studying. Other students reported other forms of note-taking which they did not class as outlining. A questionnaire on which the writer received answers from fifty college students in a

[1] Bennett, H. E.: *Psychology and Self-Development*, p. 8.
[2] Parker, S. C.: *Methods of Teaching in High Schools*, pp. 410–11.
[3] Woodworth, R. S.: *Psychology*.
[4] Charters, Jessie Allen: "How Two Hundred and Fifty-Eight Junior College Women Study"; in *Journal of Educational Research*, January, 1925.

state university revealed that the greater number of students gave first preference, among the various methods, to outlining. Another investigation which the writer made, in a graduate class in education in the University of Chicago, revealed that seventy-seven students out of one hundred and thirty-one took notes or made outlines, thirty-three marked the book, and twenty-one did neither. These procedures were entirely uninfluenced by the persons making the investigation; they represent the free choices of the students. It was found, furthermore, that those who outlined had the highest average grades, those who marked the book the next highest, and those who did neither had the lowest average grades of all three groups. In the light of these facts it seems clear that outlining is a method of study which can safely be recommended and practiced.

19. Study the text to find solutions for previous problems. If you bring to your textbook study a few questions or problems and seek answers to them, you add an element of purposefulness that is very desirable. Sometimes these problems or questions will be suggested by the teacher when the assignment is made, sometimes they will be suggested by the previous lesson or chapter, and sometimes they will grow out of your own personal experience. The ability to discover or set up problems for yourself is one of the marks of a good student, and it is one which can be cultivated. If you cannot set up problems or questions of your own, then a preliminary survey of the chapter simply to discover the real issues might be desirable, followed by a more intensive study for the purpose of finding the answers to the questions thus discovered.

20. Recite the lesson to yourself. One rule for memorizing is to test your knowledge by attempting recall, and this applies to the learning of textbook material as well as to the memorizing of a poem. There are several ways to recite the textbook lesson to yourself. One is to put the book away and recall the main topical divisions, listing them as they are recalled, and completing the list by referring to the book at the end of the process. Another way is to begin with the topic headings and recall the details which support each. A third plan is to test yourself on the author's exercises at the end of the chapter. Mrs. Charters found that some students recite the lesson aloud, some in a whisper, some in the mind only, and some make a written summary from memory and check up by referring to the book.

21. Study the text orally in certain cases. Although silent reading is usually distinctly superior to oral reading, the latter sometimes has value for certain special purposes. Occasionally a very difficult sentence can be better comprehended when read orally than when read silently. Sometimes the nature of the lesson is such as to call especially for memorizing, in which case oral repetition may have merit. When your recitation on the material learned is to be oral, oral methods of studying are usually best. Certain subjects by their very character call for oral study of the textbooks — foreign languages, for example. A warning, however, should be extended against promiscuous resort to oral study, for it has a distinct tendency to slow down the rate of reading, it greatly tires the muscles of the diaphragm, and it largely diverts attention from the thought to the word-calling — all to such a degree that it should not be employed except for some very obvious reason.

22. Use the text in certain cases for drill purposes. Textbooks in certain subjects are largely exercise books, or student guides for drill and practice. For example, the usual mathematics text is largely a book of drill exercises intended to make automatic the skills which are desired. Similarly, foreign-language texts contain a large amount of practice material. It is a good idea to consider well the real purpose of the particular text being studied, and then to adapt the procedure to that purpose. Certainly the study technique appropriate to a text whose major purpose is drill should be different from that employed with one whose major purpose is to impart information or insight into principles. For detailed treatment of the procedure to be employed on the drill type of textbooks, see the chapters on skill and memory.

23. Follow up class work by further study in the text. Most of us have acquired the bad habit of studying the text to get ready for the class, when as a matter of fact there is equally as much reason for studying the subject in class as a preparation for effective use of the text afterward. By the modern plan of supervised study the class work ordinarily precedes rather than follows the individual work, because this order produces better results. It is only reasonable that the more you know about the subject to begin with, the more you should be able to get out of the text. The plan of procedure might well be to study the text both before and after the recitation period rather than concentrate all the work into one period before it.

24. **When in difficulty study the same lesson in two different textbooks.** Just as two photographs of a person tell more about the person than two copies of the same photograph, so reading two textbooks on the same subject is more profitable than reading the same textbook twice. The writer has had occasion several times to advise students who were failing in chemistry, French, and similar subjects, and has found that the advice to use a second textbook has been distinctly helpful. A second author covers the same ground in a somewhat different way, using different illustrations and different terms of explanation, and repeating the same things in different words. In fact one school goes so far, it is said, as to have students who fail enroll in two sections of the course in order that they may get a double exposure for each lesson, because it has been proved that, although the content of the two courses may be identical, the individuality in the methods of the teachers will make the second exposure constitute, for the pupils, the difference between failure and success.

25. **Get study-suggestions for the particular lesson from the teacher.** Since the instructor knows what he intends to do with a given chapter or lesson, he is in an excellent position to suggest the method by which it should be studied. The natural time for this suggestion is in connection with the making of the assignment, when the discussion of what to study can naturally and easily be made to include how to study it. If you do not feel satisfied with your study technique, it is a simple matter to ask for more detailed directions. Further individual requests for guidance or suggestions during the progress of the work may bring forth additional help.

26. **Increase your speed of reading.** Fast reading is better than slow reading. You learn more from each page when you read rapidly than when you read slowly, to say nothing of the fact that in reading fast you cover more pages. In rapid reading you receive several words at one glance and thus take in the material in thought units rather than word units. The result is that comprehension is improved as speed is increased. If you read very slowly, the material is supplied to the mind so slowly that the attention wanders off upon irrelevant associations while waiting for the next idea to be presented by the eye. The mind is capable of receiving ideas much more rapidly than the eye is capable of supplying them, therefore rapid reading requires primarily a training of the eye to do its work at a better pace. That this can be done is

clearly shown by numbers of scientific experiments by investigators in the field of reading. In fact, the statement is made on good authority that the average student can double his rate of reading without at all sacrificing the quality of his comprehension.

Methods and devices for increasing the reading rate are here indicated:

(1) Keep a record of the time required for reading each chapter, and try to reduce the time.

(2) Read under pressure of a time limit, trying to read as much as you can before time is called.

(3) Read words in groups instead of one word at a time.

(4) Practice for speed on very easy material, such as fiction, where there is no difficulty at all in getting the meaning.

(5) Practice by the tachistoscopic method — that is, uncover a unit of printed matter for a second or less and see how many words you can recognize at one glance.

(6) Reduce vocalization, moving the lips, and inner speech to a minimum. The eye can move much more rapidly than the voice, and if you say the words you limit your speed of reading to the speed of your voice.

There are a few limitations to the speed at which you should read. They are as follows:

(1) When reading for enjoyment a leisurely reading is preferable because it will allow time for the imagination to play on what is read.

(2) In reading difficult material it is necessary to take time to figure out meanings.

(3) Unnaturally fast reading is inefficient.

When you reach the point that you are skipping and skimming, or when you get into a state of nervous haste, your reading inevitably becomes unsatisfactory.

QUESTIONS AND EXERCISES

1. Classify the points in the chapter under three heads as follows: (*a*) Those which apply only to textbooks; (*b*) those which apply to any kind of printed matter; (*c*) those which apply to material presented in oral form.
2. Write out very briefly what you consider the best way to study a textbook chapter for the usual type of school situation.
3. List the subjects in which you study textbooks and under each state the principal points in textbook study technique which are peculiar to that subject.
4. Arrange the points in this chapter under the following heads: (*a*) Those which you regularly practice; (*b*) those which you sometimes practice; (*c*) those which you never practice; (*d*) those which you never expect to practice.

MATCHING TEST

Directions: Write beside each number the number of the paragraph in the chapter which discusses it.

....   1. Title-page and preface.
....   2. Acquiring skill.
....   3. Hasty preview.
....   4. Storage of knowledge after school.
....   5. Bold-faced headings.
....   6. Purpose of recitation.
....   7. Buying books.
....   8. Page assignments.
....   9. Parallel texts.
....   10. Value of outlining.
....   11. Putting knowledge to use.
....   12. Advantages of silent reading.
....   13. Attempting recall.
......   14. Editing the book.

.... 15. Correlation of text and recitation.
.... 16. Hunting for the answer.
.... 17. How to read rapidly.
.... 18. Directions for study.
.... 19. Collateral reading.
.... 20. Contents, index, etc.
.... 21. Visual aids.
.... 22. Writing in the book.
.... 23. Reviewing.
.... 24. Main points.
.... 25. Number of times to read lesson.
.... 26. Textbook authorship.

TRUE–FALSE TEST

Directions: Indicate which statement is true and which is false, using plus (+) for true and zero (o) for false.

....+... 1. To read the text twice is usually unwise.
....+... 2. You should approach a text with a receptive mind to assimilate what it has to give.
....o... 3. Studying a topic in two books is likely to cause confusion.
.... 4. The free textbook law is a handicap to study.
....o... 5. The general reader tends to skip bold-faced headings.
....o... 6. Pictures in books are for ornament more than use.
....+... 7. Fast reading is usually good reading.
....o... 8. The textbook lesson should be prepared at one study period.
.... 9. Textbooks should usually be studied silently.
.... 10. Textbooks are for knowledge and not for skill.
.... 11. You should make up illustrations of your own as you read.
....o... 12. Textbooks are almost always written by the very best scholars.
....+... 13. Outlining is commonly approved by educational writers.
....o... 14. Each text assignment should be of uniform length.
....o... 15. Who wrote a book is unimportant; it is what he wrote that counts.
....o... 16. Indexes are not worth the paper they are printed on.
....o... 17. Collateral reading should be resorted to only when the text is entirely inadequate.
....+... 18. To try to recall the substance under various topics is good procedure.

.... 19. Textbooks usually are rich in suggested applications.
.... 20. A textbook is usually quite condensed.
.... 21. To have your book open in class is pedagogically wrong.
.... 22. You should never leave a passage until you understand it.
.... 23. The text is your best storage place for knowledge not remembered.
.... 24. Practically all textbook lessons are to be studied alike.
.... 25. To mark your book indicates poor taste.
.... 26. Texts are inadequate bases for review.

SHORT–ANSWER TEST

Directions: Answer each question or complete each statement by inserting a word, phrase, or brief answer.

1. An important essential in acquiring speed of reading is to reduce ....
2. What do scientific studies show as to the value of outlining texts? ....
3. How reliable is the material of the average textbook? ....
4. Why should you learn something about the author? ....
5. How does marking the text affect its value? ....
6. What law is illustrated by reading a text several times? ....
7. What is the main function of footnotes? ....
8. What should be the relation of textbook study to collateral reading? ....
9. When is the best time to get study helps for a lesson? ....
10. For what purpose are the exercises in textbooks? ....
11. What should you do with a text after the end of the course? ....
12. What is the result of using two textbooks? ....
13. To what extent should texts be studied aloud? ....
14. How should the text be used in reviewing? ....
15. Why is a regular page assignment undesirable? ....
16. When is reading aloud in textbook study justified? ....
17. Why is reciting to yourself good? ....
18. How can you add to a textbook? ....
19. At what time should the text be studied as compared with the class period? ....
20. Taking books to class permits longer ....
21. With what mental attitude should a text be approached? ......
22. Owning your text gives greater freedom to operate your ......
23. Finding the main points requires considerable ....

24. How does the value of tables compare with that of regular printed matter?........
25. How can you fit a textbook principle to your own individual needs?........
26. What are bold-faced headings intended to do?........

READINGS

1. Adams, John: *Making the Most of One's Mind*. Geo. H. Doran Co., New York, 1915.

Chapter VI, "Reading." Chapter VII, "Textbooks and Books of Reference."

2. Book, W. F.: *Learning How to Study and Work Effectively*. Ginn & Co., Boston, 1926.

Chapter XVII, "How to Prepare an Assignment in a Text."

3. Dearborn, G. V. N.: *How to Learn Easily*. Little, Brown & Co., Boston, 1918.

Chapter IV, "Books and their Educative Use."

4. Earhart, Lida B.: *Teaching Children to Study*. Houghton Mifflin Co., Boston, 1909.

Chapter IV, "Relation of Rational Study to Textbook Study."

5. Headly, Leal A.: *How to Study in College*. Henry Holt & Co., New York, 1926.

Chapter X, "How to Read."

6. Lyman, R. L.: *The Mind at Work*. Scott, Foresman & Co., Chicago, 1924.

Chapter IV, "Reading to Understand and Remember." Chapter V, "Reading as an Active Process." Chapter VI, "Evaluating What We Read and Hear."

7. May, M. A.: *How to Study in College*. Syracuse University Press, Syracuse, New York, 1923.

Chapter VI, "The Reading Type of Study."

8. Parker, Samuel Chester: *Methods of Teaching in High Schools*. Ginn & Co., Boston, 1915.

Chapter XVII, "The Use of Books."

9. Tryon, Rolla M.: *The Teaching of History in Junior and Senior High Schools*. Ginn & Co., Boston, 1921.

Chapter III, "Special Methods of Procedure: Textbook."

10. Wiley, J. A.: *Practice Exercises in Study and Assimilative Reading*. Published by the author at Cedar Falls, Iowa, 1922.

Contains definite drill exercises for improving speed, comprehension, finding main points, etc.

CHAPTER V

ACQUIRING SKILL

THE law of habit is fundamental to all effectual study and learning. Practically every subject in the curriculum has something that involves habit-formation or the acquisition of muscular skill. Learning to pronounce foreign words, to draw geometrical figures, to manipulate laboratory apparatus, to speak before a class, and to write on the typewriter are a few common illustrations. The following principles and methods may be of some service as guides in this form of learning.

1. **Get a clear idea of the act to be performed.** Make a conscious and purposeful analysis of the act, and see what in particular you are to accomplish. You need to realize your objective, else you will not reach it, and practice will be blind and wasteful unless specifically directed toward that definite goal by a thorough understanding of the nature of the act which is to be learned.

2. **Learn the underlying principles and theory of the act.** You can learn to drive an automobile without the theory of gears, clutches, or carburetors, but it is sometimes rather hard on the car, to say nothing of your own patience. A brief explanation of the mechanism involved in shifting gears greatly facilitates learning to shift without producing the common rasping noise. Knowing the "why" of

a task often contributes much to the "how" of accomplishing that task. If you have mastered the general theory of the act you can often see the similarity of two different steps, and thus learn how to take the second by applying what you had previously learned about the first, while without a knowledge of the theory you would take as long to learn the second step as you took to learn the first. Judd found that boys learned to hit a target under water much more rapidly when they were given the theory of refraction than when they were left in ignorance of it. It is a good idea to read or study about the scientific or theoretical aspects of an act, as a preparation for attempting the actual practice. Cooking classes, in which the principles are taken up before any actual attempt at cooking is made, offer a good illustration of this rule.

3. **Perform the act yourself.** A man may learn much *about* an act by watching some one else do it, but in order to learn how to do it it will be necessary to do it himself. In other words, we learn to do by doing. The actual muscular performance of the act is necessary if you are to achieve skill. Being told or shown how to do a thing may greatly simplify and shorten the learning process, but it cannot complete it. This idea is involved in the proverb, "Experience is a dear teacher, but a fool will learn from no other." Undirected experience is a most expensive teacher, hence books and teachers are provided as guides and models are given to copy from; all these things the wise man uses to the max-

imum.   After all these means have been exhausted, he must complete the process of learning by actual practice of the process in the school of direct experience.   We learn by our own responses.

4. Give yourself a chance to succeed. In learning to dive, begin practicing from the water's edge instead of from a high tower, and, in learning to speak in public, begin by practicing before small audiences.   Each failure is in a sense a punishment, and has an inhibiting effect upon your practice.   If the failure assumes the proportions of a major disaster, it becomes practically impossible to proceed.   Whenever in learning you can arrange so to simplify the situation as to make success easier and reduce the seriousness of the failures, and at the same time keep the essential conditions typically the same, you make the learning more certain.   In a sense this is the hothouse idea applied to education, but then, some of our most beautiful flowers and most useful plants would never exist if we did not provide hothouse advantages to enable them to survive in their infancy.

5. Analyze the nature of your successes and failures. If you succeed in any attempt, even though by accident, note what it was that brought success and try to profit by the knowledge next time.   If you fail at something, try to see the why or how of the failure instead of being satisfied simply to acknowledge it a failure.   The more keenly conscious you are as to the nature and the causes of your success or failure, the more certain will be your progress in the business of learning. It has been found that teachers can greatly improve their skill in classroom instruction by the use of self-rating scales which help them to analyze the specific causes of their failures, or the specific things on which further improvement is needed.

6. Get constructive criticism from others. Self-analysis is good so far as it goes, but it does not go far enough. You cannot hope to see yourself entirely as others see you. For this reason it is well to have some one observe you at practice and point out the errors which you cannot detect. By submitting your methods to the inspection of those more expert than yourself, you obtain constructive criticisms and suggestions which will prevent perhaps many repetitions of the same errors. You also avoid reducing to habit some act or procedure which achieves the result, but by a round-about or wasteful way. It has been found that teachers increase their skill in classroom technique more rapidly if they are rated by their supervisors by means of an analytical teacher-rating scale, and are shown exactly where they need improvement, than if they are simply left to their own devices.

7. See how others do the same act. One of the remarkable things about most operations involving skill is that there are so many possible and different ways of doing them, and the more complex the act the greater the variety of methods which may be employed. If you become acquainted with the methods used by several persons, you can pick the one which seems best to you.   Certainly you cannot be sure of finding the best method when you know only one.   In adopting methods used by others you at least know that they have been tried out and have proved reasonably successful.   To go a step farther, however, and adopt the methods used by experts, is to have a reasonable assurance of having found the best methods.   It is, of course, one thing to know how a champion golf player hits the ball, and quite another thing to hit it that way yourself; nevertheless, knowing how the champion hits it should be of some service.

8. Find out what constitutes good form in the task, and then adopt it.   Each task or act of skill has its own particular elements of good form.   There is a best way to stand, a best way to sit, a best way to hold your instruments, and other ways of doing these things are productive of inferior results. Good form in golf is not the same as good form in baseball or tennis, nor is good form at the piano the same in all respects as good form at the typewriter. The handwriting specialists have found quite definite connections between success as a penman and such qualities of form as position in front of the table, manner of holding the pen, placement of the paper, etc.   In order to obtain the best results in learning any act of skill, it is necessary to find out what constitutes good form in that particular act, and then to adopt it.

9. Start right.   First impressions are more lasting than later ones, and the associations that are formed first tend to endure longest. These first impressions are hard to erase and exercise an important influence in directing the channels through which nervous energy flows in later experience. When a word is seen for the first time misspelled, it is far more difficult to learn, since the old association has to be dissolved before a new one can be substituted. The degree of ultimate skill attained depends very much upon the kind of beginning that is made. The first attempt should be reasonably correct and in line with the final results to be reached.

10. **Keep out of "blind-alley" methods.** There are many methods of procedure which look good at first, but which lead to certain failure at the end. If you choose them instead of more genuinely sound procedures, you simply waste a large amount of time and effort and eventually have to come back to the point from which you started. The unfortunate thing is that such wrong procedures do not always merely waste your time. They may even leave you in worse condition than before you began, with much to unlearn and with associations to break up which are practically indestructible. One of these blind alleys is the "hunt-and-peck" method of typewriting. Another is learning to speak a language by thinking in English and then translating the thought into the foreign tongue. Since you cannot always judge the ultimate results of a method before you have tried it out, it is a good plan to ascertain desirable methods from persons who have had experience in the particular line of

work to be undertaken, and to follow their advice even though it may not seem consistent with your own opinion in the case.

11. **Pay attention to the result rather than to the process.** As a general rule it is better to be conscious of what you expect to achieve than to be conscious of what you are doing with your muscles as a means of achieving it. An objective state of mind is more likely to obtain satisfactory results than is a subjective one, or one turned in upon itself. Particularly in acquiring skills of a somewhat social type, such as the ability to speak in public, the objective attitude is very important. If you are self-critical and self-conscious you have little mental power left to devote to the task in hand. It is better to think about what you want to say than about the kind of impression you are making or your posture or delivery while you say it.

12. **Acquire speed as well as accuracy.** To be really skillful in an act you must learn not only to perform it correctly but rapidly. If you can write the most beautiful and legible hand imaginable, but lack speed, you cannot be considered successful in handwriting. Efficiency demands not only a good result, but economical procedure in securing that result and time will be one of the foremost factors determining that economy. Before you complete your learning process, then, you must take definite steps to secure speed of performance. Throughout the entire practice period this should be kept in mind as an ultimate objective,

but it should be one of the major objectives in the latter stages.

13. Sacrifice speed in favor of accuracy in the early stages of learning a thing. However important speed may be as a final aim or objective, accuracy is a much more important element in the early stages of studying a subject. When associations are first being formed in a study, a single error does more harm than many correct performances can repair. If you try to hurry, you make so many mistakes that you may even make negative progress. The foundation for speed later on must be laid in accuracy and perfection in the beginning.

14. Learn the elements of an operation together instead of separately. To carry out the entire operation at once may seem like an impossible and wasteful method of learning, and the temptation to learn one element or process at a time and then put them all together later may at times be very great, but in this case appearances deceive. The trouble with the plan of learning the parts separately is that they do not readily assemble themselves on demand into a unified whole. They have a queer and baffling tendency to persist as separate parts. Barton reports the results of an experiment in learning typewriting in which he found it wiser to practice writing whole words in connected sentences from the start than to practice the various strokes by means of exercises involving one part of the keyboard at a time. Similar experiments in other kinds of work have shown similar results, all agreeing on the general principle that it is better to learn the elements together than separately.

15. Do not let yourself be deceived by plateaus in your learning curve. The learning curve is seldom a steady upward incline. It more often consists of a series of sudden rises followed by what have been termed "plateaus." You learn rapidly at first, then apparently make no improvement for a while, after which you suddenly begin to improve again. The causes for these plateaus are numerous and varied. A common one is loss of interest. You stop improving because you lose interest and so do not try as hard as you did before. Another cause is the transition from lower-order to higher-order skills. For example, you are likely to have a plateau in the typewriting-learning curve at the point where you begin to react to words as wholes instead of to the individual letters in words. While you are making these new adjustments your total score for speed may even suffer a temporary decline. Then there are plateaus due to fatigue, which you may later get over when you have taken a rest or have got your "second wind." The whole policy of the learner toward plateaus may be summed up in the advice which was once given to an athlete: "Remember that when you are at the point of exhaustion and feel like giving up, your opponent is probably at the same point, and if you hold out a little longer he may give up first."

16. Practice with the will to learn. Practice has little effect on the formation of nervous connections or the real development of skill unless it is accompanied by the will to learn. If you have strong pressure behind you, or if you have a powerful motive for acquiring the skill, you can materially reduce the amount of practice that will be necessary. Certain telegraphers, it is said, have been known to send messages for ten or fifteen years without any increase in the rate of sending, and then, with the work motivated by an offer of promotion conditioned upon the development of better speed, to acquire in a few weeks or months a much higher rate. Of course, it will be difficult sometimes for you to work up the desired will power or desire to learn, but a few suggestions looking toward good methods of doing this may be found in Chapter VIII, "Developing Interest."

17. Increase your skill by repetition. The old adage has it that "practice makes perfect." While this is not absolutely true, and while much depends on the kind of practice followed, nevertheless it is certain that perfection is not to be had without practice. Each time you exercise a given nervous connection you cement that connection that much more firmly. The law of exercise is a central law in all learning; and it is simply that learning takes place by performing the act to be learned. Other things being constant, your skill in a given act depends on the number of times you repeat that act.

18. Keep your mind on the act while you practice it. "Attentive repetition" is a much-used term in treatises on the psychology of habit-forming.

Simply to repeat an act is not enough; you must repeat it with your attention concentrated on it. If your mind wanders off to other things, errors are likely to occur that will set the whole process back to the beginning. Even if errors do not occur, inattentive practice lacks the pressure or intensity necessary to give it effectiveness. Some persons have acquired such skill that they can perform acts, such as playing the piano, for example, without thinking about them, but in performing those acts they are not learning. The learning has already taken place, and when the acts are carried on automatically and without attention, the learning has come to a standstill.

19. Permit no exceptions. Each departure from the regular way of performing an act breaks up the associations already formed, and tempts you to repeat the same error. The "just one little drink" is enough to overcome many months of temperance on the part of one who has made a New-Year's resolution, and the policy represented by "this one lapse doesn't count" is equally dangerous in any form of practice. Whether you count the exceptions or not, Nature does, and every one of them registers deeply in the tissue of your nervous system.

20. Distribute practice over several periods. It is better to practice in several short periods than in one long one. For instance, piano practice should be for an hour a day rather than for seven hours on one day. If a man is to become a great musician his training must be distributed over a number of years; no amount of concentrated practice after reaching maturity can completely compensate for lack of musical practice during earlier years. In practicing foreign-language pronunciation, it is better to work for six periods of ten minutes each than for one period of an hour. Each time a thing is forgotten and relearned it becomes more permanently fixed, and the short-period plan makes the most of this fact. There is a limit, however, to the value of this plan. That limit is reached when practice periods become so short that they only allow time for warming up.

21. Provide rest periods as well as practice periods. Fatigue is a serious enemy of learning, and if practice is carried to the point of serious weariness more harm than good is done. Not only does fatigue cause errors and exceptions to occur, but it has a hindering effect on interest and in that way may retard learning. Rest periods likewise accomplish more than the simple prevention of fatigue. They actually promote learning. They allow the results of practice to "set" or crystallize, very much as a rest period gives concrete a chance to harden. James's statement that we learn to swim in winter and to skate in summer is based on his recognition of the positive part played in learning by rest periods, as is also the common policy among colleges and universities of having students study several subjects for a number of months instead of a few subjects, each for a short and concentrated period.

22. Learn beyond the threshold. Unless you

carry practice beyond the point required for present performance you will be unable to perform the act at a future date because of forgetting. Even after you reach the point where you can do the thing perfectly, it will be necessary to go on and practice for a considerable length of time in order to store up a reserve fund of skill sufficient to enable you to function after considerable forgetting has taken place. In a sense this extra learning is insurance against failure through forgetting; or it may be thought of also as a reserve stored up for emergencies.

23. Employ more refined methods as you near the limits of perfection. The nearer you approach to the maximum of speed or the absolute limits of perfection, the more it costs to secure a given unit of improvement. The writer recently saw a man clear the bar in a pole vault at 13 feet 9 inches. Probably the last 9 inches had cost him more effort and practice than had the other 13 feet all combined. He was able to acquire these last marginal units of skill only by the adoption of the most refined methods known to the sporting world. If a few additional units of achievement are known to be worth the effort that gaining them requires after you have approached close to the limits of the humanly possible, then it becomes necessary to search for the more refined techniques which are known only to the few greatest experts, and to spend an enormous amount of time in mastering the artistic touches and more subtle elements.

24. Measure your progress. Plan the work so

that you can make some definite check-up or measurement of your accomplishment. Keep a record of your achievement for each attempt or for each practice period. List your achievement for each trial in a regular column or table, or possibly translate each into the form of a graph, where you can get a visual impression of it. Try not only for a high score each time but also for a higher score than you have previously achieved, thus competing with your own past record. It has been found that when school children had access to handwriting scales their penmanship improved because the scales made possible a measurement of individual progress that before that had been impossible.

25. Practice under varying conditions and situations. A skill that is extremely specific in nature is of less practical value than one which can function in a wide variety of situations. Car-driving skill that is associated only with a Buick or a Dodge is inferior to that which applies to many makes of cars. Probably it is well, in the early stages, to learn an act in one particular setting until it is thoroughly mastered there, but ultimately practice should be carried on under other conditions and circumstances which will help to generalize the skills acquired and thus produce greater adaptability. Slight variations in the setting of the act may do much to enlarge its field of possible application and thus enable it to be used in a greater number of different life situations.

26. When other sources of guidance are lacking,

experiment.   If you cannot secure directions or guidance from books or from other people, and cannot solve your problem by reasoning it out, try something and see what happens.   Passively waiting for a method to present itself to you is a futile plan; you will have to work for the method.   After all is said and done, there will always be much need of "trial and error," or of trying something and then trying it again in the light of the results of the first trial.   The successful man, however, is the one who does not resort to trial and error until other better methods have failed, and who, when he does resort to it, experiments with his eyes open and his mind alert for anything he can learn by each attempt.

27. Do not strive for a degree of skill that is not worth its price.   The development of any particular skill is subject to the law of diminishing returns. You acquire less and less skill for each additional unit of practice devoted to it.   For example, six weeks of practice in typewriting may give you a rate of thirty words per minute, but the next six weeks will not raise the rate to sixty, nor the third six weeks to ninety.   It costs more to get the second thirty words than to get the first thirty, and it may take years to secure the last few words required for winning the world's speed contest.   The question then becomes one of determining what degree of skill is absolutely essential, what additional amounts would be desirable, and when it ceases to be worth while to pay the added price.   If there were no other skills to be acquired except the one in hand there might be no limit to the amount of practice that would be worth while, but, since practice on one thing means neglect of others, you will have to distribute your efforts among the various possible skills in the proportions that will give the greatest possible returns.

28. Keep the mind off automatic acts.   Some things are better left to habit than subjected to conscious guidance by reason or intelligence.   In fact, thinking about certain things is an actual hindrance to their performance. For example, the writer has no trouble at all in tying his tie under ordinary circumstances, but a number of times he has become distinctly confused by the question of what to do with each particular hand, and has had to forget it and begin all over again in order to get the tie tied.   Typists report that if they think about their keys or their fingers they become confused and make errors.   This point is very appropriately illustrated by the following rhyme from some unknown source:

> The centipede was happy quite
> Until the toad, for fun,
> Said, "Pray which leg comes after which?"
> Which wrought her soul to such a pitch
> She lay distracted in the ditch
> Considering how to run.

QUESTIONS AND EXERCISES

1. Outline the chapter by arranging the twenty-eight points into a few major classes or families.
2. List ten specific kinds of school work which you are doing which involve primarily the development of skill.
3. Restate each of the twenty-eight points as it would specifically apply to your principal skill subject.
4. What points in the list appear to contradict each other? How can the contradiction be explained away?
5. What is the biggest thing you have learned from the chapter?

MATCHING TEST

Directions: Write beside each number the number of the paragraph in the chapter which discusses it.

.... 1. College schedules.
.... 2. Accuracy first.
.... 3. Beating your own record.
.... 4. Rate of practice.
.... 5. Self-activity.
.... 6. Regularity of progress.
.... 7. Self-consciousness.
.... 8. Hothouse education.
.... 9. Spaced repetition.
.... 10. Direct method in foreign languages.
.... 11. Self-analysis.
.... 12. Finer points of technique.
.... 13. New-Year's resolutions.
.... 14. First attempt.
.... 15. Supervision.
.... 16. Adaptability.
.... 17. Handwriting position.
.... 18. Imitation.
.... 19. Concentration.
.... 20. Trial and error.
.... 21. Motivation.
.... 22. Judd's experiment.
.... 23. Law of diminishing returns.
.... 24. Whole method.
.... 25. Law of exercise.
.... 26. Aimlessness.
.... 27. Thinking versus habit.
.... 28. Overloading.

TRUE–FALSE TEST

Directions: Indicate which statement is true and which is false, using plus (+) for true and zero (o) for false.

.... 1. Plateaus are natural and normal parts of the learning curve.

.... 2. The most profitable practice is that which you can do without thinking about it.

.... 3. Success of penmanship bears little relation to the way you hold the pen.

.... 4. One long practice period beats several short ones.

.... 5. It is better to forget yourself and think of what you expect to do.

.... 6. It is better to practice alone than in the presence of others.

.... 7. Speed is an essential element in efficiency.

.... 8. Practice makes perfect.

.... 9. It is better to learn typewriting by connected sentences than by fingering exercises.

.... 10. If you fail, try again and do not bother to find out why.

.... 11. Learning takes place even while you are not practicing.

.... 12. Speed is a minor matter in the earlier stages of practice.

.... 13. Practicing after a thing is learned is wasted energy.

.... 14. Touch typewriting is a blind-alley method.

.... 15. You should not attempt anything that is clearly beyond your capacity.

.... 16. The greater your desire to improve the less practice you need.

.... 17. Trial and error can never be entirely eliminated.

.... 18. It is better to imitate an average performer than a highly skilled expert.

.... 19. The more skill you have the harder it is to get further improvement.

.... 20. Learning from books is more economical than learning from ordinary experience.

.... 21. Knowledge of why often interferes with skill.

.... 22. It costs more to get progress when you are first beginning than when you are quite expert.

.... 23. To acquire skill you must know what you are to accomplish.

.... 24. You should allow occasional exceptions as a means of relaxation.

.... 25. A skill should be acquired in a very definite and specific setting.

.... 26. A word once misspelled is harder to spell than before.

.... 27. Thought is always a better guide than instinct or habit.
.... 28. Handwriting scales promote progress in penmanship.

SHORT–ANSWER TEST

Directions: Answer each question or complete each statement by inserting a word, phrase, or brief answer.

1. How does science aid in learning practical arts?........
2. You learn by your own ....
3. Whether you succeed or fail you should find out ....
4. Practice periods should be longer than the time required for ....
5. Why is a right start so essential to learning?........
6. Why does self-measurement improve progress?........
7. How can you be sure of getting the best method of doing a task? ....
8. What is the chief cause of plateaus?........
9. Inattentive practice is poor because it lacks ....
10. When is trial and error procedure desirable? ....
11. To be skillful you must not only do the act well but ....
12. The case of telegraphers who suddenly gained speed after years of no progress illustrates the importance of ....
13. Learning is more certain if you are reasonably sure of ....
14. Practice is blind unless you have a ....
15. What is a blind alley in study?........
16. The main essential of acquiring skill is ....
17. Learning beyond the threshold really means providing a ......
18. Why does practice under various different circumstances produce superior results?........
19. Why is it wasteful to learn the parts of an act one at a time? ....
20. How much thoroughness should you strive for?........
21. The effect of a rest period is to give associations a chance to ....
22. What is meant by good form?........
23. The best way to achieve speed is by ....
24. The effect of exceptions in practice is to ....
25. The hardest units of achievement to gain are ....
26. When is reason a poor guide for action?........
27. What principle in acquiring skill is involved in teacher-rating? ....
28. The objective attitude in practice means ....

READINGS

1. Book, W. F.: *Learning How to Study and Work Effectively*. Ginn & Co., Boston, 1926.

    Chapter IX, "The Rôle of Habit in Learning How to Work Effectively."

2. Edwards, A. S.: *The Fundamental Principles of Learning and Study*. Warwick & York, Baltimore, 1920.

    Chapter IV, "Learning and Habit-Formation."

3. Kitson, H. D.: *How to Use your Mind*. J. B. Lippincott Co., Philadelphia, 1916.

    Chapter IV, "Formation of Study Habits."

4. Lyman, R. L.: *The Mind at Work*. Scott, Foresman & Co., Chicago, 1924.

    Chapter II, Section III, "The Formation of Good Habits."

5. May, M. A.: *How to Study in College*. Syracuse University Press, Syracuse, N.Y., 1923.

    Chapter X, "The Drill Type of Study."

6. Parker, Samuel Chester: *Methods of Teaching in High Schools*. Ginn & Co., Boston, 1915.

    Chapter VI, "Acquiring Motor Control." Chapter VIII, "Practice or Drill."

7. Waples, Douglas: *Procedures in High School Teaching*. The Macmillan Co., New York, 1924.

    Chapter XVII, "The Drill Lesson."

CHAPTER VI

MEMORIZING

To many persons the terms "study" and "memorizing" have about the same meaning. Throughout the ages memorizing as a method of learning has held a prominent position in schools. While the method has often been misused and abused, and has been employed largely to the exclusion of thought and appreciation, nevertheless it is, and probably always will be, an important element in study. The following suggestions may help to improve its effectiveness.

1. Apply the general principles for acquiring skill. The procedure for memorizing and the procedure for acquiring skill are subject to the same general principles and laws. Much of the chapter on skill, therefore, should be re-read in its relation to the present chapter. For example, a correct start, the will to learn, no exceptions, spaced repetition, etc., are as important in memorizing as in habit-formation. Furthermore, much of the present chapter on memory is distinctly applicable to the previous chapter on habit, and should be studied in that light. The basis for distinguishing between principles of memory and of skill is not clearly defined in this book and no attempt at minute psychological precision has been made. Points have simply been classified under one or the other head according to their major emphasis, and some points are included under both heads when their applications are sufficiently different to justify separate mention.

2. Adapt the method of attack to the nature of the material being learned. Psychologists tell us that there is really no such power as memory, but that we have many memories. They mean that, for example, our ability to remember poetry does not necessarily help us to remember names and faces or to keep our appointments. Many persons have spent time and money on memory-training courses in the hope that they might get some kind of general formula or method of attack which would serve in all situations which demand memory. This is a vain hope. The methods of memorizing one kind of material are not equally good for memorizing all other kinds. The memory is exceedingly susceptible to training, but only in specific ways and in relation to specific kinds of material. The procedure to be recommended for memory training, then, is simply that of acquiring the specific skills and tricks for the various specific kinds of material to be memorized.

3. Understand the material to be memorized. Meaningful material is easier to memorize than nonsense material. Before attempting to memorize, then, it is best to study the undertaking in order to get the central idea. In learning textbook or lecture material it is frequently necessary to look up the meanings of unusual words in the dictionary or to translate the passages into your own terms.

If you understand the material, you can learn it by thought units, but if you do not, you have simply to memorize an enormous number of words.

4. Form associations between the new material and what you already know. What you already know may be compared to a hitching-post to which you can tie new knowledge. Since what you really know is already fixed and established in your memory, whatever is firmly associated with it also becomes fixed and established. Certain patented memory-training courses which are on the market employ this principle in a somewhat arbitrary and doubtful way by having you memorize thoroughly a hundred isolated words, to serve as hitching-posts or filing-trays, and then memorize your shopping list, for example, by associating each separate item in it with one of the hundred words, beginning with the first and proceeding in regular order. The general and fundamental principle upon which this device is based is sound, but the device itself is probably of little worth to the average individual. Whatever you expect to be able to recall later on must be associated with something which you are certain will still be in existence at that time. If you tie a knot in your handkerchief in order to remind yourself to stop at a friend's house, and then lose the handkerchief, you do not remember to stop — unless, of course, you have formed some other association. If you memorize a lecturer's words, but do not associate them with their meanings as expressed in terms of your own previous knowledge and experience, those words do not enable you later on to recall his ideas.

5. Group the elements that are to be memorized. Automobile license plates are now constructed on the plan of grouping the numbers into bunches, as 1–318–859, for example, instead of presenting a solid array of numbers, such as 1318859. The reason is that a large number can be much more readily memorized when arranged in groups than when the figures are run together. The same thing is true of other forms of memorizing. For example, try memorizing the following series of syllables as it is printed, simply as a series of twelve: *zig, baf, jer, pif, jan, fal, vek, rin, kaj, lun, mur, jif.* After you have learned these syllables, try a different method on another twelve, bunching them into three groups of four syllables each, as follows:

> *pag, kug, dal, raz,*
> *tiv, kap, pud, zab,*
> *mis, gar, fon, vip.*

If you have a number of isolated details to remember, try to group and classify them into a few main groups or patterns, and then learn these few things rather than the many parts. It is easier to remember the whole word *cat* than it is to remember the three letters, *c, a, t.*

6. Employ some logical form of association. Before starting to memorize, arrange the material into some logical sequence or order, so that the mind can take hold of it. For example, the items may be arranged in the order of their importance, either ascending or descending, or in the order of chronological sequence in the time series, or they may be classified by sizes, colors, causes, countries, etc. — any basis being employed that the nature of the materials permits. The point is simply that a miscellaneous list is much more difficult to remember than a classified list. In order to see the truth of this statement, contrast the difficulty of memorizing the series, *banana, oats, barley, celery, lemon, wheat, spinach, asparagus, apple, corn, orange, rye, carrot, turnip, apricot*, with that of memorizing the same words arranged in three natural groups — fruits, vegetables, and cereals — (1) *banana, lemon, orange, apple, apricot*; (2) *celery, spinach, asparagus, carrot, turnip*; (3) *oats, barley, wheat, corn, rye*.

7. Trust your memory. Unless you have confidence in your ability to remember, you are not likely to remember. Public speakers report that on the platform, the fear of forgetting is one of the most common causes of forgetting. One of the complaints sometimes made against note-taking is that it destroys the ability to remember without notes, because no habit of trusting the memory is formed. One of the outstanding features of some of the patented memory-training courses is the effort to build up a person's confidence in his own ability to remember. The student is given an initial exercise which appears to be very difficult, but which in reality turns out to be quite easy; his reaction is to the effect that he didn't know he could memorize so well, or that he can already see improvement in his power to memorize. If such courses succeed only in establishing self-confidence and willingness to trust the memory, they have rendered worth-while service.

8. Learn with the intention of retaining. What you learn only for to-morrow will stay with you only until to-morrow. What you learn only for final examination day will leave you after the final examination day, if not sooner. Unless you have a determination to remember, and feel a personal responsibility for retaining what you have learned, it fades out quickly. If a thing is really worth remembering, it should be learned for all time, and not for temporary recall only. A strong intention to remember has somewhat the same effect upon retention that the plan to awaken at a certain time has upon your sleep. The mental "set" persists even after conscious attention to the matter has ceased, and carries out your original intentions without your direct conscious supervision.

9. Learn under high pressure. Fast-moving automobiles wear out roads more rapidly than slow-moving wagons, even in spite of their rubber tires. The difference is due to their superior speed. Each impression that they make is made with high intensity. The same principle holds in memorizing. If you are working with vigor and intensity you make more lasting impressions on your nervous system than when you proceed in a leisurely way. Students have been known to learn more in two hours' application at high pressure before examinations than in a period many times that long when there was less pressure. Such learning probably had comparatively little permanent value, it is true, but the fault may easily have lain in the lack of any serious intention to remember permanently, rather than in the speed with which the knowledge was acquired. There is a caution which should be observed in connection with this point — namely, that when high pressure begins to produce nervousness or frenzy it begins to lessen the value of the results obtained.

10. Attempt recall as you learn. After you have made a start at memorizing something, test yourself out by trying to repeat it without looking at the book. Or put away your list and see how many items you can think of without help. This not only intensifies your mental process, but also serves somewhat as a measurement of your degree of success and as a basis for the guidance of your future repetitions. The value of attempting recall as an aid to learning is now so thoroughly established that the method has been definitely crystallized into school practice by means of examinations, surprise tests, and daily recitations.

11. Use the "whole" rather than the "part" method. It is ordinarily better to repeat the entire poem, chapter, or unit of material from beginning to end once and then go over it all again than to break it up into stanzas, paragraphs, or small units and memorize one at a time. That is hard advice to follow because with this method you do not have the sense of success or of immediate accomplishment that results from working by the "part" method. That sense of achievement is deferred until along toward the end of the process, when suddenly you seem to learn the whole thing all at once. Two reasons why the "whole" method is preferable are: (1) It embodies the principle of spaced repetition, since a longer interval lapses between each repetition of a given unit than in the "part" method. (2) It associates each unit with those preceding and following it, instead of associating the end of each unit with the beginning of the same unit. A slight departure from a strictly "whole" method, however, is often desirable. When the various parts are of distinctly uneven difficulty, it is more economical to employ a "part" method on those that are more difficult, after the others have been learned, taking care to finish up the process with a few repetitions by the "whole" method to connect thoroughly all the parts.

12. Make use of rhythm as an aid to memory. The reason that we usually think of poetry when we hear the word "memorizing" is that poetry lends itself with special ease to memorization. Rhythm has been used for ages as a servant of memory. Probably the legends and myths of primitive peoples would never have survived had it not been for their rhythm. They were put into poetic form and sung or chanted by the bards in many a festive hall, becoming so firmly implanted in men's memories that they were remembered by generation after

generation, even before they were reduced to written form. We are all familiar with such jingles as "Thirty days hath September," which represent the same device as that used by the ancient bards merely applied to more modern problems. Students dealing with statistics, or copying large numbers, find rhythm helpful in the task of remembering numbers during the interval between seeing them and writing them down. They adopt the plan of bunching the numbers and repeating them rhythmically, as, for example, 2-5, 3-4-6, 1-3, 9-4-7, instead of employing the more monotonous form 2-5-3-4-6, and 1-3-9-4-7.

13. Establish the kinds of bonds that you will need later. Learn according to the way that you are to use your material. If you expect to use it orally, memorize by reciting aloud; if silently, then practice silently. If you must meet a situation where your knowledge is to be expressed with the help of your hands, memorize it in connection with the use of your hands. Methods of memorizing the spelling of words have in recent years shifted considerably from oral to written because of our recognition of the importance of this principle and of the fact that our recall of the spelling of words is limited almost wholly to situations involving writing.

14. Establish several different kinds of bonds. The more different kinds of bonds you use in associating ideas the more likely the ideas are to remain associated. If you bind them together by

means of a visual image, then by writing them down together, then by saying them over together, then by doing something with them in an overt muscular way, all these various bonds tend to supplement one another. Not only is the total strength of the association increased by the use of a variety of ties, but the likelihood of recall under various different circumstances or situations is greatly increased. Different kinds of bonds, in other words, serve you in different situations, and if you have several types of bonds established, your knowledge has greater adaptability or greater ability to function in more than one way. There is a limitation to this principle, however, as is illustrated by Æsop's fable about the cat and the fox. The fox had a hundred tricks for escaping the hounds, and the cat only one. When the hounds appeared, the cat climbed into a tree and the fox began his tricks. He was finally captured after having tried the last one. It may be well to learn the spelling of a word by several different methods, but at least one of these methods must be learned so well that it actually works!

15. Repeat the material orally. Oral repetition in memorizing has two major advantages. One is that it involves a greater amount of muscular effort than does silent repetition. By exercising the speech muscles over and over, you literally impress the material upon your muscles in addition to impressing it on your mind. To put the matter in other words, you form kinæsthetic bonds. Another advantage of oral repetition is that it has an auditory by-product. You not only say what you want to remember, but you hear what you say. This enables you to build up auditory images which are effective aids to memory. There is one danger, however, in oral repetition. It is somewhat likely to degenerate into a purely rote-memory method. It may become merely a word-calling process without any genuine mental accompaniment.

16. Visualize. We have all had the experience of remembering a point by recalling that it was located in a certain position on the page, say near the bottom on the left-hand side. Visual images of this kind play an extremely important part in memory. Sandwick devotes one section in his book, *How to Study and What to Study*, to the suggestion, "Make a synopsis and visualize it." If there are many points in a chapter and you make a neat and condensed outline of them on paper, a clear mental picture of the page is often sufficient to enable you to recall them all.

17. Use mnemonic devices. We have all employed some such trick device for remembering isolated details as the use of "Roy G. Biv" for recalling the colors in the spectrum or "Sinking Fund Smith" for recalling the initials of the Mr. Smith who is the head of a bond house. Or possibly we recall the telephone number 2550 by thinking of it as $25.50. Such schemes often prove quite serviceable, particularly if they are reasonably simple and grow naturally out of the material learned. They may readily prove our undoing, however, when they become so elaborate as to require more mental effort than would be required to memorize the material by unaided rote memory. Some people work harder to memorize their memory devices than they would have to work to memorize the material itself.

18. **Develop your own individual methods.** You cannot hope to adopt in every detail the methods of memorizing employed by others, just as you cannot hope to copy every detail of their dress, facial expression, or personality. Each person is likely to discover or devise methods of memorizing and remembering which are peculiar to his needs and by which he can get his own good results. It is well to recognize these individual differences, and to realize that the memorizing methods which are good for persons who are quicker or slower than yourself may not be suited to you. For example, you should not be discouraged if you cannot get results by a method which is suited only to persons considerably more gifted than you. Or, if you are an auditory type of person, you need not hope to be as successful by a visual method as is a person of the visual type. Even after we learn a great deal more about methods of studying than we know now, there will still be wide room for individual initiative and choice.

19. **Memorize some things by rote.** Memory work is like most other tasks of life in that it involves a certain amount of "dirty work"; that is, work which requires just plain hard labor or brute strength. Some people spend more effort in trying

to avoid hard work than it would cost them to "get down to business" and do the work. The scramble for "white-collar" jobs in the vocational world has its counterpart in the search for "royal roads" and "master keys" and "sure things" in mental pursuits. Some things, as for example a list of German adverbs or prepositions, simply have to be memorized by main strength and effort because they do not lend themselves naturally to any "high-class" method yet known to educational experts. This fact should not, however, be taken as a justification of memorizing by rote when better methods are available.

20. Allow a fallow period between periods of learning. The permanency of an impression is determined by the impressions which immediately follow it. It has been known for many years that if the mind is forced to shift from one task immediately into another, without a moment of pause, there is an increased tendency to forget what was learned in the first period. It seems that the mind needs a little time in which to "set its house in order" or to "straighten things up" or to consolidate what has been gained, and that, if you allow a short period of idleness or free meditation under relaxed conditions after finishing a period of study, and before you take up a different kind of work, you increase your chances of mastery. To this rest period has been applied the term "fallow period," borrowed from the agricultural practice of letting land lie idle until it recovers its fertility.

21. Review at intervals.   Even with the best methods of learning, memories tend to fade with time.   It has been found that most forgetting takes place within the first twenty-four hours after learning, and that from that point on the decline is very gradual until there is practically no trace of the memory left.   After a thing has been learned and forgotten, however, it is easier to relearn than it was to learn the first time and is also more easily retained.   Each time the material is reviewed and mastered afresh, the residue that is retained after the first few hours or days is increased.   This fact explains why reviewing lessons at intervals after they are learned is so much to be desired.

22. Resort to verbatim memory only when there is a good reason.   Probably the word "memorizing" immediately calls up to most people the idea of "learning by heart," or verbatim memory.   As a matter of fact, however, this learning by heart is one of the least common of our memorizing experiences.   To memorize means to impress something upon the mind so strongly that it can be retained until a later time; the process may not even involve words at all.   For example, you "memorize" a person's face, or his house, or his automobile when you impress it on your memory so that you can recognize it or recall a mental image of it.   Similarly, you can memorize a chapter by acquiring an understanding and appreciation of its main points, even though you are unable to repeat the exact words of the author.   Verbatim memorizing in study should ordinarily be eliminated or else reduced to a minimum.   Sometimes it is necessary, as when memorizing a formula or a poem, but as a general rule it is wise to memorize ideas rather than words.   Even when verbatim memory is employed, care must be taken that ideas are learned in addition to the words, else the words are useless.

23. Forget useless knowledge.   There is no advantage in making your mind an attic or a trashpile.   There are enough live and important and necessary things to be remembered to utilize all your available brain capacity without your attempting to accumulate all the musty and useless ones.   In fact, there are many things you might like to know which you really cannot afford to know, because effort devoted to them is simply effort withdrawn from other things of greater importance.   Your memory is very much like your money in this respect: it is useful only while it is in circulation. A miser's gold is of no benefit either to him or to others, and facts stored in the memory but never used had better never have been learned.   Encyclopædias are much more desirable storehouses for mere facts than are human brains — in the first place because they have a greater capacity for content, in the second place because their contents are more systematically classified, and in the third place because they can be consulted more readily than brains by the inquiring public.

QUESTIONS AND EXERCISES

1. Show as many ways as you can in which memorizing and acquiring skill resemble each other.
2. Make an outline for the material in the chapter.
3. What points do not agree with your own experience in memorizing? How?
4. Memorize the points in this chapter, applying to the task the rules that are laid down.

MATCHING TEST

Directions: Write beside each number the number of the paragraph in the chapter which discusses it.

....	1. Speed.
....	2. Repeating long or short units.
....	3. "Common labor" in memory.
....	4. Classification.
....	5. Kinæsthetic bonds.
....	6. Relation of new knowledge to old.
....	7. Changing from one task to another.
....	8. Confidence in memory.
....	9. Law of forgetting.
....	10. Reciting to self.
....	11. Variety of associations.
....	12. Learning in the way you are to use it.
....	13. Meaning as an aid to memory.
....	14. Special tricks for memorizing.
....	15. Learning by heart.
....	16. Mental images.
....	17. Combination.
....	18. General faculty of memory.
....	19. Individuality.
....	20. Relation between habit and memory.
....	21. The mind as a rubbish pile.
....	22. Remembering primitive legends.
....	23. Will to remember.

TRUE–FALSE TEST

Directions: Indicate which statement is true and which is false, using plus (+) for true and zero (o) for false.

.... 1. Rhythmical material is more easily memorized.

.... 2. It is better to memorize anything by rote than by memory devices.

.... 3. One of the chief services of patented memory courses is establishing confidence in your ability to remember.

.... 4. If you must use knowledge in muscular ways you should learn it by muscular practice.

.... 5. It is better to learn a thing well through one of the senses than to attempt exposure through several senses.

.... 6. Remembering depends upon method of memorizing and not upon intention to remember.

.... 7. Some things should be learned by purely mechanical methods.

.... 8. It is better to learn a selection as a unit than a few lines at a time.

.... 9. Miscellaneous items are harder to memorize than homogeneous items.

.... 10. Most forgetting takes place in the first twenty-four hours.

.... 11. Nonsense material is the easiest to memorize.

.... 12. Trying to recall as you memorize aids learning.

.... 13. If you have an idea in your head you can recall it.

.... 14. Learning the exact words of a piece of material is usually undesirable.

.... 15. Training to memorize poetry aids remembering facts.

.... 16. High-pressure learning before examinations gets more than ordinary results.

.... 17. To try to recall something by its position on the page is poor technique.

.... 18. Bunching items into groups aids memory.

.... 19. The psychological lines between memory and habit are very sharply drawn.

.... 20. You should not try to retain everything you learn.

.... 21. The auditory results of oral study are more a hindrance than a help.

.... 22. A period of idleness between two different tasks aids learning the former task.

.... 23. There is no real difference between the method best for bright and for dull students.

SHORT–ANSWER TEST

Directions: Answer each question or complete each statement by inserting a word, phrase, or brief answer.

1. After a few repetitions you should ....
2. Why is written spelling preferable to oral? ....
3. Why are automobile license numbers bunched by three's? ....
   ....
4. How does rapid learning affect retention? ....
5. Learning through visualizing, speaking, and writing illustrates the use of ....
6. The thing that makes poetry easy to memorize is ....
7. Before starting to memorize you should first ....
8. Why do speakers on the stage forget their speeches? ....
9. How do the rules for memorizing relate to those for acquiring skill? ....
10. To learn a fact you should connect it with ....
11. Why is what you learn just before an examination often soon forgotten? ....
12. The part method should be resorted to for ....
13. What is implied by the statement that we have many "memories? ....
14. Why does classification aid memory? ....
15. What should be one's attitude toward verbatim memory? ......
16. Why cannot all people memorize a thing alike? ....
17. When should rote memory be used? ....
18. What is the effect of turning immediately from one task to another? ....
19. The danger in oral learning is that it is likely to be ....
20. When is knowledge valuable? ....
21. What should be one's attitude toward mnemonic devices? .....
22. What is the main service of reviews to memory? ....
23. What is the best way to use visualization to remember the points in a chapter? ....

READINGS

1. Adams, John: *Making the Most of One's Mind.* Geo. H. Doran Co., New York, 1915.

   Chapter III, "Manipulation of the Memory."

2. Book, W. F.: *Learning How to Study and Work Effectively.* Ginn & Co., Boston, 1926.

   Chapter XIX, "How to Memorize or Fix in Mind the New Knowledge and Facts Learned."

3. Cunningham, William H.: *Character, Conduct and Study.* G. P. Putnam's Sons, New York, 1926.

   Chapter XIV, "How to Go about Memory Work."

4. Edwards, A. S.: *The Fundamental Principles of Learning and Study.* Warwick & York, Baltimore, 1920.

   Chapters X–XI, "Memories and the Permanence of Acquisition."

5. Headley, Leal A.: *How to Study in College.* Henry Holt & Co., New York, 1926.

   Chapters VI–VII, "How to Remember."

6. Lyman, R. L.: *The Mind at Work.* Scott, Foresman & Co., Chicago, 1924.

   Chapter IV, "Reading to Understand and Remember."

7. McMurry, F. M.: *How to Study and Teaching How to Study.* Houghton Mifflin Co., Boston, 1909.

   Chapter VII, "Memorizing."

8. May, M. A.: *How to Study in College.* Syracuse University Press, Syracuse, New York, 1923.

   Chapter VII, "The Memory Type of Study."

CHAPTER VII

THINKING

THE ability to think is one of the outstanding traits which distinguish man from the lower animals. Without thinking, adaptation and ready adjustment to new situations are very difficult. Much school work consists of some kind of thinking or problem-solving. The aim of the following paragraphs is to help to secure not only more thinking, but a better quality of thinking as well.

1. **Define the problem.** All thinking originates in a problem, a doubt, a perplexity, or a difficulty. If you have no choice or decision to make, or no goal to reach, or no obstacle in your path, you do no thinking. In other words, you think only when you have to. The quality of your thought life depends upon your ability to discover and to define problems. The poor thinker does not see the problem until it is immediately before him, and even then he does not know exactly of what it consists. The good thinker sees the problem more quickly and particularizes, or localizes, or defines it exactly and precisely, then proceeds to attack it with a definite plan of procedure.

2. **Do your own thinking before consulting other people.** Unless you think your problem through as far as you can, before reading or talking with others about it, you sacrifice the opportunity to make

original contributions to it.   A minister was asked
how he managed to preach an original sermon on a
well-known text upon which thousands of other
men had already preached.   His reply was that he
outlined his own sermon before reading anything
on the subject, and then read all available sermons
that had bearing on it.   He said that, in preparing
his sermons, if he did his reading first he could only
follow the course of one or more of the other writers,
but that by doing his own thinking first he could
preserve his originality.   A scientist who has directed numbers of research investigations reports
that his directions to his workers are first to perfect
and file with him a complete and detailed outline of
the plan of procedure to be followed, then to read
what other investigators have done, and finally
to revise the original plan in the light of suggestions
gained from others.

3. **Recall what you already know about the problem.**   The best source from which to procure new
ideas is the supply of old ones with which you start.
If you want to be a good thinker, accumulate a
worth-while supply of information and organize it in
such a way that you can recall it readily when you
face a problem.   If you recall the solutions of previous problems, you are able to start on the new
one where the old ones left off; if not, you have to
go back and solve the problem from the beginning.
It frequently happens in geometry classes that the
proof of a proposition is long and difficult because
preceding theorems have been forgotten; it becomes

necessary to work out again what should be easily quoted as having been previously demonstrated.

4. Obtain an abundant supply of material with which to think. Thinking does not take place in a mental vacuum. You must have some facts or information with which to work. If you are to become a good thinker, you must first acquire a rich and varied fund of experience and accumulate a large body of facts. The material for thought may be compared to that used in building construction. The contractor requires brick, mortar, lumber, nails, and such things; without them all his technical ability would be useless. The mere possession of information, however, is not enough to produce a good thinker. A knowledge of medicine does not qualify you for thinking in the field of law, nor does a knowledge of geometry theorems enable you to solve any of the political problems that confront the Nation. Quite often some man of prominence makes himself ridiculous by expressing his opinions on matters of which he really knows nothing. Your knowledge must be associated and organized if it is to serve you well in thinking. You must not only have ideas, but have them in a usable form. Nor should all your material for thinking be stored in the memory. It will usually be necessary to hunt up new material having a bearing on any problem of importance that confronts you.

5. Secure stimulation from a variety of sources. Do not become a slave to one particular system of thinking or take all your mental food from a single source.   Compare different viewpoints on the matter under consideration and try to see all sides of the question.   If you borrow a given number of ideas, they will do you better service if they come from different types of writers or thinkers than if they all come from a single type.   Ideas obtained from books are not likely to offer the same kind of contribution as that offered by ideas obtained from interviews or observations; scientific books generally provide a different type of stimulation from that secured from popular books.

6. Collect and evaluate all available suggestions. You are not prepared to accept one solution of a problem until you have collected several other solutions with which to compare it.   In a sense every solution of a problem divides itself into two stages — collection and evaluation.   In the first stage you gather together the whole array of possible answers, or as nearly complete an array as you can, and in the second stage you undertake to evaluate them. Probably a more definite and conscious distinction between these two stages would improve the quality of thinking.   The specialists in research have gone so far as to devise elaborate and systematic procedures for these steps, and the usual research report treats the collection and the evaluation procedures separately.

7. Do not expect to develop ideas in perfect form at once. The associative process is not particularly systematic or orderly.   Ideas do not come into your mind in outline form, neatly classified and arranged in groups. That is characteristic of the final result of the thought process rather than of the process itself. You must catch every good idea that floats through your mind, reduce it to record, and finally arrange, classify, compare, organize, and refine these ideas and reduce them to definite form.

The importance of unsystematic and imperfect suggestions as aids to originality may be illustrated by a case taken from the field of art. A professor of art, who was himself a successful painter, was asked how he conceived original ideas for his paintings. His method is as follows: He takes a piece of paper and makes at random a number of meaningless marks, continuing until the space is well filled with a network of tangled lines. He then lets his imagination play on these lines — in much the same fashion as you let your fancy see the clouds as representing birds, camels, or lions — until some idea is suggested which seems worthy of being elaborated into a painting. For instance, a sharp point where the pencil reversed its motion may be imagined by him as the tip of a dragon's tongue, and immediately other lines seem to stand out from the rest as representing his back, feet, or tail. When the idea has taken definite form in his mind, he deepens the lines for these main features and then copies the whole in more perfect form on more permanent materials. The parallel between this process and ordinary thinking is very close. You cannot produce an original intellectual product in perfect form without some kind of raw material to begin with. You have to gather some kind of ideas together, however crude they may be, and work them over into more refined form.

8. Adopt some definite plan for covering the field systematically. Unless you work systematically, you may go over and over one phase of a problem and never touch on some of the other phases at all. Chance or impulse will guide you in weighing or judging no better than in gathering the original data. It will be necessary to adopt some systematic scheme for focusing your attention upon all the essentials, so that you will know when you have covered the whole field. Benjamin Franklin's method was to write the factors for and against the question to be decided on opposite pages of his notebook, then to study them for several days in order to be sure that he had given each its due share of attention, and finally to make his decision by canceling off opposing arguments that were of equal weight and noting which side had the uncanceled residue. Some such plan as his is very much to be recommended, since it insures careful consideration of all the data and prevents basing the decision on a part only.

9. Employ active methods of forming new associations. Original ideas seldom come as the result of passively waiting for them to present themselves. Most great inventions are due to active effort. The inventor focalizes his attention on the problem and works at it for a long period of time. If you dwell long enough on a problem, keeping your mind actively engaged all the time, something new is obliged to present itself. One way to do this is to thrust the topic into contact with other fields or problems and try to see at least some connection between it and them. This might be called the "rolling snowball" method of thinking, since the thought starts with a nucleus and grows by absorbing whatever it comes into contact with. Incidentally, some of the apparently irrelevant or inappropriate suggestions that are met with in the course of this type of thinking turn out, on later examination, to be most helpful, just as even the sticks and grass that are rolled into the snowball help to give body and strength to the mass. A graduate student who is working on a thesis finds, after a period of time, that almost any topic which comes up has some kind of relation to his thesis topic. There are many possible associations or bonds between almost any two topics; your part in thinking is to go out actively in search of them and actually establish them.

10. Analyze the problem into its parts and think on one at a time. Split the topic up into its elements for a simplified attack, and work on each element individually. Analysis aids fertility of ideas. When you break the problem up into five parts, you can think of as many different things about each part as you originally could about the undivided whole. Then, having treated each of the parts, you can work back and forth between them all and make each suggest new things with regard to the others. This point may be illustrated by what happens when pebbles are thrown into a

pond. If you want to break the water into ripples as thoroughly as possible, throw the pebbles into several different places on the surface rather than all in at the center. Each wave thus caused starts a series of waves from its own center, and the interference of all these sets new waves going in still different directions. Similarly in order to cover the whole area and scope of a problem, it is necessary to start at several different focal points.

11. **Make use of writing as an aid to thinking.** Writing is a very effective ally and servant in original thinking. Its values are numerous and varied. What you have written down serves to stimulate new ideas. The written record of previous thoughts serves to prime the pump and start the flow of new thoughts. Writing things down facilitates comparing them later on and thus aids originality. The effort to find a word to express an idea often clarifies the idea itself, or perhaps stimulates a new and better one. The concreteness and the muscular activity involved in writing tend to hold the mind on the problem, and thus aid concentration and persistence in solving it. The writing helps to keep the whole problem before you and to prevent your thinking in fragments. It has been compared to the nails which a carpenter uses in building to hold things together while he works on another part of the structure. By the use of writing you get all your ideas recorded, and then have them kept safe for you until they are needed. Moreover, the method insures the leaving of a cue by which to take up the

thread of the thought after it is broken. You can more effectively judge and evaluate the elements in a problem if they have been reduced to definite and tangible form. Writing is also helpful in this connection in that it enables you, to a certain extent, to separate the collecting from the evaluating process, and thus permits you to do one thing at a time.

12. Stimulate your thinking by talking with others. A good way to think a subject through is to talk it over with some one else. Not only does the other person's comment suggest to you new ideas, but what you yourself say causes new ideas to take form in your own mind. Talking has many of the same advantages as writing as an aid to thinking, in that it involves a definiteness of formulation that greatly promotes the crystallization of clear thinking. It is for this reason, in part, that governments are carried on by means of parliaments, committees, and cabinets, where talking things over can make for more adequate thinking on the problems discussed.

13. Use questions to stimulate and direct your thinking. The use of the question as a teaching device is very old indeed, and its persistence in service has been in large measure due to its value as a stimulus to thinking. The questions which are asked by the teacher or the textbook are useful, so far as they go; then come questions which you yourself originate. If a subject is to be covered thoroughly, a good plan is to start by listing every question which you might reasonably hope to answer, and then to add new ones as they come to mind during further study of the problem. Each new question may shed some light on previous ones, and as questions are answered the answers will suggest new questions. A good test of your ability to think on a given topic might well be to list all the pertinent questions that you can ask about it.

14. Rearrange and reclassify your ideas from several different viewpoints. A good way to do some new thinking on a special subject is to write down on a separate card each main fact or idea that comes to you, shuffle the cards thoroughly, and then try to classify the ideas. The process helps to break up certain old associations and to allow new ones to be established in their places. This point may be illustrated by the fact that it is easier to secure the beautification or improvement of a city after a major calamity, such as an earthquake or a fire, than in normal times. Ideas take on new meanings when they have a new environment. Robinson [1] calls attention to this fact under the caption "Necessity of Resynthesizing Knowledge." He also points out that the progress of scientific discovery in certain fields was retarded for years simply because, in certain classifications of knowledge by libraries, those fields were given obscure rank. If you want to cover a field thoroughly, go over it according to one classification, then reclassify it according to some different plan, and continue in

[1] Robinson, James Harvey: *The Humanizing of Knowledge*, p. 69. Geo. H. Doran & Co., New York.

this way until a proper degree of thoroughness has been attained.

15. Promote thinking by means of comparison and contrast. Comparing or contrasting two things is an excellent way to analyze them into their elements. The search for likenesses and differences results in a more complete grasp of the relationships of the various elements involved. Many things cannot be evaluated except in comparison with other things. A man is not handsome, nor a woman fair, except in terms of comparison with other human beings. There are few musicians who have a sense of absolute pitch, but almost any one can tell whether one note on the piano is higher than another. The essence of good thinking, therefore, is to be able to make good comparisons. Many errors of thought are traceable to neglect of this point. For example, certain people have decided that all the students in a school should be required to study a particular subject because it has been clearly shown to have value, but they have not taken the trouble to compare the value of that subject with other subjects which it is expected to displace. A thorough realization that everything in the world is relative would make for considerably greater accuracy in thinking.

16. Employ tabular and graphical aids to thinking. A central concept in the statistical form of thinking is the reduction of a number of individual cases to an average or single number which is representative of what they all have in common, but which omits or discards what is peculiar to an individual case. The first step in arriving at such a general measure of all your cases is to tabulate them. As soon as you get all things of a kind together, you are in a much better position than you were at first to study them and to see their real significance. When the facts are not only arranged in tabular form, but also translated into charts or graphs for visual analysis, their interpretation is still further improved. The writer has found that graduate students think more clearly regarding their thesis problems when they employ graphs to represent their data than when they do not. Possibly there may be a question as to which is cause and which is result, but it is quite apparent that the two things are related.

17. **When the importance of the problem justifies it, solve it by means of specialized methods of research.** Research is simply a systematic and refined technique of thinking, employing specialized tools, instruments, and procedures in order to obtain a more adequate solution of a problem than would be possible by ordinary means. It starts with a problem, collects data or facts, analyzes these critically, and reaches decisions based on the actual evidence. It involves original work instead of mere exercise of personal opinion. It evolves from a genuine desire to know rather than a desire to prove something. It is quantitative, seeking to know not only what but how much, and measurement is therefore a central feature of it. It involves,

furthermore, the use in the natural sciences of special instruments of precision, such as telescopes, barometers, and stop watches, and of rotation experiments, correlation coefficients, or internal criticism of documents in the social sciences. The ordinary unspecialized student should at least know that such specialized instruments and procedures are possible, and that the ultimate solutions of problems must be checked and verified by careful research. Incidentally, it might be well to mention the importance of putting more faith in the conclusions of men who have done such scientific thinking, than in those of men who bid for popular support on the strength of their unsupported opinions.

18. **Do some thinking as idle meditation or free association.** There are some problems that are more readily solved under conditions of freedom and relaxation from purposeful work than under a vigorous form of direct application. Mere reverie, musing, meditation, fancy, or daydreaming may not solve many of the urgent practical problems of an industrial age, but neither will the work-type of mental procedure produce the inspiration for some of the greatest things in the realm of art. The more highly original forms of creative thinking may not readily be harnessed to systematic and methodical techniques.

19. **Give time a chance to aid your thinking.** Time aids thinking in two ways, by letting you forget some things, and by letting you discover some other things. In the first place, it makes possible

the severance of the old associations, so that your ideas may make new combinations or assume new arrangements. "Sleeping on a problem" is good, because it enables you to free yourself from the obsessions of yesterday, or to free yourself from bondage to a single overpowering idea. In the second place, time permits new associations to form and new ideas to arise which cannot be forced at one sitting. The solutions of some of the world's greatest problems have come as the seemingly spontaneous fruits of uncontrolled idle meditation. When a problem has once become definitely fixed in mind, and the search for its solution actively begun, it never completely rests. When you are off duty or thinking of other things, this problem still acts as a magnet and draws to itself any related idea which passes through consciousness.

A great many successful thinkers report that they consciously let their problems "soak" or "simmer" or "stew" for a while as a means of thinking them out. Several professors report that they prepare their addresses for scientific conventions by starting on them early, then letting them "soak" for a long time, and finally organizing them shortly before they are to be given. A dean of a large university reports that he always carries around several weighty administrative problems in the "soaking" stage, and prefers to leave each about two weeks before taking it up finally for definite solution. A college student who has an extraordinary record reports that he keeps a list of "things to be studied over" on his desk and adds new ones as they develop, checking off the old ones as they are solved.

20. Enlarge your vocabulary. The superiority of man over animals along intellectual lines is in large measure due to his possession of language. The larger our vocabulary, the greater our capacity to think. In fact, the psychologists have found that size of vocabulary in itself constitutes a fairly satisfactory intelligence test. A word is a sort of abbreviation for an experience or set of experiences that one has had. For example, the word "good" stands for all the experiences of one particular type that a person has had, and the word "cold" stands for another set. If our thinking had to be carried on in terms of the actual experiences themselves, instead of through the medium of their condensed abbreviations, the whole thing would be so slow and so cumbersome that only the simplest forms of reasoning could be completed. Yet that is exactly what happens when one does not have a large vocabulary. He must simply confine his thinking to the more concrete problems of the immediate environment and neglect the more complex and abstract problems. Our vocabulary might be compared to the carpenter's tools. The carpenter who has only a hammer and a saw can do certain simple labors, but before he can become an expert workman he must have chisels, augers, planes, squares, levels, plumb lines, and so forth. Each new word in a person's vocabulary corresponds to a new tool in a set, and opens up that many more possibilities of skilled workmanship in intellectual things.

21. Be sure that your terms are clearly defined.
Thinking is carried on by means of words, or symbols, with which your ideas are associated. If the matter that is associated with a given word is uncertain, or if it varies from time to time, the result is comparable to that which would be produced by measuring objects with a rubber tape-line. One of the very common errors in thinking is just this failure to define terms, or, as one writer expresses it, the tendency to use "woolly ideas." In employing technical terms it is very essential that you use them in their technical sense rather than according to your own choosing. The content of a given word should remain constant, furthermore, throughout the whole thinking process, instead of expanding and condensing at different times as you proceed. For example, if you are reasoning with regard to the values of "science" and at one time let the term mean about the same as "education," at another, limit it to "natural science as studied in schools," and then later use it as synonymous with "scientific method," you will very likely reach unsound conclusions. To define is to set the limits of the thing defined, and the more definite and precise your terms the more dependable will be the reasoning that results from their use.

22. Be sure you have all the data before you.
Conclusions should not be drawn until all the facts are considered. One of the serious weaknesses in a great deal of thinking is the tendency to make decisions without adequate data, or, which is worse,

without any data at all. It is very easy to make the error of generalizing before all the evidence is in, or of generalizing on the basis of one or two cases, or of generalizing on the basis of selected cases which are not truly representative of the real situation. Two or three coincidences regarding the transference of thoughts will not establish mental telepathy as an actual process, nor does the fact that many red-haired people are high-tempered establish any real connection between red hair and high temper. If you are not in possession of all the facts required for a judgment, either hold your judgment in tentative form or else secure the necessary data. Governmental problems will serve to illustrate this point. The President has a large number of extremely important problems to solve, and he must not make mistakes, yet he cannot possibly know all the facts required for their solution. Consequently he has a large staff of experts whom he can consult for data in the various specialized fields. He does not consider it necessary to make snap judgments and so cover up his lack of familiarity with certain subjects, but freely consults those who are in a position to know. Surely the average student is no more expected to know everything than is the President of the United States.

23. Beware of substitutes. There are as many kinds of substitutes available in the field of thinking as there are in the commercial field, and the scholar must exert the utmost care to avoid confusing the genuine with the substitute. You usually think only when you are forced to do so for lack of any other means of meeting the situation confronting you. Frequently these other means of making your adjustments are entirely adequate, and there is no particular value in using the higher mental processes. In other cases, however, you have all the feelings of satisfaction without the real justification for it, and are content with substitutes without knowing the difference. The process in such cases may be classified under the general head of "rationalizing," or hunting up excuses for doing what you are going to do anyway. When you rationalize you are not conscious that you are deceiving yourself. You think you have arrived at your decisions by sound reasoning, and that your action is based on logical justification, when as a matter of fact you have been deceived by a mere substitute for thought. There are so many of these substitutes that a few of them are treated in the next six paragraphs.

24. Eliminate the emotional factors. It is hard for a person to reason clearly when he is angry or in love because his emotions smother the rational faculties. The same is true with regard to the other emotions. When we turn on the emotions we almost automatically turn off the intellect. A good rule to follow is never to make any important decision while under the influence of some powerful feeling, whether anger, grief, or exultation due to success. Certain shrewd salespersons know how to appeal to emotions of vanity, greed, or even to parental love to such an extent that they can sell

customers what they do not need, the victims being
skillfully induced to base their decisions upon emotional rather than intellectual considerations. Of
course the emotions have their place in the guidance
of conduct, and they are important factors in our
evaluations of things and propositions; the purpose
here is simply to warn against giving them complete
control and then making reason assume the responsibility for the results.

25. Discount your prejudices. If you already
have dogmatic notions or prejudices about a question, you are not likely to give it a fair consideration.
For example, if you are a Republican your mind is
more or less closed to any merits that might lie in
the Democratic Party. We all have a considerable
body of fixed ideas of this sort which are constantly
being used as substitutes for genuine thinking. The
meaning of prejudice is "judging beforehand," or
determining your course of action before considering
the facts in the case. Although self-analysis is
rather difficult for most people, it is at least worth
while to suggest that, when you are faced by a problem about which you have strong convictions, a
good policy is to make a considerable allowance for
your bias and give the other side the benefit of the
doubt.

**26. Distinguish between facts and your own
personal interest.** It is difficult to arrive at a decision which you know will be contrary to your own
selfish interest. You can almost convince yourself
that black is white, or that north is in reality

straight up if it is sufficiently to your advantage to reach such a decision.   This fact explains why the quality of the thinking that is done on the subject of governmental legislative problems is so poor.   The persons who do the thinking are often actuated primarily by selfish interests and, however honest they may be, their decisions are seriously influenced by unconscious considerations of the probable profits or losses to self or to the special groups represented.

27. Do not surrender yourself to the power of suggestion.   It is a trait of human nature to accept as true whatever we hear or read, even when it is presented without evidence or competent authority. We all believe we should buy Ivory Soap because it floats and is 99 44/100 per cent pure, but we have little knowledge, if any, as to how Ivory Soap really compares in value with other brands.   We learned during the World War that suggestion is a thing of tremendous power in the control of human be-havior, causing a great many men to give their lives willingly without knowing exactly why.   We ad-mire the heroism and patriotism of those men, but we can hardly refrain from asking whether that war would have taken place if those millions had been more disposed to ask for the evidence and to make decisions of their own instead of accepting uncriti-cally the decisions handed down to them.   Students have a noticeable tendency to accept as true what-ever appears in the textbook, or, still worse, what-ever the teacher says.   Their faith is almost as great as that of the boy who had become engaged in an argument of the "'Tis so, 'Tain't so" type and was challenged for his authority. His reply was: "'Tis so 'cause pa said so, and if pa said so it's so even if it ain't so."

28. Do not base decisions on chance. Some people dodge the difficult task of thinking by flipping a coin. Others do a similar thing less openly when they unconsciously let their decisions turn on very trivial incidents. The tenderfoot "just happens" to meet the swindler and "just happens" to lose his money, as he sees it, but it was not a chance with the swindler. There is really no such thing as chance. Everything has a cause. We use the word "chance" to signify causes which we have not analyzed or do not understand. Whether a penny falls heads or tails is simply a matter of the combinations of forces which have operated upon it. Likewise there is a reason back of everything you do, and if you do not know what it is it would be a good idea to find out. The causes operating to influence your decisions may be random and unselected, or they may be accidentally or purposely selected to mislead you. In any event, there are so many more ways to go wrong than there are to go right that chance is a poor substitute for thinking.

29. Use analogies and figures of speech cautiously. Figures of speech are like fire in that they are extremely valuable servants but dangerous masters. They help to direct attention to the particular elements they represent, but they do this so well that they frequently take it completely away from some of the other features that should not be over-looked. The fact that two situations are alike in some striking way — or even in several, for that matter — does not necessarily mean that your responses to the two should be identical. A single factor in one of the situations may call for a striking difference in your response to the two cases. Yet the natural tendency is for you to assume that, since the two are alike in a few points, they are alike in all. For example, hundreds of superstitions have been due to this false use of analogy. Take the idea that it is wise to plant potatoes "in the dark of the moon" and beans "in the light of the moon" because one vegetable develops its fruit beneath the soil and the other above. The analogy between the behavior of the moon and of the two plants is very loose indeed, but numbers of people have been content to base their thinking and action upon it.

30. Criticize your thought process according to the rules of logic. In olden times the scholars hoped to produce great thinkers by teaching formal logic, but they failed because they did not teach their students any facts or content to which to apply their logical steps in thinking. The fond hopes of the early enthusiasts for logic have not been realized. Knowing the nature of the thought process or the rules for good thinking has not produced good thinkers. And yet, while we may not hope to carry out our thought process strictly according to formal rules of logic, there is probably much to be gained by checking the final solution or proof against those rules as a part of the verification process. At least a number of good scholars report their own formulas for doing this, such as the following: What is given? What is wanted? What is done? What is found? What is shown? This is a somewhat home-made formula, but any systematic list of steps by which to check up your results is probably better than none.

31. Always check or verify your solution or else hold it as a tentative one. Test it out first in the imagination. Write down or repeat your decision, along with the reasons upon which it is based, and see if it seems of true value after reaching its final form. Then try it out and see if it works. There are too many possible sources of error in reasoning for you to rely upon your logic without an actual verification of some kind. The main difference between philosophy and science is that the former asks whether a thing is reasonable and in harmony with sound logic, while the latter asks whether it will work out in actual fact. When it is impossible to verify your solution by actual experiment, keep it in mind as a tentative solution only, and keep on trying to verify it. Some of the world's greatest problems are still in this unverified stage. For example, the atomic theory has never been completely verified. If a case demands immediate action before a perfect solution has been found and verified, go ahead and act on the most plausible solution possible, but do so with the definite realization that you have been forced to compromise and that your act is subject to revision.   There is no more excuse for idleness and inactivity, because you have not reached a perfect solution, than there is for considering a question eternally settled merely because practical necessity has forced you to adopt a course of action before reaching a final solution.

32. Avoid the tendency to be academic by constantly checking your thinking against actual cases. In mediæval times the greatest scholars gave days and even years of their time to the consideration of such questions as how many angels can stand on the point of a needle, yet they were the very people who would persecute such a man as Galileo for daring to make a telescope for more accurate and refined observation of the real nature of the universe.   The old story of the two boys who were quarreling about the color of the horse's tail, and found on going to the stable that both were wrong, has its counterpart in the thinking of many people who build elaborate intellectual structures only to have them topple when they try to apply them to actual situations.   The quality of thought is improved when observations replace suppositions as the chief foundation.

33. Summarize the results of the thinking in a few words.   The test of your clearness of thinking is your ability to express the meat of the whole thing in a nutshell.   If you really see plainly what is involved, you can condense it to a few words, and if not, you have to go round and round.   As a means of clarifying your own thoughts it is a good plan

to take stock, at intervals, of all that has been accomplished up to that point, and then to summarize the whole matter at the end. After an unusually interesting and thoughtful class discussion, on one occasion, the writer congratulated the members of the group on the excellent thought they had given the question under consideration. One student, a bit more discerning than the rest, or a bit more bold, ventured to ask, "But just what have we decided on?" This question was the greatest contribution that had been made to the class during the whole period, because it brought out the summarization of the thought which would otherwise have been overlooked.

QUESTIONS AND EXERCISES

1. Outline the chapter by classifying the thirty-three points into four heads as follows: (a) Problems, (b) Material, (c) Procedure, (d) Miscellaneous suggestions.
2. Make a new outline of the chapter, this time classifying the material under the following heads: (a) How to get more thinking, (b) How to get better thinking.
3. What are the three most valuable and the three least valuable points in the list?

MATCHING TEST

Directions: Write beside each number the number of the paragraph in the chapter which discusses it.

.... 1. Part versus whole.
.... 2. Technical terms.
.... 3. System.
.... 4. Influence of feeling on thought.
.... 5. Forcing new associations.
.... 6. Orderliness of association processes.
.... 7. Bias.
.... 8. Likeness and differences.

.... 9. Collection versus evaluation.
.... 10. Visual aid to thinking.
.... 11. Selfishness.
.... 12. "Thinking it over."
.... 13. Speech as an aid to thought.
.... 14. Recitation method of teaching.
.... 15. Short circuits in thinking.
.... 16. Manysidedness.
.... 17. Taking things on faith.
.... 18. Information.
.... 19. Science of thought.
.... 20. Scientific thinking.
.... 21. Final inspection.
.... 22. Memory.
.... 23. Reverie.
.... 24. Pedantry.
.... 25. Originality.
.... 26. Superstitions.
.... 27. Having facts available.
.... 28. The value of writing.
.... 29. Supply of words.
.... 30. Locating the difficulty.
.... 31. Luck.
.... 32. Condensing.
.... 33. Loose-leaf thinking.

TRUE–FALSE TEST

Directions: Indicate which statement is true and which is false, using plus (+) for true and zero (0) for false.

.... 1. If you wish to be original you should not read what others have thought.
.... 2. The meanings of facts vary according to their classifications.
.... 3. A large vocabulary aids thinking.
.... 4. Figures of speech are unreliable instruments for thinking.
.... 5. Prejudices hinder thinking.
.... 6. New ideas usually come from those you already have.
.... 7. Ideas come into the mind in logical order.
.... 8. If you really understand anything you can state it in a few words.
.... 9. If you decide a thing by chance you are as likely to be right as wrong.

.... 10. Emotions should be suppressed because they interfere with thinking.

.... 11. Questions stimulate thinking.

.... 12. The results of thinking should be tested out chiefly on the basis of internal consistency.

.... 13. Logic has been the greatest instrument for improving thought.

.... 14. Human nature demands a reason for every action.

.... 15. You can think more effectively if you write your thoughts down.

.... 16. The highest type of thinking is rationalizing.

.... 17. When you start solving a problem you should not stop until you are through.

.... 18. It is better to break a problem up into its parts when thinking on it.

.... 19. Research aims primarily to prove something.

.... 20. Idle daydreaming never produced a worth-while thought.

.... 21. Thinking is impossible without facts.

.... 22. To define a word means to quote its dictionary meaning.

.... 23. It is easy to bribe the intellect.

.... 24. You should never act on a decision until you know it is sound.

.... 25. Saying what you think clarifies your thought.

.... 26. Everything is relative.

.... 27. Thinking is better if based on a single stimulation than if based on several.

.... 28. The test for soundness of a decision is whether it is based on two or more cases.

.... 29. Benjamin Franklin's method of thinking was one of allowing free play to his impulses.

.... 30. Meditation is the best way to stimulate new ideas to arise in the mind.

.... 31. Getting all things of a kind together facilitates thinking about them.

.... 32. Thinking is impossible unless there are at least two possible courses of action.

.... 33. Collection should precede evaluation of suggestions.

SHORT–ANSWER TEST

Directions: Answer each question or complete each statement by inserting a word, phrase, or brief answer.

1. Why are governments conducted by parliaments and committees?........
2. Before making a decision you should have .... before you.
3. Written procedures for thinking are good because they make for ....
4. Why is the recitation so much used in teaching?........
5. What is the term for finding excuses for doing what you want to do?........
6. Aside from permitting you to think of new points, how does time aid thinking?........
7. The order in which thoughts arise in the mind is very ....
8. Why can you not think clearly about a love affair?........
9. What type of thinking is best suited to the fine arts, as contrasted with practical arts?........
10. What should you do in thinking on a problem about which you have a strong bias?........
11. You are not justified in accepting a solution until you have ....
12. Why can politicians honestly disagree so radically as they do? ....
13. Research differs from ordinary thinking in that it is more ......
14. Why do we buy Ivory Soap?........
15. If you borrow ideas you should borrow from ....
16. What is chance?........
17. Writing your ideas down on cards is good because it permits ....
18. To what extent does ability to think in one subject aid thinking in other subjects?........
19. Why are analogies often misleading?........
20. The chief value of tabulation as an aid to thinking is that it promotes ....
21. In order to be a good thinker you should remember the results of previous ....
22. What is the final step in the thought process?........
23. The value of any object or idea can only be arrived at by means of ....
24. A good way to prevent thinking in fragments is to resort to ....
25. What is the relation between words and experiences?........
26. The best check on the results of thinking is through ....
27. To be original you should think the problem through for yourself, then ....
28. Thinking is unsound unless the content of the terms used remains ....

29. How much has logic contributed to the improvement of thought?........
30. Before leaving a problem its solution should be briefly ....
31. You can think of more ideas on a given subject if you ....
32. You cannot think unless you have a ....
33. In thinking on a subject your procedure should be .... rather than ....

READINGS

1. Book, W. F.: *Learning How to Study and Work Effectively*. Ginn & Co., Boston, 1926.

   Chapter XX, "Learning How to Reason or Solve New Problems Effectively."

2. Boraas, Julius: *Teaching to Think*. The Macmillan Co., New York, 1922.

   The entire book is an excellent analysis of thinking and how to improve it.

3. Columbia Associates in Philosophy: *An Introduction to Reflective Thinking*. Houghton Mifflin Co., Boston, 1923.

   The book as a whole deals with thinking from the standpoint of logic and scientific method.

4. Cunningham, William H.: *Character, Conduct and Study*. G. P. Putnam's Sons, New York, 1918.

   Chapter XI, "Think."

5. Dearborn, G. V. V.: *How to Learn Easily*. Little, Brown & Co., Boston, 1918.

   Chapter V, "Is Your Thinker in Order?"

6. Dewey, John: *How We Think*. D. C. Heath & Co., Boston.

7. Earhart, Lida B.: *Teaching Children to Study*. Houghton Mifflin Co., Boston, 1909.

   Most of the book is devoted to thinking as a form of study.

8. Edwards, A. S.: *The Fundamental Principles of Learning and Study*. Warwick & York, Baltimore, 1920.

   Chapter VI, "Ways of Thinking and Pitfalls for the Student."

9. Headley, Leal A.: *How to Study in College*. Henry Holt & Co., New York, 1926.

   Chapter VIII, "How to Judge." Chapter IX, "How to Reason."

10. Kitson, H. D.: *How to Use Your Mind*. J. B. Lippincott Co., Philadelphia, 1916.

    Chapter VII, "How We Reason."

11. Lyman, R. L.: *The Mind at Work.*   Scott, Foresman & Co., Chicago, 1924.

    Chapter III, "Thinking and Learning to Think."   Chapter VI, "Evaluating What We Read and Hear."

12. May, M. A.: *How to Study in College.*   Syracuse University Press, Syracuse, New York, 1923.

    Chapter IX, "The Problem-Solving Type of Study."

13. McClure, Matthew T.: *How to Think in Business.*   McGraw Hill Book Co., Inc., New York, 1923.

    The whole book is an application of John Dewey's *How We Think* to the field of business.

14. Parker, Samuel Chester: *Methods of Teaching in High Schools.*   Ginn & Co., Boston, 1915.

    Chapter IX, "Reflective Thinking."

15. Sanford, Fernando: *How to Study Illustrated through Physics.*   The Macmillan Co., New York, 1922.

    Deals with the scientific method of thinking.

16. Waples, Douglas: *Procedures in High School Teaching.*   The Macmillan Co., New York, 1924.

    Chapter XV, "The Process of Reflective Thinking."   Chapter XVI, "Teaching Pupils to Think."

CHAPTER VIII

DEVELOPING INTEREST

JUST as trains do not go without engines nor street cars without electric currents, so study is impossible without interest and motivation to furnish the driving power. There is hardly any limit to what a human being can accomplish if only he is sufficiently interested. Since interest is so fundamental to every kind of study, any suggestions which will help you to secure it, even in a small degree, should be worth while. The following paragraphs present such devices and methods as have been mentioned by writers on the subject, or suggested by students who have wrestled with the problem in their own work.

1. **Know exactly what you are trying to do.** An automobile trip of a hundred miles to a definite place may be very enjoyable, but there are few persons who would care to ride for a hundred miles around one block, or wandering aimlessly on the highways from village to village. Lack of interest in school work is frequently due simply to a lack, on the part of the students, of any definite objective. Before starting a task, stop and ask exactly what you are going to try to accomplish. You may have to get help from the teacher here, but it is hopeless to try to become interested in an undefined and aimless piece of work.

2. **When not interested, ask for a reason for the work.** If you see no relation between your task and your goal, ask to have it pointed out. You have a right to know why you are doing any given piece of work, and you owe it to yourself to find out. Unpleasant work done without a reason is pure drudgery. Tell your instructor what your ambitions and aspirations are, and ask how you can use the present work to achieve them. Often a few minutes of personal conference between student and teacher can accomplish a meeting of minds that transforms the entire course from drudgery to purposeful and interesting work.

3. **Stimulate your interest by remote incentives in addition to immediate ones.** In practicing the reading of German for the Ph.D. language examination, the writer found the interest problem of considerable importance. Two procedures were tried. One was to read short stories, and the other to read novels. The latter method proved much the more satisfactory. In the reading of short stories one story would be finished in a short time and then it usually took a genuine struggle to begin a second one; but in the novel-reading the first chapter stimulated a desire to continue into the second one. So it is with the interest in school work. With only immediate ends to strive for, you have to fight your interest battle anew every day; but if there are larger and more remote ends to work for, each day's achievement will only add zest to the next day's efforts. There is also likely to be greater con-

tinuity of effort and greater conformity to some reasonable standard of work when you move toward a major objective than when you plan each unit separately, just as there will be fewer wasted miles of traveling when the whole journey is planned as a unit than when it is decided each day how far is to be traveled the next.

4. **Decide on your purpose in life as a means of getting interested in your studies.** The student who expects to be a physician or an engineer has a more favorable opportunity for becoming interested in his work than does the one who has not the slightest idea as to what he is going to do. When once you set up that major life objective, the intermediate steps, such as chemistry, English, or mathematics, become much more interesting, because they are clearly seen as steps leading to a desired goal. Having a life purpose in mind makes much more probable the choice of a proper course and adds enormously to its interest.

5. **Choose your studies with due regard to your interests.** It will be easier to become interested in what vitally concerns you than in a subject that is unrelated to your life or experience. In choosing your course of study it is important to consider carefully what your interests are and then adapt the course to them. One caution, however, is in order. Your education should not be entirely adapted or adjusted to your present interests, since one aim of education is to help in acquiring new interests. To this end you are sometimes required against

your choice to take courses which will provide a new point of view and open up new fields of interest.

6. **Keep interested from a sense of duty.** Bear in mind that the good student is one who shows an interest in his work, and determine to do your part to make your contribution or to raise the standard of your class or school by putting its work on as high a plane as possible. Arouse an interest in the work through an ideal of service, realizing that the more you do to help enliven the course, the easier you make it for both teacher and fellow students. If for no other reason, you can afford to put forth your utmost effort to become interested because of the personal satisfaction there will be in having done what is right.

7. **Surround yourself with suitable stimuli which will encourage you.** It is possible to set the stage, so to speak, for promoting the sort of thing you want to do. A motto posted over your door will serve as a constant reminder of your worthy resolution and an encouragement to live up to it. A convert who proclaims his new decision in church is more likely to live up to it than one who makes a silent and secret resolution to live a better life, because he has the expectations of his fellow men to meet, and that fact stimulates his determination. If you surround yourself with an environment of good books, busy and studious companions, and the paraphernalia of study, it will be much easier to keep up your interest than otherwise. This fact explains why so many who start correspondence courses do not finish

them. They lack the necessary environmental stimuli to maintain interest. It also explains why a well-ordered library is such an excellent place for study: the necessary stimuli are there.

8. **Wherever possible, use positive interests in preference to negative ones.** Spontaneous interest is preferable to forced interest. Interest in a reward is a better motive than fear of punishment; hope of success is more stimulating than fear of failure. Negative interests tend to cause a paralysis of effort, while positive interests tend to create a certain buoyancy or general feeling of well-being which is favorable to achievement. It is said that it is easier to keep up the morale in an offensive army than in a defensive one, since the former is inspired by hope of victory while the latter is inspired by fear of defeat. It is also said that the chessplayer who plays a defensive game is seldom the winner. It is much more conducive to interest to look to the desirable outcome of your task and forget, for the present, the undesirable consequences of failure to do the task.

9. **Make your studies interesting by applying them to everyday life.** Apply what you learn in the classroom to situations outside. Look for practical ways of using the subject, and ask yourself constantly what you can do with the things you are studying and learning. Do not let a subject be learned in a logic-tight compartment containing purely academic notions and concepts and shutting out the world of practical affairs. School work is

often lacking in interest just because of this scholastic or academic tendency to intellectual aloofness, or pursuing knowledge for its own sake and avoiding any contact with the "sordid affairs of practical life."

10. **Develop the ability to be interested in things in a purely intellectual way.**   To be interested in a problem which involves no practical application and no emotional satisfaction ordinarily requires a development as a scholar far beyond the rudimentary stages.   It is not possible in the case of ordinary untrained individuals.   The genuine scientist, philosopher, or scholar is able to dwell for hours or days on matters which to the ordinary layman are of no interest whatever.   In other words, these persons derive an intellectual satisfaction from their work which is denied to less thoroughly developed minds. The difference between pure science and applied science is largely one between an intellectual motive and a practical motive.   Civilization and education are in large measure due to the intellectual contemplation, meditation, and "idle curiosity" of a few keen thinkers who were able to detach themselves temporarily from pressing matters of present and local importance and mull over problems of a more general and abstract type.

11. **Increase interest by the exercise of your originality and individuality.**   Work out things for yourself instead of waiting orders from the teacher. Express your own choice about what you would like to do, and get the privilege of following it occasion-

ally instead of waiting for the teacher to plan something for you and take a chance on its appealing to your interest. Prepare term papers or special studies in connection with your courses, thus turning a portion of your time and energy into topics particularly suited to your own interest. In doing assigned tasks invent your own personal way of doing them, and thus make it possible to turn in a piece of work that expresses your individuality. There is no good reason for thinking that you must do the same thing that other people do, and in the same way. A blind attempt to copy another's style is deadening, and greatly lessens any enjoyment that could come from the work. Be yourself and do things your own way; the freedom of self-expression will make the result of much greater interest.

12. **Secure interest by means of the newness of experiences.** As a general rule we are more interested in the unusual than in the commonplace. New or striking facts are more interesting than what we have known for years. In choosing subjects and courses of study, therefore, select those that explore fields of which you are totally ignorant, so that there will be a freshness or novelty of experience. Exercise your originality in doing an assignment, and explore obscure portions of the field or try to put things into relationships that others have not yet discovered. The fact that the inventor gets such keen interest from his search for something new suggests that seeking new things in school studies will increase your interest in them. The stimulus that

normally arouses the instinct of curiosity is the presence of something new or unfamiliar which tempts to study and exploration.

13. Increase your interest in a subject by learning more about it. The more you specialize on a subject, the more interested you become. It is a common observation that teachers of particular subjects grow so interested in them that they lose interest in the other branches of knowledge. You will find a lecture of special interest if you study the subject beforehand and are sufficiently familiar with the topic to be able to say to yourself here and there, "That is my idea exactly." Further study on a subject of which you already know something gives you, at frequent intervals, an experience comparable to seeing a familiar face in a crowd composed chiefly of strangers. It is not to be understood that complete familiarity with a subject is the best way to develop interest, for when you have learned about it all there is to know, it becomes commonplace and uninteresting. But it is important to go thoroughly enough into the thing to discover the wonders and mysteries; then those wonders and mysteries will lead the mind on.

14. Derive interest from the sense of success. "Nothing succeeds like success," according to the old proverb. On the other hand, no greater obstacle to interest can be imagined than the knowledge that failure is certain. Next to the idea of certain failure is the idea of uncertain success as an interest-killer. If you do not know what you are trying to do, and do not know when you have finished it, or what really constitutes completion of the task, it is very improbable that you will have any sense of success. To be aware that progress is being made is a tremendous aid to interest. It is for this reason that you are usually most interested in the studies in which you are doing your best work. Avoid undertaking work beyond your capacity, since a failure in one piece of work is likely to create a feeling of failure in general and make it hard for you to keep interested in any of your work. Likewise, avoid taking more work than you can do well, since the knowledge that you are not doing good work will have a depressing effect and make all study more difficult and less interesting.

15. Undertake tasks which are difficult enough to offer a real challenge. In order to enjoy a rest, it is necessary to do enough work to get tired; and in order to have a keen sense of success in your work, it is necessary to face obstacles which really test your ability. The very fact that a thing is difficult makes it interesting, unless, of course, the difficulty is so great as to prevent success. A fisherman enjoys the sport much more when a fish puts up a vigorous battle than when it is easily landed. Some very bright and capable students have little interest in school because they have never undertaken anything that was difficult enough to challenge their ability.

16. Assume or pretend interest as a means of developing it. There was considerable wisdom in

Polonius's advice to his son, "Assume a virtue if you have it not"; for by the very effort to give outward evidence of the virtue it is easy to arouse the inner reality of that virtue. This is true, particularly, in connection with interest. If you sit up and look and act as though you were interested, soon you discover that it is not pretence, but that you have actually become absorbed in the task at hand. A task may be very uninviting, and yet, if you plunge in vigorously, it is likely, in a little while, to assume a different aspect. There is a close relation between external posture or attitude and its internal emotional accompaniment, and a change in one can bring on a change in the other.

17. Arouse and maintain interest through self-measurement. Keep a record of your results or accomplishments, so that you may have a sense of progress and of definite gains. Plot your curve of results, or post your best record and try to beat it. Compete with yourself by trying to beat the best that you have ever done before. Try to find where your strong and weak points are, in order to discover your interests and select the line of work in which you will be most likely to succeed.

18. Distinguish between lack of interest and low physical condition. Students frequently blame their subjects for being dull and uninteresting when the real difficulty lies with themselves — in a torpid liver, eye-strain, indigestion, lack of sleep, or over-fatigue. The highest degree of interest and mental vigor is impossible without a robust body and a normal and vigorous functioning of all its parts. Certain schedule adjustments, such as studying an uninteresting subject at a favorable time of day, frequently solve the interest problem to a surprising degree.

19. **Safeguard interest at the critical points.** Human nature is the same, in general, the world over, and to a large extent the same kind of thing that will cause trouble for one person will cause trouble for all. Accidents on highways tend to occur most frequently at certain critical points; it is necessary to erect danger signals at those points. So it is with interest in school work. Each task has its critical points at which interest is most likely to lag. Some of these may be briefly mentioned, although they are different for different types of work. One such critical point is at the very beginning. Before you get warmed up or thoroughly started on a task, it is very likely to lack interest. The old proverb, "Well begun is half done," concisely expresses this thought. A second critical point is where the novelty of first impression wears off. A third is where you have to change from lower-order to higher-order habits in the learning process, as when you shift from letter units to word units in typewriting. A fourth critical point is where you reach the point of relatively slow progress due to having approached the limit of perfection. It is very difficult to keep up interest in the advanced stages of drill work when it takes large amounts of drill to produce small increments of progress. Each

subject or task has its particular and individual critical points at which interest is likely to wane, but being aware of these dangers makes it easier to overcome them.

20. Make use of habit as an aid to interest. Many interests must be learned, acquired, or secured through the formation of habits. There are some persons who much disliked olives the first time they tried to eat them, but who learned, by persistence, to like them. The same kind of thing can be done in the field of study, by starting with a distasteful task and doing it so often that it becomes a habit, after which each repetition may bring keen enjoyment. Each repetition makes the nervous resistance less, and thus increases the satisfaction resulting from the act.

21. Let your emotions contribute to interest. The matter-of-fact, or prosaic, is usually less interesting than the emotional, or poetic. There are some people who lose much of the joy of living because they feel constrained to repress their emotions and keep entirely within the bounds of the conventional and prosaic. Education in general is suffering from specializing on things intellectual and neglecting to cultivate proper emotional or "feeling" states. If you will give yourself an opportunity to respond whole-heartedly to your subject, both intellectually and emotionally, you will be more likely to find joy in the work than if you repress all but the intellectual responses.

22. Borrow interest in school work from the fine

arts. Help to make the classroom attractive and interesting by coöperating to secure pictures and ornaments. Help to adapt such artistic elements to the kind of work that is to be done in the room. For example, if you are studying Spanish, help to dress up the Spanish room to radiate the atmosphere of Spain or South America; or, if the study is physics, help to secure for that room pictures that show great examples of engineering and of similar applications of science to the service of man. Take advantage of opportunities to see your subject in its artistic form, by attending plays, musical concerts, architectural exhibits, art galleries, industrial expositions, county fairs, and so on, as the case may be.

23. Utilize present interests to acquire new ones. Things that are intimately related to your present interests tend to be more interesting because of the association, just as a young man tends to develop an interest in music or in amateur photography if the girl whom he admires particularly is a musician or an amateur photographer. Any new interest can be acquired if it is properly connected with interests already possessed. To like one's teacher is in all probability to enjoy the subject she teaches. If the recitation period is particularly interesting, the assignment for the next lesson tends to be more attractive. Whatever you can do to associate an uninteresting subject with something in which you already have a keen interest will be of help in transferring your interest to it.

24. Secure interest by relating your work to your

instincts. Human beings are all endowed with certain inborn tendencies or instincts, such as the impulses to eat, to fight, to be afraid, to seek approval, to mate, to make things, to be with the crowd, to do as the crowd does, and so on. Acts that directly relate to one of these original tendencies are more interesting and enjoyable than those that are altogether new and only acquired. If you can adopt a method of study procedure which gives you a chance to express one or more of your innate instincts, your interest in the subject in hand is greatly improved. Some of the principal instincts and their applications to school work are discussed in the remaining paragraphs of this chapter.

25. Use your collecting instinct as an aid to interest. A squirrel collects nuts when he does not need them, and seems to get keen satisfaction out of each addition to his pile. Human beings have this same general tendency, which is capable of being adapted to the collection of many kinds of things, both physical and intellectual. If in your science work you will begin collecting specimens, such as butterflies, insects, geological fossils, minerals, etc., the subject will become fascinating and rousing your own interest in it will cease to be a problem. The same principle may be utilized in collecting ideas or experiences. If you are keeping a record of new facts, laws, principles, experiments, etc., and once develop a pride in your notebook, adding to the collection becomes an extremely satisfying experience. As an illustration of the power of such a collecting

hobby the writer's boyhood experience of counting
gray horses may be cited.   The game was to count
a hundred gray horses, and then to watch out for
the first girl walking down the lane, who was to be
his future wife.   He counted the hundred horses,
but he could not make himself stop at that point,
and the list grew to about a hundred and seventy-
five before it was possible for him to break up the
obsession.   This is a case of specialization on a
trivial or foolish sort of collecting, but the collecting
instinct can be turned to useful purposes as well as
trivial.

   **26. Increase interest by manipulation or construc-
tion.**   Muscular experiences are usually more interesting than those that are purely mental, such
as we get through reading books.   As a rule we enjoy handling an unfamiliar object more than we enjoy reading about it.   The reason manual training,
shop work, and laboratories in general are interesting is that they involve such a large amount of
manipulation and construction.   In order to put
interest into the abstract or non-laboratory subjects, therefore, try to introduce more of this manipulation element.   Making a neat and attractive
drawing to represent something in the lesson is one
way to do this.   Keeping a notebook is another.
Making a model, or a cast, or a chart to show the
relations of abstract things to one another will help
to serve the same purpose.   Developing an intellectual theory, and preparing a long paper to set
forth the results of your study of a given topic,

represent specialized forms of the application of the instinct of construction.

27. Use your pride in your own ability as an aid to interest. Try so to distinguish yourself as to gain the commendation of your teacher or classmates. Try to get good marks and grades, which give you, in turn, a feeling of success and of personal self-satisfaction in your work. Try for the honor of doing what others cannot or will not do. Try to win a place for your work in such school or classroom exhibits as exist, where you will be able to let others know what fine work you can do. Even if you are of lesser ability, a sense of personal pride should stir you to supreme effort to avoid being the poorest student in the class, or having the poorest specimen of work in the school exhibit.

28. Enter into various forms of competition. Pick out some person of about your own ability and try to surpass him. Compete against your own previous record or achievement. Try for rewards, prizes, or victory in contests. In contests between groups, coöperate to the utmost with your own group. When work is to be exhibited, try to win a place in the exhibit for yourself or your group. Competition is one of the greatest sources of motivation in life outside of school, and if properly used it is a splendid means of cultivating interest in school work.

29. Develop interest by means of imitation. Watching others do something worth while is likely to cause one to want to do the thing himself. In the story of *The Great Stone Face*, we read that constant observation of the face caused a transformation in the countenance of a certain observer. While this incident is purely imaginary, nevertheless it is quite true that we tend to pattern our life and conduct after the models we see about us. When we imitate or dramatize something, we make it a part of us. It becomes a reality embedded in the fiber of our muscle and nerve. This explains why we are more interested in Shakespeare when we dramatize his plays than when we read them.

30. Associate with others who are interested. It is much easier to become interested in a thing if your associates are interested in it. The herd instinct makes you want to do what your associates are doing, and to like or approve what they like. If you pick your associates from the studious and interested, you can be studious and interested yourself with little effort. Frequently it is possible to join a club or a society composed of students who are particularly interested in a given line of study, such as music, debating, botanizing, or speaking a foreign language, and thus provide for yourself a stimulating social environment that will increase your own interest in the subject. It should also be said that when there is a choice of teachers it is wise to choose one who is himself thoroughly interested in the subject to be studied, since his interest will go far toward stimulating yours.

31. Utilize social factors to promote interest. Do your best to make a good impression on the teacher. Try to show up well before your fellow students. Take part in group coöperative work. Coöperate with your group in order that as a whole it may achieve its objectives. Try to help it to surpass those competing with it. Assume responsibility for group leadership, or undertake a task in which you are conspicuous; the fact that the eyes of all the rest are turned on you will force you to do your utmost. Make use of all possible opportunities to apply the principle that man is a social being and inherently prefers social life to life as an isolated individual.

32. Increase interest by resorting to oral speech. An important characteristic of man as a social animal is his pronounced tendency to communicate with others. The fact that billions of hours are wasted annually in "just talking" illustrates the keen satisfaction that comes from talking. Class discussions are usually more interesting than lectures or reading for the reason that they involve talking. Speech can so readily transform drudgery into interest that it would be unfortunate to overlook it as an interest asset. And the more variation in talk, the better. Asking a question sometimes changes a discussion from an impersonal and purely academic affair to one that is highly personal and, for the moment, intensely real to the asker. The more you talk in class, and the more you discuss your work with others outside of class, the more likely you are to become genuinely interested in it.

33. Increase interest through concreteness.

Concrete experiences, involving actual sensory impressions, are usually more interesting than abstract ones which depend on words or imagination instead of on actual sight, touch, and hearing. Seeing a single battleship is likely to prove more interesting and educative than reading about a whole fleet. Take every opportunity to get actual first-hand experiences in order to enrich and vitalize what you read about. Go on field trips, excursions, and observation tours to points of interest that are related to your school work. Study the pictures included in your textbook, instead of skipping over them as extraneous material. Study objects and exhibits in school or public museums. Even go so far as to draw sketches or diagrams of things that you are studying about, in order to reduce them to concrete form, which will give them clearness and interest. Contribute such materials as you have to the class group so as to help the other students. A little mutual coöperation can go a long way toward making concrete the subject under investigation.

34. Improve your interest by means of variety. "Variety is the spice of life," according to the old proverb. You can overwork any successful device or procedure of study if you use it endlessly without giving it a rest. Change of subject and change of the method of studying offer a certain relief. Simply turning from one study to another when you have reached the point of boredom is an effective device for continuing to work without at the same time straining the interest.

35. Do some things as work instead of trying to reduce them to play.   Even though you do not feel an interest in a task, turn in and do it anyway, for the sake of the good you will get out of it.   Many things that are unpleasant in themselves are distinctly worth while because of the ultimate or later rewards that come from them.   The policy of doing only what is pleasant at the time would mean reducing everything to play, and would rob us of the greatest satisfactions of life, which come only as rewards for labor that is not particularly pleasant at the time it is being done.

QUESTIONS AND EXERCISES

1. Outline the chapter.
2. List the subjects you are studying and under each list by number the points in this chapter that seem most helpful in developing interest in that subject, giving after each the particular reason why you think it especially applicable.
3. Classify the methods given in the chapter into two groups, as follows: (a) Those which are definite and easy to apply; (b) those which are rather general and difficult to apply.

MATCHING TEST

Directions: Write beside each number the number of the paragraph in the chapter which discusses it.

....   1. Plateaus.
....   2. Instinct of workmanship.
....   3. Resolutions.
....   4. Rivalry.
....   5. Selecting courses.
....   6. Coöperative tasks.
....   7. Long units of work.
....   8. Change.
....   9. Interest through difficulty.
....   10. Not attempting too difficult work.
....   11. Health.

.... 12. Definite purpose.
.... 13. Emotional repression.
.... 14. Self-expression.
.... 15. Companions.
.... 16. Direct experience.
.... 17. Interest versus effort.
.... 18. Asking why.
.... 19. Æsthetics.
.... 20. Transfer of interests.
.... 21. Class discussions.
.... 22. Competing with self.
.... 23. Acquired interests.
.... 24. Self-advertisement.
.... 25. Helping others to get interested.
.... 26. Dramatizing.
.... 27. Vocational decisions.
.... 28. Practical uses.
.... 29. Hope versus fear.
.... 30. Instinct of ownership.
.... 31. Novelty.
.... 32. Native interest.
.... 33. Pure science.
.... 34. Familiarity.
.... 35. Make believe.

TRUE–FALSE TEST

Directions: Indicate which statement is true and which is false, using plus (+) for true and zero (o) for false.

.... 1. The school exhibit is a very artificial basis for interest.
.... 2. The more you know about something the more interested you become.
.... 3. Success is essential to interest.
.... 4. To face obstacles often increases interest.
.... 5. If you act interested you are.
.... 6. Education has neglected the emotions.
.... 7. School subjects lose educational value when dressed up in artistic form.
.... 8. "Love me, love my dog," is unsound psychology.
.... 9. All interests are based ultimately on instincts.
.... 10. Work with the hands is naturally more interesting than work with the mind.
.... 11. It is easier to do work if you have a reason for it.
.... 12. If you have only immediate incentives to work for your interest is more difficult to maintain.

.... 13. Interest is a smaller problem if you have chosen a life work.

.... 14. One should never select courses because they are interesting.

.... 15. Your being interested is a service to your fellow students.

.... 16. A public reform is better than a private one.

.... 17. Knowledge should be pursued for its own sake.

.... 18. Human nature rebels at doing what everybody else is doing.

.... 19. Dramatizing is more interesting than reading.

.... 20. A task is more interesting if several persons work together.

.... 21. The more you talk about your work the more you like it.

.... 22. Reading is more natural than observation.

.... 23. Turning from one task to another usually taxes one's interest.

.... 24. You should not do anything unless you are interested in it.

.... 25. A record of progress is an aid to interest.

.... 26. Interest can sometimes be secured by taking a nap.

.... 27. Warming up is prerequisite to the maximum interest.

.... 28. Reward is a better incentive than punishment.

.... 29. The collecting instinct does not apply to things intellectual.

.... 30. Oft-repeated acts are certain to be uninteresting.

.... 31. The presence of a purpose in work robs it of interest.

.... 32. It is impossible to get interested in a subject unless it has practical application.

.... 33. Self-directed work is more interesting than teacher-directed work.

.... 34. The stimulus for the instinct of curiosity is something new.

.... 35. Contests are based on an original trait of human nature.

SHORT–ANSWER TEST

Directions: Answer each question or complete each statement by inserting a word, phrase, or brief answer.

1. What makes easy tasks interesting?........
2. To acquire a new interest attach it to ....
3. What instinct is especially utilized by laboratories?........
4. Why does a fisherman like for a fish to fight back?........

5. Why does success beget success?........
6. What you see frequently you tend to ....
7. What is a learning curve?........
8. What is the result of pretending interest?........
9. Why is "well begun, half done?"........
10. Why are the fine arts interesting?........
11. Why do you like a song better after singing it a few times? ....
12. Why is poetry more interesting than prose as a rule?........
13. How does the effort to make knowledge practical affect interest?........
14. How does a life objective affect interest?........
15. What service does a motto render?........
16. When is an unpleasant task work as contrasted with drudgery? ....
17. The world's most common pastime is ....
18. Individual work is not as interesting as ....
19. When is an unpleasant task not drudgery?........
20. Laboratory work is more interesting than textbook work because it is more ....
21. The things that are most interesting are those which are most nearly ....
22. Why does the modern workman take less pride in his output than formerly?........
23. Why is it easier to read novels all day than to read short stories?........
24. Why is going somewhere more enjoyable than riding around? ....
25. A good way to spoil a good procedure is to ....
26. Why is it one's duty to develop interest in his work?........
27. A good way to get interested in music is to ....
28. What effect does novelty have on interest?........
29. Uninteresting courses should sometimes be taken in order to ....
30. Why are group contests better than competition for prizes? ....
31. What instinct is responsible for the purchase of encyclopædias? ....
32. What characterizes the pure scientist as regards his basis for interest?........
33. Why is the regular assigned lesson often less interesting than term papers?........
34. How may the schedule be made to aid interest?........
35. How can you get interested in a lecture you are to hear?........

READINGS

1. Bode, B. H.: *Fundamentals of Education.* The Macmillan Co., New York, 1921.

   Chapter IV, "The Development of Ideals." Chapter V, "Interest, Duty, and Effort."

2. Book, W. F.: *Learning How to Study and Work Effectively.* Ginn & Co., Boston, 1926.

   Chapter XVI, "Developing an Interest in Your Work and in Your Own Advancement and Success."

3. Dewey, John: *Interest and Effort in Education.* Houghton Mifflin Co., Boston, 1913.

4. Headley, Leal A.: *How to Study in College.* Henry Holt & Co., New York, 1926.

   Chapter III, "How to Concentrate."

5. Kilpatrick, W. H.: *Foundations of Method.* The Macmillan Co., New York, 1925.

   Chapters VI–VII, "Coercion and Learning." Chapters X–XII, "Interest."

6. Kitson, H. D.: *How to Use your Mind.* J. B. Lippincott Co., Philadelphia, 1921.

   Chapter XI, "How to Become Interested in a Subject." Chapter XII, "The Plateau of Despond." Chapter XIII, "Mental Second-Wind."

7. Parker, Samuel Chester: *Methods of Teaching in High Schools.* Ginn & Co., Boston, 1915.

   Chapter XIV, "Interest."

8. Strayer, G. D.: *Brief Course in the Teaching Process.* The Macmillan Co., New York, 1911.

   Chapter VII, "The Appreciation Lesson."

9. Thomas, F. W.: *Principles and Technique of Teaching.* Houghton Mifflin Co., Boston, 1927.

   Chapter VII, "The Principle of Interest."

10. Waples, Douglas: *Procedures in High School Teaching.* The Macmillan Co., New York, 1924.

    Chapter V, "Motivation."

CHAPTER IX

BUILDING A VOCABULARY

IT was pointed out in a previous chapter that ability to think well is dependent upon the possession of a large and choice supply of words. The psychologists have quite clearly demonstrated a genuine relationship between language, or words, and the higher mental processes. Throughout the ages of history the effort to master words has been one of the objectives of schools and scholars. Ability to study consists, in considerable measure, in the possession of a good supply of words with which to handle the ideas that study presents and involves. The paragraphs composing this chapter are intended to help in acquiring such a supply.

1. **Make conscious effort to enlarge your vocabulary.** In order to enlarge your vocabulary, you must be alert to discover new words. You should keep a sharp lookout for words which may be added to your present list. A "don't-care" attitude toward increasing your vocabulary is certain to retard its development. The mere consciousness of the importance of being the master of many words will make you more alert and receptive to new ones. A will to learn is as important in acquiring a vocabulary as in any other type of learning. Some persons make vocabulary-building an interesting game, setting a goal of a certain number of new words to be

definitely mastered or added each day. Others report that they resolve never to let a new word pass unnoticed, but to write it down for later investigation. Numbers of other methods of carrying out this suggestion are given in succeeding paragraphs in the present chapter.

2. **Acquire a rich and varied personal experience.** The words you use depend very much upon the kind of experiences you have had. The meaning that a word has for you is definitely limited to the experience background which you have for interpreting it. In fact, a word is simply an abbreviation for a set of experiences, and cannot have a meaning for you unless you have had the experiences basic to it. For example, the word "cold" is for you an abbreviation or condensation of all those experiences you have had which involve shivering, huddling up in your wraps, hurrying to get into the house, thawing out frozen ears, stepping under cold showers, and so on. For a person who had lived all his life in a tropical climate the word could not have the same meaning that it would have for an Eskimo. Similarly, all the words we use are dependent upon our experiences. A person who lives in a simple rural environment, never travels, never sees new places or things, and never reads, will have a very limited vocabulary indeed, because his experience-background will not support many words.

3. **Read good literature extensively.** An extensive reader has, as a general rule, a large vocabulary. Different writers use different words, and if you

read the work of many authors you inevitably come into contact with an extremely broad range of vocabulary. Furthermore, the best writers are the possessors of the best supplies of choice words, and they use words with a high degree of precision, thus setting for you the best possible example. Another advantage of reading as a vocabulary-builder is that it gives the words in their natural settings instead of as isolated units. The reader learns each word in its relation to other words in the sentence, and hence is better able to use it in sentences of his own. After all, the clearest idea of a word's meaning is frequently to be derived from the context in which the word is found rather than from the formal dictionary definition. Foreign-language students who work by the direct method find that their vocabularies naturally grow very rapidly through reading and purposely refrain from reference to the dictionary.

4. **Secure intellectual contacts in many different fields of knowledge.** Though each field of knowledge employs a fund of general words that are common to all fields alike, in addition to these it has a special list of words which are peculiar to itself. For example, such words as "capillarity," "osmosis," and "convection" are more closely associated with physics than with mathematics. The student of physics will acquire them much sooner than will the student of geometry. The more different branches of learning you explore, the more special words of this type you master. By contact with

these various fields, then, you will be enabled to understand, and to speak or write intelligently on, a wide range of topics, and enabled also to maintain interests in many subjects which would otherwise be closed to you because of your ignorance of their terminology.

5. **Listen to good lectures and addresses.** Lectures and addresses offer a number of peculiar contributions to a vocabulary. In the first place, they are oral, and thus tend to add words to your speaking vocabulary rather than simply to your reading and writing vocabularies. In the second place, they carry a certain color or expression which is lacking in printed material. The speaker not only utters the words but puts a certain expression and inflection into them which enrich and clarify their meanings. Finally, lectures have an advantage, in vocabulary-building, over informal oral speech because they are usually prepared with considerable care, and hence involve a more choice collection of words than the student is likely to meet anywhere else except in good literature.

6. **Associate with persons of large vocabulary.** The words we use are limited as a rule to those with which we and our associates are familiar in everyday life. For this reason a constant association only with small children, or only with persons of limited education and intellectual interests, tends to hamper vocabulary growth. If a word which is perfectly familiar to you is not familiar to your associates, you are likely to drop it for fear they will consider

you "highbrow."   On the other hand, if your associates use a larger number and a better quality of words than you do, you unconsciously imitate them and soon feel natural in using words which it formerly made you self-conscious to use.

7. **Use oral methods of adding new words.** Knowing the meaning of a word that you hear or read does not make you a master of it.   The word is not truly yours until you can use it in your own speech with a feeling of naturalness.   This feeling in using a word rests on a double foundation, auditory and muscular.   The word must actually sound natural to your ears and feel natural to your vocal organs.   In order to acquire this sense of naturalness you will have to repeat the word orally many times.   Reading aloud is one way of doing this; that provides both the muscular and the auditory element.   It is not enough, however, because what you read aloud does not involve the element of self-choosing.   Another plan is to write a passage which contains the words to be mastered, and then say it aloud to yourself or to others.   A big word will not seem quite so awkward if you have used it first on paper, where you have a greater sense of privacy and freedom from self-consciousness; but eventually some kind of oral practice with the new words used extemporaneously will be necessary for establishing them finally as your own.   Public speaking and debating are excellent ways of accomplishing this. The writer well recalls his experience, in his high-school days, of adding the word "suffrage" finally

and fully to his natural vocabulary by being obliged to use it repeatedly in debating the question of woman suffrage.

8. Study definite word lists. In addition to employing various informal and indirect methods of enlarging your vocabulary, it may be well at times to devote attention to the study of definite formal lists of words. For example, lists of synonyms, opposites, similar words with different meanings, or words frequently misused may be distinctly serviceable as guides to study. The study may be of especial value if the lists are made up to suit your own particular needs, or chosen from the subjects or fields in which you are working. For example, a list of leading terms in psychology or physics or rhetoric may well repay formal study.

9. Look up new words in the dictionary. The dictionary habit is much to be encouraged. A faithful user of the dictionary is likely to have a good vocabulary. When you are reading and meet a new word which you do not know, either stop and look it up, or else make a note of it and consult the dictionary later. Good intentions are not enough. Most of us silently wish that we knew the meaning of the word, and then forget all about it. The dictionary may not be at hand when we need it, and the effort required to go to it may seem too big a price to pay for a single word. The remedy for this particular difficulty may be secured in either or both of two ways: (1) by having a dictionary in easy reach of your study desk, (2) by having a pocket notebook in which to record the doubtful words until there is a sufficient collection to justify a trip to the dictionary.

10. **Learn pronunciation as well as meaning.** You may know the meaning of a word perfectly well, but unless you know its pronunciation you naturally will not be able to use it as a part of your speaking vocabulary.   A good illustration in point is the name of the Egyptian king whose tomb was opened a few years ago, and about whom much was printed in the papers.   Such uncertainty prevailed regarding the pronunciation of this name that conversation was seriously hampered until by common consent it was agreed to call him King "Tut." There are numbers of words which we should like to use but deliberately shun because we do not know how to pronounce them.   Certain words which are commonly pronounced two ways, such as "route," are deliberately shunned by the person speaking because he does not know which pronunciation his audience would sanction.   A few minutes spent with the dictionary would remove any ordinary uncertainty and enable such words to be used with much more self-confidence.

11. **Study the derivations of words.**   Some words are simply combinations of other simpler words and can readily be understood if we think of them in terms of their parts.   For example, the word "overseer" may be readily interpreted by this method as one who looks over the work done by others. Oftener, however, all the parts of the word are taken

from some other language, and then the task is somewhat more complicated. For example, take the word "supervisor," composed of the words "super," meaning over, and "visor," meaning one who sees or looks. A person who already knows the foreign words from which the English word is derived may get some real help from tracing it back to its elementary beginnings. There is some doubt, however, or at least it is still a debatable question, whether the minute study of derivations is a better method of vocabulary-building than more direct methods which are available.

12. **Make notes and outlines from lectures and printed material.** There are two situations in which you may express yourself. One is when you have something to say, the other when you have to say something. In ordinary theme writing, letter writing, or conversation, you are in control of the situation and so can dodge a special vocabulary difficulty by saying something slightly different from what you had set out to say; but in taking notes on the thoughts of some one else, you have no such freedom. The result is a much more rigid standard for you to meet, and you are forced to use words which under certain other circumstances you could avoid. Note-taking is an excellent kind of vocabulary training for another reason; it involves much juggling with words in order to shorten long statements and still preserve the essential ideas.

13. **Memorize literary selections.** Occasionally a writer chances to put together an unusually fine

combination of words which expresses a thought so precisely and so forcefully that others dare not hope to improve on it. These gems become famous, and are often quoted by other writers who wish to express the same ideas in other connections. Perhaps it would be worth while for the average student to devote special effort to memorizing passages of this kind. . Poetic stanzas or striking prose quotations which you memorize and retain become your permanent possessions, and serve as excellent standards by which to choose words. It is possible to buy books of quotations, or "forceful sayings," or "expressive lines," made up of clever and well-expressed thoughts. Such compends are very good sources of suggestions for new words.

14. Associate words with foreign words whose meanings you already know. There is a close relation between English and foreign vocabularies. All languages are more or less related in families, and certain languages are very nearly akin. For example, English has many close parallels in Latin, French, Spanish, and German — so close, in fact, that knowing the foreign word almost guarantees knowing the English word which is related to it. This relationship of the English language to other tongues has suggested to many minds that students should take foreign languages as a means of increasing their English vocabulary. Probably all will agree that this method has some effect on the student's vocabulary, but whether it is the most *economical* method for improving it is by no means

certain.   It is extremely doubtful whether time spent on foreign-language study will add as much to one's English vocabulary as will the same amount of time spent directly on English itself.

The writer would suggest, if for some other reason you have studied or expect to study a foreign language, that you might well make an effort to get improvement in English vocabulary as one of the by-products of such study.   Nor is this recommendation made without evidence of its worth.   A thesis study by one of the writer's pupils, Mr. F. E. Shaw, secured data on this question by correlating various factors with scores on a standard vocabulary test. The factors correlated were: (1) years of English studied, (2) years of Latin studied, (3) years of all foreign languages studied, (4) intelligence, (5) age, (6) college class.   He isolated the effects of each of these factors from those of all the others by means of partial correlation, and found correlations with size of English vocabulary as follows: years of English studied, correlation was .71; years of Latin studied, correlation was .48; years of all foreign languages studied, including Latin, correlation was .39.   These results show that the study of English adds more to a vocabulary than does the study of Latin, and that Latin adds more than any of the other foreign languages, which, because of its closer relationship to English, is to be expected.

15. Study the finer shades of meaning in words. The difference between the ordinary person's use of words and that of the artist lies largely in the

latter's mastery of the niceties of vocabulary, or the subtle differences between words. There is a vast difference between passable words and select words — as much as between ox carts and automobiles. To find a word which not only expresses the general idea that you have in mind, but also the exact shade of meaning that you want, you must have a large number of words that are nearly alike from which to choose. Without a close study of the fine distinctions between closely similar words, the best you can do is merely to use words that approximately express your thoughts — or, to be more exact, you can have only an inexact thought. A good way to master these more subtle differences between words is to practice paraphrasing your ideas, or restating them in other words. Note-taking serves the same purpose somewhat, especially if you restate the lecturer's points in your own words. Translating from a foreign language has much of this same element in it, since there is often no exact English equivalent for a given foreign word and it is necessary to exercise considerable discrimination in choosing the one which will serve best. A dictionary of synonyms is helpful also, since it offers a wider variety of words from which to choose than you can ordinarily call up from memory.

16. Practice using words you have learned. There is a large difference between an effective vocabulary and a potential vocabulary. You have a large supply of words which you could use but do not. Just as the churches have learned that the best way to keep a convert in good standing is to put him to work, so we know that new words must be put to use if they are to be retained in an effective vocabulary. You should seek for opportunities to use new words, and see in how many different ways you can use them, not only in writing, but in reciting or in informal conversation. Play with them by putting them into new combinations or in different sentences. Try them out at home, on your roommates, in writing which is not to be kept, and as a means of preparing for more formal situations. Whatever the particular method you employ, the general principle is that a word is not yours until you have used it sufficiently to make it natural and automatic.

17. Get criticism of your use of words. It is not only important to add new words to your vocabulary, but also to add them correctly and to eliminate any false usages which may have been previously learned. You are fortunate if you can get an able friend to notice your ordinary speech and call to your attention such words as you use incorrectly. Without such criticism you are likely to go on, entirely unconscious, making the same error over and over. A group of friends or certain members of the family would do well to band together for mutual criticism, each helping the others to see their errors. The next best thing to criticism by others is self-criticism after an interval of time. If you write a paper early and let it wait a few days before handing it in to the instructor, you will al-

most certainly be able to improve on your choice of words when you take it up for final revision.

18. Measure your vocabulary. In vocabulary-building, as in other forms of learning, knowing how you compare with others and with your own previous record is a decided aid to progress. Standardized tests have been devised to measure the size of a person's vocabulary, and they can be taken in a comparatively short time. An excellent one is the *Inglis Vocabulary Test*, published by Ginn & Co., which contains one hundred and fifty words selected to be representative of the "intelligent general reader's vocabulary." This list consists of "those words which belong neither to our everyday vocabulary of commonest words, nor to special and technical vocabularies, but which constitute a large part of the educated person's vocabulary." By means of the two forms of the test, which are of equal difficulty, it is possible to measure yourself at two different times and to determine the amount of progress that you have made. Similar vocabulary tests are also included as parts of general intelligence tests.

QUESTIONS AND EXERCISES

1. Outline the chapter.
2. Arrange the points in the order of their importance.
3. What experiences or practices do you think have been most helpful to you in increasing your vocabulary?
4. Give every reason you can why a large vocabulary is to be desired.

MATCHING TEST

Directions: Write beside each number the number of the paragraph in the chapter which discusses it.

....   1. Condensing.
....   2. Companions.
....   3. Importance of vocabulary.
....   4. Vocabulary tests.
....   5. Foreign languages.
....   6. Wrong use of words.
....   7. Special words.
....   8. Quotations.
....   9. Potential versus actual vocabulary.
....   10. Learning words in sentences.
....   11. Subtle differences between words.
....   12. King "Tut."
....   13. Basis of a word's meaning.
....   14. Foreign roots of words.
....   15. Direct and formal word study.
....   16. Reading aloud.
....   17. Definitions.
....   18. Listening.

TRUE–FALSE TEST

Directions: Indicate which statement is true and which is false, using plus (+) for true and zero (o) for false.

....   1. Translating a foreign language contributes more to vocabulary than does studying it by the direct method.
....   2. Size of vocabulary is largely a matter of desire to learn new words.
....   3. Memorizing poetry has little effect on vocabulary.
....   4. Lectures contribute more to vocabulary than informal speech.
....   5. It is profitable to study foreign languages for their service to vocabulary.
....   6. The more varied the subjects you study, the more rapidly your vocabulary grows.
....   7. Words must be learned on the vocal organs as well as in the mind.
....   8. A dictionary loses most of its value if not close at hand.
....   9. Words are seldom picked up by imitation.
....   10. The best way to learn a word is to go back to its derivation.

.... 11. A word is simply an abbreviated experience.

.... 12. Vocabulary varies inversely as amount of reading done.

.... 13. Lists of synonyms and opposites are of small value in vocabulary-building.

.... 14. The Inglis test is a measure of your technical vocabulary.

.... 15. You should correct what you write immediately after writing it.

.... 16. Note-taking does not permit you to dodge your vocabulary difficulties easily.

.... 17. A word does not belong to you until after you have used it.

.... 18. Words with two pronunciations are less frequently used than others.

SHORT–ANSWER TESTS

Directions: Answer each question or complete each statement by inserting a word, phrase, or brief answer.

1. How many words are in the Inglis test?........

2. Why are special word lists good for vocabulary study?........

3. How much value has the study of derivations of words?......

4. For what type of vocabulary is knowledge of pronunciation most essential?........

5. What service can a pocket notebook render to vocabulary building?........

6. What does oral speech contribute in adding words to your vocabulary?........

7. Why does translation aid vocabulary?........

8. How does the study of English compare with the study of Latin in effect on size of vocabulary?........

9. What type of vocabulary does the word "osmosis" illustrate? ....

10. Why are memory gems of service to vocabulary?........

11. It is better to learn the meaning of a word from .... than from the dictionary.

12. Words heard in lectures have their meanings explained by the aid of the speaker's ....

13. How can incorrect words be eliminated from your vocabulary? ....

14. Upon what does the meaning of a word depend?........

15. Your oral vocabulary is largely limited to that of your ....

16. How are words like converts?........

17. If you want a large vocabulary you have to put forth ....

18. What phase of foreign language study most closely resembles note-taking?........

READINGS

1. Boraas, Julius: *Teaching to Think*.   The Macmillan Co., New York, 1922.

   Chapter XII, "Size of Vocabulary as a Measure of Thinking Ability."

2. Fenton, Norman: *Self-Direction and Adjustment*.   World Book Co., Yonkers-on-Hudson, 1926.

   Pages 83–86, Vocabulary, includes a vocabulary test.

3. Headley, Leal A.: *How to Study in College*.   Henry Holt & Co., New York, 1926.

   Pages 395–96, Record form for unfamiliar words.

4. Schwesinger, G. C.: *The Social-Ethical Significance of Vocabulary*.   Teachers College Bureau of Publication, New York, 1926.

5. Ward, C. H.: *What is English*.   Scott, Foresman & Co., Chicago, 1925.

   Chapter XIII, "Vocabulary Work."

CHAPTER X

USING THE LIBRARY

THE library is the scholar's workshop, and whoever wishes to take up scholarly pursuits must be a master of the art of using it. It is much more than a storage place for rare and sacred volumes. It is more than a mere collection of novels which may be read on week-ends. It contains information on an infinite number of topics, and has almost innumerable special facilities for finding out about almost any imaginable subject. In order to be an artist at using the library, instead of a crude workman, it is necessary to know something of its special facilities and how to utilize them. The following paragraphs point out a few of these things.

1. **Get acquainted with the different departments in the library.** The usual library consists of an order department which selects and purchases new books; a catalogue department which numbers, classifies, indexes, and stamps the books; a binding department, which binds periodicals at the end of the year when the annual volumes are complete, and which also rebinds or repairs books that are worn from use; a loan department, which delivers books to students and keeps records of the loans; and a reference department which helps you to find what you want by giving advice and assistance and by

providing selected reading lists on various topics. It will be well, at the beginning of the school year, to locate those departments with which you are to come in contact as a student. One university asks each freshman to draw a map of the library, showing what is to be found in each room, and what type of books is to be found on the shelves in each portion of the room. The least that you can reasonably expect to do is to find the loan desk, the periodical room, the readers' guides, the encyclopædias, the card catalogue, and such points; and a definite trip through the library at the opening of the school year for this purpose is not too much to ask.

2. **Get acquainted with the scheme of call numbers used by your library.** Two major systems of call numbers are used by libraries — the Dewey Decimal system, and the Library of Congress system. It is not the purpose of this paragraph to give details of these systems, except to tell how they can be identified. The Library of Congress numbers are preceded by letters, as, for example, LB 118 T 25, while the Dewey Decimal numbers use decimals instead of letters — as 379.171 J73M. There is one suggestion on using the call numbers that may be helpful here and that is to get acquainted with the numbers assigned to the major fields of knowledge in which you are working. For example, the Dewey Decimal system numbers 370 to 379 deal with education, as do the Library of Congress numbers LA, LB, and LC. This kind of information not only helps you to locate books on the shelves, but also

to judge the nature and the desirability of a book to which you have seen a reference.

3. Get acquainted with library regulations, and follow them. Each library has its own individual plans and procedures with regard to the use and withdrawal of books. Certain cards must be signed for certain purposes. Certain books may be withdrawn for one length of time, and others for longer or shorter periods. Special regulations as to books on the reserve shelves are necessary in order to meet local conditions. Some books may be used only in the room, while others may be taken from the building. You owe it to yourself, to the library, and to your fellow patrons of the library to give a few minutes to a definite study of the library regulations, so that you will be able to coöperate with the library staff in the best possible way. Some schools find this coöperation so necessary that they print the library regulations in the annual catalogue, or distribute printed sheets to all new students at the opening of the year.

4. Make a definite study of the art of using a library properly. Probably a course in how to use the library would be one of the most valuable courses that the average student could take. This art of using a library properly is one of the essentials in life outside of school, just as it is an essential in successful school work. The man who expects to succeed in business or professional life must continue to study, and the library will be the chief source of material that will help him with his problems. When you use the library in school, it is well, therefore, to be aware of your particular and immediate purpose, and also to be alert to learn anything you can about library technique that will be of service in later situations.

5. Get accurate and definite references. Find out exactly what you are to do, and then do that particular thing. If possible, obtain from your instructor the actual titles, authors, and pages that are to be consulted. If the assignments are by topics rather than by authors and pages, make sure that you have a clear idea of the boundaries of the topics. Asking for the key word under which to look for material will often greatly facilitate finding it as well as increase the certainty of finding the right kind. There is no virtue in random searching if a better method of procedure is possible. It is legitimate for you to insist on being provided not only with references, but also with specific directions as to how to locate materials or how to search for additional references. Students sometimes complain that they lack proper guidance for their library work, when in reality the whole trouble lies in their own carelessness in failing to copy down such important items as the name of the author or the publisher, or the name of the journal — or the edition of that journal — in which an article appeared. The bibliographies which students sometimes prepare are so incomplete in regard to these matters that many of the references are practically useless.

6. Make use of prepared book lists instead of

compiling your own. In these days, when modern rifles are available at moderate prices, it would not be economical for a man to invent a new kind of bow and arrow. Neither can a student afford to neglect the remarkable work that has been done to prepare ready-made lists of references on almost every conceivable topic. Aside from the practice that you get in bibliographical technique, there is no particular value in making your own reading list rather than using a ready-made one. Teachers frequently hand out mimeographed lists of references for their courses; libraries have printed or mimeographed reading lists for many topics; reports on special investigations such as theses contain extensive lists of references on their particular topics; and such special institutions as the United States Bureau of Education publish bibliographies on numbers of topics. A good way to start the search for material on your subject will be, therefore, to search first for the lists or bibliographies that have already been prepared by others, and to make one of your own only after you are sure no one else has made one. It is particularly valuable to secure reading lists that have been prepared locally, since they are likely to take into consideration the limitations and the facilities of the local library.

7. Locate references by means of bibliographies in textbooks. Frequently you require for your purpose not a complete list of references, but a selected list. In that case the references given at the ends of chapters in textbooks are more helpful than references secured from the card catalogue. If you wish to obtain a fairly brief list of selected titles, it will be better to follow the guidance of some one who has written a chapter on your subject and included in it what he considers the most helpful references than to attempt to select suitable material yourself. When you have found one good book or chapter on the topic, of fairly recent date, it will be easy to secure from it quite a dependable list of additional references. In fact it is the writer's belief that a recent book will offer you more material on your subject than any other source; that is, if you want to do only a limited amount of reading on the subject.

8. Use the card catalogue to find books that are in the library. There are two kinds of situations in which you have to make bibliographies. The first is when the bibliography is to be for your own use in later reading on the subject, in which case a title is worthless unless the book is in the library. The card catalogue is a good place to go for books in such a case. The second situation is when you are making a bibliography for the use or guidance of others, not necessarily to be used in connection with a particular library. In this case the card catalogue is inadequate as a source of references, since it contains only the references to books in this particular library. If you want a complete list of books regardless of whether they are accessible or not, do not depend on the card catalogue. There is another serious limitation of the card catalogue which many students do not realize: that is, that it contains only books or bulletins, and does not list periodical material. A student who uses only the card catalogue automatically excludes from consideration some of the very best literature on his subject; simply because it did not happen to appear in book form he misses it.

There are a few hints on finding references by means of the card catalogue that should be given here. One is to look under more than one letter or guide card for material. If you do not know the name of the author, look for the material under the title of the book; if you do not know either, look under the subject or topic. This is sometimes difficult, since there might be several different words which would express the subject and you do not know which one the library has used, but if you look for the subject under all the names you can think of, your search is likely to be successful. Another suggestion is to look for books under a more general heading than your particular subject in the hope that you will find yours covered as a single chapter in the more general work. Incidentally it is well to study the scheme of indexing that is used for the cards in the trays. For example, names beginning with "Mc" are classified as if spelled out "Mac," and there are numerous other specific details of the kind that will bear studying.

9. Use the *United States Catalogue* to find what books have been published on your topic. Sometimes your problem is to find what books are in

existence on your subject regardless of whether they are in your local library or not. For this purpose the *United States Catalogue* is most helpful, since it lists all works published in book form during the period covered. The scheme of indexing is alphabetical, by subjects and authors, and abundant cross-references are supplied. Publishers are listed, and also prices in most cases, which makes it easy to order any book desired. In making a complete bibliography, this work is absolutely indispensable. It is kept up to date by monthly volumes, cumulated at intervals into semi-annual, annual, and larger units. These monthly supplements carry the name *Cumulative Book Index*.

10. **Use the *Reader's Guide* to find periodical material of general interest.** The magazine or periodical material which appears in the journals of a general type, such as appeal to large numbers of readers, is carefully indexed and classified by author and subject in the *Reader's Guide*. If you wish to read something on a given topic, simply find that topic in the alphabetical index, and under it you will find listed all articles bearing on it which were published during the period covered. Systems of cross-references help in locating material on similar and related topics. Two cautions should be observed in using the *Reader's Guide*: one is that it is limited to a particular list of journals of general interest, and therefore omits material, however good, that was published in other journals; the second is that it is limited in time to the particular period covered.

The dates are given on the volumes, and tell exactly the limits for each volume. The *Reader's Guide* dates only from 1900, having been begun at that time as a continuation and extension of a similar work of somewhat lesser merit known as *Poole's Index*.

11. **Use the *International Index* to find periodical material of a more specialized type than is listed in the *Reader's Guide*.** It commonly happens that you need material of such a very specialized nature that it appeals to only a limited number of readers, and which appeared in journals of limited circulations serving highly selected groups of readers. In such cases the *International Index* is of more service than the *Reader's Guide*. The two are published by the same company, constructed on the same plan and style, and differ only in that they index different periodicals. What appears in one is automatically excluded from the other. In order, therefore, to obtain a complete list of references on your subject, it is necessary to consult both, since they are mutually supplementary.

12. **Find out what special-subject indexes are available, and how to use them.** Aside from such general indexes as the *Reader's Guide* and the *International Index*, there are numerous special indexes which classify works bearing on particular fields. Some of these are mentioned here, but this list does not attempt to include all. The following will illustrate the kind of facilities available in the average library:

(1) The *Annual Magazine Index*, specializing in history, travel, and fine arts.

(2) The *Book Review Digest*, listing reviews which have been published about books, and indicating whether they are favorable or unfavorable.

(3) The *Dramatic Index*, devoted to the drama, as the name suggests.

(4) The *Industrial Arts Index*, specializing in engineering, business, and trade articles, including government bulletins and pamphlets.

(5) The *Engineering Index*, covering periodical material and the publications of engineering societies.

(6) The *Agricultural Index*, devoted, as the name implies, to agriculture.

Similar indexes are available for other fields; in many cases they go into a very minute analysis of the material indexed, as in the case of certain reference works in law, which classify thousands of court cases and give digests of each.

13. Learn how to make a complete bibliography, as well as a working bibliography. It is one thing to be able to find something to read on a subject, but quite another to find all that has been written on that subject. To make a complete or exhaustive bibliography is, of course, a somewhat difficult task and calls for specialized bibliographical training, but it would seem that at least by the time one graduates from college, if not by the end of the sophomore year, this art should have been acquired. You can find *some* references by crude and unsystematic methods, but in order to be able to find *all* references you must learn what are the specialized bibliographical aids that are available and must use them systematically. For example, the crude worker may say he has exhausted the *Reader's Guide* when he has "looked up the references" in it, but the expert will state what rubrics he had looked under in the *Reader's Guide*. The expert will make a definite plan of procedure for his search, and when he has finished he will be able to tell with such precision and definiteness where he has searched that another worker, taking up the search to extend it, need not duplicate any of the work that has been done.

14. **Select good books in advance, and keep a waiting list.** Some of the readers of the world's best literature have their books picked out to read weeks or months before they get time to read them. Instead of waiting until ready for a new book, and then scrambling about for it, they make note of good books that come to their attention from time to time, and then, when the time comes, pick one from the eligible list. This will be a good idea for you to bear in mind. One college professor reports that he regularly and systematically goes through the lists of "new books received" as they are prepared by his library and picks out the titles he wishes to examine. Then, as he gets time, he reads or reviews them one after another and always has the feeling of being sure he has not missed anything in which he would be interested. Another professor,

in an institution where all new books are exhibited for a week before being put in the stacks, makes it a practice to visit the library every Wednesday afternoon to look over the new volumes.

15. **Learn how to use encyclopædias.** Unless his attention is directly called to it, the average student does not discover what a wealth of convenient and authoritative material is included in encyclopædias. Even persons who have learned to depend on them frequently do not know how to obtain the maximum of value from them. Two points in this connection need special attention. The first is the use of the index volume, which many students do not even know exists. If interested in aviation, they look in the "A" volume, or if interested in motors, in the "M" volume; but they never think of looking up "aviation" in the index volume to find treatments of it in connection with such topics as war, transportation, or engines. The second point at which many students fail in their use of encyclopædias is in the failure to select encyclopædias which specialize on the particular field involved. There are encyclopædias of biography, of quotations, of commerce, of poetry, as well as general works of the *Encyclopædia Britannica* type. Possibly a general encyclopædia is a good place to begin the search for a piece of information, but the search need not end there.

16. **Make use of stack privileges, if possible.** There is something to be gained from direct contact with books on the shelves that cannot be gained in

any other way. Simply browsing around in the stacks and picking out books that interest you is distinctly educative. It gives you somewhat the same kind of contact with books that you get with people as you lounge in the lobby of the hotel at a convention. You will meet many books "socially" in this way which you would never definitely look up and call for at the loan desk. That school is fortunate which is able to operate on the plan of opening the stacks to the students and letting them choose their books directly from the shelves; but, because of certain shortcomings in certain students, some schools cannot use that plan. Little matters of honor and thoughtfulness in putting books back in their right places are very important in determining the success. If the careless students realized the value of the stack privilege, they would coöperate to make it available to all instead of to a few select honor or graduate students. Possibly you can help to bring this about.

17. Practice the art of finding material within a book. It will not be necessary for you to locate a book or article bearing directly on your subject, if you know how to use books that treat other subjects in the same or related fields. For example, if you want material on how to use the library and do not happen to have a book dealing directly with that subject, you can get a book on methods of teaching and find, for your purpose, the chapter or pages that treat of library technique. To be able to use the table of contents or the index of a book to locate speedily what you want, skimming and skipping to find what bears on your topic, is a great asset. This ability does not come without effort, however, and it is not easily acquired. Probably the most helpful suggestion as to how to acquire it is that you go to the shelves, take down one book after another, and hunt through each until you find at least one contribution to your subject. A careful analysis of several books will show you the various types of hiding-places that there are for valuable material and how to uncover them.

18. **Practice the art of skimming and skipping.** Bacon said that some books are to be tasted and others chewed and digested. This is especially true in obtaining library material, since so much depends upon getting exactly what you want for the particular occasion. You cannot afford, on account of the time it requires, to read certain books, and yet you cannot afford to neglect them entirely. It is very necessary at times to turn the pages and scan the material, stopping occasionally when something of unusual value is found. In doing this it is well to remember that the first and last paragraphs, and the first and last sentences in a paragraph, are usually of the most importance. With a little practice it becomes possible to obtain from a page, almost at a glance, whatever on it most concerns you.

19. **Make a thorough acquaintance with the library books you use, and remember them.** As a general rule students are satisfied with the con-

sideration of the material in a book, and give little thought to the book itself. As a matter of fact, you will not be able to read a book intelligently and critically until you have learned something in regard to who wrote or who published it. Before you begin to read or take notes on a new book, you should make a preliminary study of the title-page and the preface, and then review the table of contents in order to get a sense of perspective. An introduction is as important in meeting new books as in meeting new social or business acquaintances, and should not be neglected. Another important asset is the ability to remember the books which you have used. To recall that a given topic is admirably covered in a book written by a given author, who is a professor at a certain university, is not only a very useful but a very satisfying experience. Next to knowing all about any given subject is knowing who is an authority on it and where that authority can be readily consulted.

20. **In making up a working bibliography, list more titles than you will need, and choose the best.** One of the serious weaknesses of library work is the tendency to use materials that are ill-adapted to your purpose when better ones could have been secured. You are not really ready to choose a given book until you have a number of other possible books with which to compare it. A good policy is to make up a fairly large list of possible references, pick out several titles which seem to be suitable, call for all of the books, and keep the one or two which

after a brief scanning appear to be really the best. Another reason why you should make a larger list than you can read is that several of the books will probably be out of the library at the time you want to use them.

21. Judge the value of materials before reading them. The fact that a book or article is in the library indicates that it has some value or merit, but not that it is necessarily valuable for your particular need or purpose. Economy of time demands that you estimate the worth of a work before you read it, and frequently that you do so before you see it. There are several ways to make such a judgment. For one, there is usually a certain amount of information given on the card which lists the books in the card catalogue. If you will note the year and the publisher, it will be much easier to judge of the value that the work will have for you. The general nature of the contents is frequently indicated on the card. Also the number of pages tells you, in a general way, how thorough the treatment is. You can tell something about the material, furthermore, by noting who sponsors it — whether a commercial publisher, or a learned society, or some one else. The reputation of the author and of the publisher are also of service. Articles in journals may also be judged, in some measure, by the journal in which they appear, since it is well known that each journal selects material according to its own special requirements and standards.

22. Ask the librarian for assistance in finding

material. Most libraries provide assistants who devote a part or all of their time simply to helping the patrons find what they want. The writer has heard librarians express genuine regret that the patrons do not make use of such assistance as is provided. It is rare indeed that a sincere request for help is not rewarded by a most courteous response by members of the library staff. When you are in trouble or cannot find what you want, feel free to call for help, but out of courtesy to the librarian you should observe two suggestions: first, do what you reasonably can yourself, so that your request for help, when it does come, will be really necessary; second, remember the information and help which you get so that one request in connection with a given problem will be enough. Possibly there is a third suggestion, also, to be followed, namely, to learn as well as you can how to use the library by reading books or chapters on library technique, so that you will reduce the burden which individual assistance puts on the library staff.

23. Use the city or public library to supplement the school library. The books for a public library are not usually selected on the same basis or for the very same purpose as are those for a particular school or college. Consequently it is often possible to secure a book at the public library which is not in the school collection, and *vice versa*. Furthermore, congestion of readers in one particular department or along a given line of subject-matter at the school library is not so likely to be duplicated at the public library, and the latter can be used to relieve the congestion. There is likely to be much greater individual freedom in obtaining books through the public library, since it is often possible to withdraw a book there for two weeks when at the school library it is available only for overnight use. Every student should make use of the public library to supplement the school library, if for no other reason than to learn the arrangement and facilities of at least two libraries. They all differ in some respects, but when you have learned the ways of at least two of them you are likely to be able to use any of the others.

24. Read works that represent many different viewpoints. One man's treatment of a subject, however comprehensive, is nevertheless just one man's treatment, and is colored by his individual interests and attitudes. The library provides an excellent corrective for this situation, since it offers you a chance to compare many authors and works which give other sides of the subject. For any course you study, or for any textbook you possess, there are usually a number of excellent library works which throw a different light on the material. One book may treat the topic from a factual or statistical angle, another from a common-sense or philosophical viewpoint; one from the specialist's viewpoint, another from that of the layman. An educator and a business man may write on the same question, each from the point of view of his particular vocation, and each supplement the other. Until you have read up on the subject from many angles, you can hardly be said to have exhausted your opportunities for broadening your vision with respect to it.

25. Read several short treatments of a subject, as well as one long treatment. Short and long treatments differ qualitatively as well as quantitatively. The short article may be either a very condensed outline of the topic as a whole — a form which gives an excellent sense of perspective — or else a more complete analysis of a particular phase of the entire subject. The longer treatise usually attempts a complete and more or less proportionate survey of the various parts as they fit together into the whole. If you read only a comprehensive treatment, you will obtain a nice sense of perspective, but you will miss the color and vividness of experience that is to be had from the shorter and more specialized treatments. It will be impossible to exhaust every subject you take up, and therefore it is necessary to get the most that is possible out of what you do read. Several short articles are likely to give more returns in mental expansion than one unified treatment of greater length. Even if they repeat one another to some degree, this repetition is often distinctly effective in making clear just what the writers agree in considering the essential elements of the subject. The ideal procedure would seem to be to read one long treatment and several shorter ones.

26. Use materials from periodicals instead of depending on books alone. Students who have not had the matter called especially to their attention neglect one of their most helpful sources of information because they do not make use of periodical material to any great extent. The usual procedure of an untrained worker is to go to the card catalogue and take the best he can find there, making no attempt to get material that has appeared in periodicals; yet articles of that kind are preferable in many ways to corresponding material that is found in books. For one thing, they are short, and therefore give the meat of the matter in brief form. In the second place, they are likely to be somewhat more specialized than are books, since each deals with a single thing and therefore offers a different viewpoint from that which would be found in a book. In the third place, these articles are written for the general reader rather than for study in school classes, and are likely to be more interesting and practical than books. In the fourth place, factual or scientific material is more likely to be found in articles than in books, since research studies are ordinarily published in article form and only a few are later reported in books — and those usually in an abbreviated form. Finally, the periodical material is more recent. The time required for writing and publishing books makes it impossible for them to contain the very latest knowledge. The only way to get the very latest information on a subject is to consult the contents of periodicals.

27. Keep up with current and recent publications. Many libraries keep new books on a special shelf for a time after they have been received, especially for the inspection of those who appreciate the importance of being well informed about the recent books. Keeping our knowledge up to date is difficult at best, but it is practically impossible unless some conscious, purposeful, and systematic plan is adopted. Simply choosing the more recent of several books is a good measure so far as it goes, but it does not go far enough. It is necessary to make some regular provision for contact with the material in the current numbers of journals. Most libraries carry newspapers, the *Literary Digest*, *Review of Reviews*, and other such publications, as well as the specialized journals in education, engineering, law, etc. Each student should set aside a definite amount of time for reading these materials. One hour a week spent in glancing through the *Literary Digest*, and another in scanning the journals in your specialized field, would go far toward making you an up-to-date person. Surely this is little enough for one to expect of himself.

28. Use the library for contact with original sources of information. Original sources are those which give the actual facts or evidence; secondary sources, those which repeat or discuss the facts secured from original sources. Textbooks are usually secondary sources, and many times they represent several repetitions of a story without any check-back to the original evidence on the question. Persons who have never had contact with original sources can hardly realize how much of the matter in the average textbook is mere unsupported opinion. One of the great values of the library is that it offers a corrective for this evil by providing the original documents and statistical data upon which textbook writers based their statements. In choosing materials for library study, it is well to include a reasonable amount of original material, such as actual historical documents or research reports written by the actual scientific investigators, instead of relying wholly on books which present personal opinions.

29. **Divide up the references or topics among the class and let each student work on a different one.** There are two main advantages in the plan of distributing class energy in doing library reading. One is that it enables each student to keep out of the other students' way, which eliminates the congestion that is caused by several persons trying to get the same book at the same time. The second advantage is that the group as a whole comes into contact with a wider range of materials and many different viewpoints than it would otherwise, with the result that the class discussions which follow are greatly enriched. For a large class to attempt to work in the library all on the same materials or on exactly the same topics not only puts a great strain on the library facilities and makes it difficult for the various members of the class to work, but also fails to develop many of the educative possibilities of library work. A good plan is to divide the field and distribute class energies, and then to plan

some definite procedure whereby each member will report to the group as a whole what he has derived from his reading.

30. Work on definite topics instead of merely reading at random.   A large amount of student time is wasted in library work through aimlessness. The writer has known graduate students to read volumes of material in a library and to spend weeks of time in connection with masters' theses, and at the end have little to show for their work because their reading lacked the unity or order which is obtained only by having a definite topic.   Your idea as to what you want should be so clear that you will know when you have finished.   The ideal procedure is to have certain questions in your mind, and then go to the library for answers to them.   Next in importance to a definite question is a definite subject or topic; without at least that much of a guide the whole task of reading is likely to be for the most part wasted effort.

31. Do something with what you read in the library.   Work-type or study-type library reading should involve some supplementary activity if it is to be really effective.   You must do something with what you read.   You may recite on it at class or prepare for an examination covering it, or follow some other plan, but some kind of definite responsibility for putting to use the subject-matter that you read is necessary.   Making notes or outlines of the individual articles or chapters has much in its favor, as is pointed out elsewhere.   Probably, however, the most valuable thing to do is to combine the material gained from reading several articles or chapters into a single outline or paper. Your paper may not have as great scholarly or literary merit as had the poorest one which you used in making it, but it will represent your own mental reactions on the subject. Moreover, your thinking on the subject will be all the more clear from having written the paper.

32. Take notes on materials studied. Note-taking is more necessary in connection with library study than in connection with textbook study, because you cannot refer to the library books so easily as you can to those books which you own. Furthermore, study in a library is usually for a more definite purpose than is textbook study; you go there for something specific and you must take it away with you. Since you get your material, as a rule, from a number of different books or articles, it is particularly important that you have some way of fusing these diverse and independent bits into a unified whole. Having a note or a record of each bit makes it possible, after the reading is completed, to organize your ideas. The practical test of the value of note-taking in library study is whether or not experienced students do it; as a matter of fact, this test corroborates the suggestion made above. The writer has made observations of what students actually do in library study, covering, in his investigation, hundreds of individual students in three different universities and in several public libraries, and has found that sixty-three per cent of all persons found working in the reading-rooms were doing some kind of note-taking in connection with their use of library books.   Some suggestions on methods of taking notes on library readings are presented elsewhere in this book.

33. Help to increase the supply of books.   A library is by its very nature a somewhat philanthropic institution.   Seldom indeed is one able to pay for all that he gets from it.   The books which you use and enjoy are available to you through the time, labor, or money of others before you.   It is only reasonable, then, that you do your share to promote, by such reasonable methods as you can, the welfare of those who are to come after you. For one thing, you can increase the supply by taking care not to injure, destroy, or lose any of the books. You can coöperate in campaigns or projects to raise funds for the library.   Probably the most effective single thing, however, which advanced students can do, is to donate some of their books to the library when they finish the course or the year.   Frequently it is known that a given text will not be used the following year, and consequently that its sale to another student will be impossible.   If in such cases copies of the book are donated to the library by students, a good supply of duplicate copies of standard works can easily be accumulated.   This plan has been found of great value in small colleges, where funds for libraries are limited.

34. Help to increase the number of persons which

a given supply of books can serve. One of the most common obstacles to library work is the fact that books are often out when you need them. There are several remedies for this situation, however, if students will coöperate to put them into effect. One remedy is to use the library at odd hours. Libraries are like street cars in that they are subject to "rush hours," and any one who can go at other than peak-load times not only helps to relieve the congestion but also gets better service. A reserve shelf for books that are frequently used is another remedy for the difficulty; this plan prevents books from being held out for a long period without being used. Frequently a little voluntary coöperation in bringing books back with promptness completely solves the problem. Sometimes the congestion can be relieved by turning to other books of a similar nature that did not happen to be included in the reading lists, but which really serve the purpose as well. Sometimes, by a little coöperation between students, the books can be routed in such a way that each student sees them all and no student is without one at any time. It is much better to follow this rotation system than for the whole group to center on getting one book and then try for another. Waiting until the last minute to do assigned reading in the library is a common cause of failure to make books go around to all. The remedy for that is obvious. The efficiency of a library is comparable to that of a factory, in that all of the facilities of each must be utilized to the maximum. Idle machinery and idle books are both expensive, and anything that helps to increase the amount of service rendered by a book naturally increases the library's efficiency.

35. Give library books proper physical care. If students realized how many books have to be rebound every year and how much is spent to repair injured volumes, they might appreciate the importance of proper treatment for them. There are many ways of mistreating books. For example, opening a volume a little too forcibly breaks the binding at the back and does permanent injury. Publishers appreciate this fact so thoroughly that they sometimes insert a card directing the buyer to open the book by pressing down a few pages at a time from alternate sides. Students injure books by dropping them on the floor, by exposing them to rain while crossing the campus, by turning down the corners of pages, by writing in the margins and underlining words, and in many other ways. These are only little things, to be sure, but, when hundreds of students are doing them constantly, a real lover of books finds the total effect almost heartbreaking.

36. Help to make the library a place for study. It is unfortunate that in some schools it is necessary to have officials police the reading-rooms in order that quiet and good order may be preserved for the sake of those who wish to study. A reading-room is not intended as a social gathering-place, nor as a match-making institution, though some of them seem to serve these purposes. All who go to the library to study should have seriousness of aim and respect for the rights of others.   A few conscientious students can do much, through their example and personal influence, to uphold and disseminate these ideals among the student body.   Sometimes very little things will help to establish the proper atmosphere — such as replying in a whisper when spoken to in a loud voice or terminating a conversation as quickly as possible.

37. Use the library as a study place even when you are not using library books.   The library reading-room should be a general laboratory, work place, or study hall where you can go to look up an answer, prepare an original theme, or solve your problems in mathematics.   The quiet, scholarly, and purposeful atmosphere of a large reading-room constitutes an unconscious encouragement to serious and concentrated effort.   If it is difficult to work with concentration in your own room, try working in the library where the atmosphere of busy application and the example of other students will prove helpful. It is a good plan to form a regular habit of spending free periods between classes in the library, and of always having on hand at such periods some kind of work that lends itself to the circumstances or conditions of library work.   A habit of this kind may prevent the waste of much valuable time between classes.   Of course if the library is to be used in this way, all must coöperate to make it a place where study is actually possible.

38. Spend your leisure time in library reading.

While most of the discussion of library reading in this chapter has been with respect to the study or work type of reading, the other type should not be overlooked. There is genuine enjoyment to be gained from going to the local library and reading, for the sake of pastime, such literary materials as fiction, poetry, biography, and travel. It is unfortunate that most students are introduced to the library in connection with some work assignment, and so do not discover its recreational possibilities. It will be a good idea to get out of your regular field of study occasionally and go on a mental spree into new realms. You may well form the habit not only of spending some time browsing in the library for enjoyment, but also of going there at intervals for books of the recreational type to take home for leisure reading.

QUESTIONS AND EXERCISES

1. Prepare a bibliography on how to use the library.
2. Draw a floor plan of your library and indicate the location of the various departments, reference books, and bibliographical aids.
3. Classify the rules in this chapter under the following heads: (a) How to find materials; (b) what kinds of materials to find; (c) how to coöperate with the library.

MATCHING TEST

Directions: Write beside each number the number of the paragraph in the chapter which discusses it.

.... 1. Exhaustive bibliography.
.... 2. Organization of libraries.
.... 3. *Cumulative Book Index.*
.... 4. Active versus passive work.
.... 5. Public libraries.
.... 6. Direct access to bookshelves.

....   7. Magazine articles.
....   8. Length of selections.
....   9. Ready-made bibliographies.
.... 10. Agriculture.
.... 11. How to locate books.
.... 12. Reading for pleasure.
.... 13. Study hall.
.... 14. Specialized magazine material.
.... 15. *Poole's Index.*
.... 16. References at ends of chapters.
.... 17. *Encyclopædia Britannica.*
.... 18. Number of volumes in library.
.... 19. Coöperative work.
.... 20. Note-taking.
.... 21. How to open a book.
.... 22. Rules for borrowing books.
.... 23. Rate of circulation.
.... 24. Permanent acquaintance with books.
.... 25. The latest information.
.... 26. Superficial reading.
.... 27. Getting help.
.... 28. Browsing at large.
.... 29. New books.
.... 30. Estimating the value of books.
.... 31. Picking the best.
.... 32. Using contents and index.
.... 33. A course on the library.
.... 34. Spending free periods.
.... 35. Dewey Decimal System.
.... 36. Supplementary treatments.
.... 37. Primary and secondary sources.
.... 38. Complete references.

TRUE–FALSE TEST

Directions: Indicate which statement is true and which is false, using plus (+) for true and zero (o) for false.

....   1. To keep a list of "books to be read" is a commendable practice.

....   2. The life of books is largely dependent upon factors beyond human control.

....   3. A complete bibliography should be accompanied by a statement of the sources from which it was compiled.

....   4. You should avoid reading books which conflict with each other.

.... 5. Library reading should be limited to serious work.

.... 6. You should not read a book until you have compared it with others.

.... 7. Librarians should not be troubled to give personal help to students.

.... 8. All students should read the same library books if possible.

.... 9. One long selection is preferable to several short ones.

.... 10. Periodical material is of little value as a rule.

.... 11. The *Reader's Guide* is a continuation of *Poole's Index*.

.... 12. Textbooks are usually secondary sources.

.... 13. The preface is not as important in a library book as in a textbook.

.... 14. The most profitable reading is that done as undirected browsing.

.... 15. There are few indexes or library facilities to locate materials on technical subjects.

.... 16. The library should be used only for reading library books.

.... 17. In skimming a book the first and last parts are the most important.

.... 18. The efficiency of a library depends on the rate at which its books circulate.

.... 19. A reading list prepared by another person is seldom as good as one you work up yourself.

.... 20. The card catalogue is chiefly for periodical material.

.... 21. Library technique is primarily a school art.

.... 22. The card catalogue is of no value in judging the value of a book.

.... 23. The *United States Catalogue* and the *Cumulative Book Index* are really the same thing.

.... 24. Library rules are intended primarily to protect the books.

.... 25. Library work should generally be of a relaxed and passive type.

.... 26. The only effective way to add books to the library is by direct purchase.

.... 27. The student has more contact with the catalogue department of a library than with any other.

.... 28. The *International Index* overlaps the *Reader's Guide* considerably.

.... 29. The Dewey Decimal System is more generally used than any other.

.... 30. It is a simple matter to find what you want when once you get the book.

.... 31. For a working bibliography a recent book on the subject is usually the best source.

.... 32. The best way to locate material in an encyclopædia on "war" is to look in the "W" volume.

.... 33. Library work should not be burdened by note-taking.

.... 34. Public libraries consist chiefly of fiction and are worth little to students.

.... 35. A bibliographical reference should be as complete as possible.

.... 36. Stack privileges are of little real value.

.... 37. The library is primarily a storage place for books.

.... 38. The current publications are of little value because they are not yet tested and seasoned by time.

SHORT–ANSWER TEST

Directions: Answer each question or complete each statement by inserting a word, phrase, or brief answer.

1. How many references should you list in making a working bibliography?........

2. What does the library offer besides serious works?........

3. How should a new book be opened?........

4. Why are references in textbooks especially valuable?........

5. How many departments does a library usually have?........

6. To what extent is ability to use the library important outside of school?

7. How can you keep your information up to date?........

8. How would you locate all material in an encyclopædia on a given topic?........

9. Where can you go to get a library book which is too much in demand by other students?........

10. What is the main purpose of rules regarding the time books may be kept out?........

11. Where would you locate periodical material on an industrial subject?........

12. The reading-room should be a regular ....

13. What does the card catalogue contain?........

14. What is listed in the *United States Catalogue?*........

15. Why is coöperative reading by a class on a topic desirable? ....

16. What per cent of persons using library books take notes on them?........

17. What is the ideal way to get the most from library reading? ....

18. Of what value is the publisher's name in judging a book? ....

19. In locating material to read on a subject where should you go first? ......

20. What kind of sources do you call statistics and research reports? ....

21. What should you do when you cannot find what you want? ....

22. Why is a library a good place to study? ....

23. When is skimming desirable? ....

24. How does making a complete bibliography differ from making a working bibliography? ....

25. If you read several works they should represent different ......

26. How can you keep posted on recent books? ....

27. In order to get the most from library work your attitude should be .... rather than ....

28. What is the chief characteristic of material listed in the *International Index?* ....

29. In addition to books you should read ....

30. What is listed in the *Reader's Guide?* ....

31. What can students do to help build up the library? ....

32. What parts of a book should be read first? ....

33. Why are students not more generally given the stack privilege? ....

34. When is random searching for material justifiable? ....

35. How are libraries like street cars? ....

36. How can you find book material on a subject if no book is written on it? ....

37. How many systems of call numbers are in general use by libraries? ....

38. What is preferable as to length of selections for reading? ....

READINGS

1. Adams, John: *Making the Most of One's Mind.* Geo. H. Doran Co., New York, 1915.

    Chapter VI, "Reading." Chapter VII, "Textbooks and Books of Reference."

2. Book, W. F.: *Learning How to Study and Work Effectively.* Ginn & Co., Boston, 1926.

    Chapter XVIII, "How to Make an Investigation or Critical Study of a Particular Topic or Subject."

3. Dearborn, G. V. N.: *How to Learn Easily.* Little, Brown & Co. Boston, 1918.

    Chapter IV, "Books and their Educational Use."

4. Fay, L. E., and Eaton, A. J.: *The Use of Books and Libraries.* The Boston Book Co., Boston.

5. Headley, Leal A.: *How to Study in College.*   Henry Holt & Co., New York, 1926.

   Chapter XI, "How to Use the Library."

6. Kerfoot, J. B.: *How to Read.*   Houghton Mifflin Co., Boston.

7. Lyman, R. L.: *The Mind at Work.*   Scott, Foresman & Co., Chicago, 1924.

   Chapter II, Section II, "Taking Notes on References."   Chapter V, "Reading as an Active Process."   Chapter VII, "Reading for Enjoyment."

8. Reeder, Ward G.: *How to Write a Thesis.*   Public School Publishing Co., Bloomington, Ill., 1925.

   Has several chapters on library and bibliographical work.

9. Thomas, C. W.: *The Teaching of English in the Secondary School.* Houghton Mifflin Co., Boston, 1917.

   Chapter XII, "The Problem of Outside Reading."

10. Tryon, Rolla M.: *The Teaching of History in Junior and Senior High Schools.*   Ginn & Co., Boston, 1921.

    Chapter IV, "Topical, Source and Problem Procedure."   Chapter IX, "Library and Collateral Reading Problems."   Chapter X, "Teaching Current Events."

CHAPTER XI

PREPARING PAPERS

ONE of the distinguishing marks of a real student or scholar is his ability to handle ideas or knowledge on a large scale. It is comparatively easy to memorize small units of subject-matter, but quite a different thing to be master of a complex and comprehensive subject which includes a number of diverse elements. A tangible and definite example of large-scale dealing with ideas is the task of preparing papers. We refer here primarily to what is commonly called "term papers," or papers based on extensive reading and note-taking from a variety of sources. The following paragraphs offer a few suggestions looking toward improvement of this kind of work.

1. Select a suitable subject. Selecting a subject for a paper is similar in many ways to selecting the subjects or courses which you are going to study. In the first place, you should select a subject in which you are vitally interested, and which appeals to you sufficiently to justify the effort required. Next, your previous preparation must be considered; select a subject with which you are already familiar enough to be able to proceed intelligently. Avoid choosing a subject from a field of which you are totally ignorant, and be careful not to choose one that will require special research training which you lack. On the other hand, you should choose a subject that is reasonably new to you, in order to profit from the pursuit of it. It may be easier to prepare a paper on a subject which you know thoroughly than to prepare one on a comparatively new subject, but you will learn less from the work. The subject should also be important enough to be worth the time involved. There are many subjects upon which it would be easy to prepare papers, but which are not worth the time required. The availability of materials or books on the subjects in question should be another consideration. A little acquaintance with your local library will be a great help in judging whether you will be likely to find there what you will need for a given subject. Probably the most important essential of a good subject for a paper is definiteness. If your topic is very widespread, you are likely to waste considerable time working on irrelevant materials and to find, when you start to write, that you have little to show for your effort after all. This quality of definiteness should not be overdone, however; it is possible to select a subject so specific that it has no relation to other subjects and does not lead into broader problems or associate itself at all with other fields of knowledge.

2. Set up your objectives as thoroughly as possible before you begin. A good method of procedure in preparing a paper is, before you begin either to read for material or to write, to make a definite written outline of the points you expect to cover, and then read for material on these specific points. This is not always possible, however, because sometimes you will not know what the field includes and cannot tell what will be needed until you have made some survey of the subject in general. You should not let this difficulty, however, prevent your doing your best to make a plan beforehand, since an imperfect or incomplete set of objectives is better than none at all. Nor should the preliminary plan for the paper be so rigidly followed as to exclude the consideration of valuable material which is discovered unexpectedly. The definite plan is a good ideal to strive for; it usually improves the final quality of the paper.

3. **Revise the plan as the reading progresses.** However well you may have worked out the preliminary outline for your paper, revisions will be necessary after some reading has been done. A good method to follow is to read, as the first step, a few general articles or chapters which cover your subject as a whole, and then to revise the original plan in the light of the new topics or elements discovered. After this, it will be well to read articles that are more specialized and that analyze the individual topics in the revised outline. As the work progresses, each unit that you read will tend to shed more light on the remaining units to be worked out, and you can proceed step by step in the light of information secured in previous steps. Certainly it is well to keep up a constant search for new standards of selection and evaluation, and to continue this se-

lective process throughout the entire period of reading.

4. In some cases take down whatever you can find and organize later. In writing on some subjects you are not able to visualize the final outcome or plan of organization until you have practically finished the job. In fact, there may be some justification for going off at tangents, during the work, when you feel like it, and just exploring whatever dark corners your curiosity tempts you into. If you have plenty of time, and are more concerned about the information you get than the paper you write, it may be well to consider the plan of simply reading until you are full of ideas and information on the subject, and then sitting down to organize the material in hand, whether or not you have completely and systematically covered the field. This plan will allow freer reading, promote the enjoyment of it, and enable you to pick up some gems of rare value while wandering around on the by-paths. It makes an especial appeal to some students who like to browse, and it involves less of the business-like or work-type attitude than do the more systematic procedures. As a general rule, under this scheme you will have to do much more reading to produce a paper of given quality than you would under the more systematic and purposeful method.

5. Make plenty of provision for writing. Writing a paper is not a very serious task if you really have something to say. If you have read sufficiently and taken notes properly, there should be an abundance of material to go ahead with. If these requirements have not been met, no literary flourishes and rhetorical flights can avail to make something out of nothing. A paper that contains real meat will not need bombast to make its merits evident. Students often account for their inability to write by the fact that they have no command of the English language, when in reality their whole trouble lies in their lack of material and ideas. There is a great difference between having to say something and having something to say.

6. Take notes in a form especially adapted to the task. The form and quality of the notes you take have much to do with the value of the paper you write from them. If they are not clear and meaningful, you will have little material to put into the paper. If they are not mechanically easy to handle, the organization of the paper will suffer. If references to sources from which the material was taken are not included in the notes, you will be unable, in your paper, to give credit or to compare views of different authors. A few specific suggestions with regard to term-paper notes follow:

(1) The notes should be in comparatively short units, sometimes even with only one point on a card or sheet, in order to facilitate flexibility of rearranging, classifying, and organizing.

(2) The notes should be on only one side of the paper, so that you can spread them out on your table and see all of them at once.

(3) For some kinds of term papers it is well to use

a large paper ruled into rows and columns, and to enter the notes in the first place in the appropriate squares.

(4) Whenever more than one point is written on a page, it is well to leave a blank space between the points in order to be able to cut them apart for separate use.

(5) The notes taken should not be limited to what you read, but should also include good points which occur to you as you read, or even as you think of the question between study periods. Your thinking should be freely recorded all along during the process, and not left for recording at the end of the task.

7. Give considerable thought to the major outline. Making the plan for the paper as a whole is more than a mechanical or routine task. You should devote a great deal of careful study to your notes and should try to work out several possible bases for classification from which to choose. You should not finally adopt any major outline until you have made up several outlines for the same material with which to compare it. The major outlines used by different writers on the subject may serve as sources of suggestions for one of your own, or you may combine several authors' outlines and so make a composite outline of your own. Some topics can be classified according to conventional outlines, such as "What, Who, Where, Why, When, and How"; or, "Problem, procedure, results, conclusions"; but quite often the task is not so simple and outline schemes of your own must be made. A very good method is to write a number of possible main heads, each on a separate card, and then shuffle them around until you hit upon a satisfactory scheme of classification. Frequently several cards will be classified under one main topic, and this will suggest other coördinate main topics. If your original notes are in fairly short units, they may be sorted into piles according to subject, and you can thus build up a major outline directly; if they are in long units it may be necessary to go through the stack and copy off the possible main points and then concentrate on those until a scheme of classification suggests itself. Whatever the particular plan adopted, it will not be a success unless it involves considerable thought and meditation. In fact, in the organization of a paper, there is no substitute for hard study.

8. Outline the paper in detail before writing it. Making an outline should always precede the actual writing of a paper. It is as necessary to the preparation of the paper as are blueprints to the building of a house. This detailed outline should contain a statement for each paragraph which is to be included in the finished paper, and frequently it is desirable to make an even more detailed outline for the material within the paragraph. There are two radically different policies for the student regarding the use of the detailed outline in writing. One is to continue the classification and arranging of notes until they are in the exact order for writing, with each point fitted exactly into its proper place in the outline, and then to rewrite the whole paper in connected form from this outline. The other policy is to study and meditate until fully imbued with the spirit and essence of the subject, then write from memory a brief outline and from this outline write the paper, trusting to inspiration for details. The latter plan may result in greater originality, and may be somewhat more enjoyable because it makes the process seem less like work, but this plan usually produces a less orderly and less systematic paper than does the other.

9. **Profit from the procedures employed by people who write books.** In a general way the procedure of writing a long paper is comparable to that of writing books for use in schools. It is therefore of some interest to know how authors of books do their work. The following quotations are based on actual interviews with college professors in regard to their own personal methods of study while writing books and articles for publications:

(1) I get charged with emotion, so that I would rather write than do anything else in the world at that time. I have a nucleus of an idea in my mind to begin with. I spread my notes out all around me, and go through them to find anything that will stick to my idea. I do not force anything, but just write as I feel.

(2) I classify my notes by piles according to topics, and write up each little pile completely before starting the next.

(3) I go through my notes and copy each big topic on

a sheet of letter paper. I start a new sheet for each new topic. I write sub-topics on their appropriate sheets until I have all my material written down under these main topics. Then I arrange the material on each sheet into a neat outline. Finally I write the whole thing out from this outline.

(4) I put each idea I consider worthy of a place in my paper on a separate card. When all my ideas are thus jotted down, I arrange them in the order I want them and write the paper out in full from the cards.

(5) I cut my notes up into little strips with one point on a strip, and clip these little strips to the edge of a sheet of paper in the order I want them. Then I write it all out in good form.

(6) In preparing my first book I read everything that had been written on the subject; indexed the points I wanted to use so I could refer to them in the books; then took up one topic at a time, reread the indexed parts, and laboriously wrote out what I wanted to say.

(7) I read over my notes and underline with a colored pencil the parts I want to use. Then I write from reference to the underlined parts, keeping the outline in my head.

(8) In writing one of my books I made a complete outline of the entire book in order to clarify my thinking, and then put it aside and wrote the book just as I felt.

10. Embody your own original contributions in the paper. A paper should be more than a mere compilation. It should evidence your own mental effort as well as your ability as a collector of the thoughts of others. Mere tabulation and compilation result in an inferior paper. College professors who were interviewed unanimously stated that they grade term papers in part upon the evidence of the original thinking which they reveal. Your own thinking on the paper is in a sense comparable to the mortar which holds the bricks together in a wall — it is impossible to build much of a structure without it.

11. **Make the paper give evidence of wide reading.** As a rule term papers are graded or rated by instructors partly with reference to their scope, or, in other words, upon the evidence which they give that the writer has actually come into contact with the best literature on the subject. A long bibliography will not make up for lack of such evidence in the body of the paper. It should be apparent from your paper not only that you have read several works on the subject in hand, but that you know who are the foremost authorities on it, and that you know also something of their individual viewpoints and special contributions to the topic. In fact a term paper should ordinarily indicate very clearly the status of the thinking and writing that has been done by others on the subject under treatment.

12. **Maintain an objective attitude toward the subject.** In writing a term paper a special effort should be made to present the views of the various writers as their views instead of mixing them up and presenting them as your own. If you wish to use a certain statement made by William James, present it as James's view or belief rather than as if it were your own mental offspring. The general as-

sumption is that whatever you give without mentioning another source is your own thought; therefore you will have to be responsible for it. If you are not an absolute authority on the subject, you are on much safer ground if you put the responsibility upon the man who actually made the statement, and stand from under it yourself. In dealing with debatable questions, a good plan is to quote leaders on both sides of the argument instead of making up your own mind and dogmatically stating that one side or the other is right. Even if your judgment is unusually good, it is more likely to be respected after you have presented the factors or considerations upon which it has been based.

13. Include an outline or a detailed table of contents. Every paper should be preceded by a brief statement of its main points so that the reader will be enabled to view it as a whole before and after reading it in detail. Frequently the outline, owing to its concentration on main points and their relationships, will reveal more than the paper itself. The ordinary college term paper should have an outline of about a page in length, and this outline should be in such a form as to indicate the actual substance of the paper rather than merely give the topics treated without any indication of what is written about them.

14. Set forth the outline in clear form throughout the paper by means of prominent headings. A dozen or so heads and subheads, distributed at intervals in the body of a paper, add enormously to its readability.   If you actually cover two main aspects of a topic, a simple mechanical statement of that fact in the form of prominent center headings, assigned numbers I and II or letters A and B, will greatly aid the reader in finding the two lines of thought.   Not only should the major divisions of the outline be shown by center headings, but the minor points which constitute the separate paragraphs should be stated in terse form and underlined or italicized so that they will stand out.   If the substance of a paragraph is summarized in the topic heading, the reader will be more likely to get it than if he is forced to dig it out himself.   The style of writing in a paper as regards heads and subheads should normally be patterned after that of high-school and college textbooks rather than after that of works of fiction, since in the preparation of the paper clearness is the aim rather than beauty or some other consideration.

15. Include a bibliography.   You should make it possible for the reader of your paper to know what you have read, so that he, too, can avail himself of those works.   The bibliography which you include may be either a list of the works which you actually used in preparing the paper, or else a more extensive list of works which includes those, the latter being indicated by an asterisk or some similar device. The form for listing references is a matter of some importance, and especial care should be exercised to give the reference so completely that all necessary information about the work is included.   This information should include title, volume, pages, etc., and data regarding author.   The form employed in the *United States Catalogue* is a good model for this purpose.

16. Cite sources of borrowed material by means of footnotes.   If you quote a man you should furnish a footnote reference so that the reader can look up the source and read what comes before and after the part quoted.   If you credit a man with a point but state the point in your own words, it is well to cite volume and page so that the reader can check up on the accuracy of your allusion.   You should take care, however, not to cite authors and sources in footnotes when the importance of the points does not justify it.   To resort to the formality of a footnote for a very trivial matter shows a poor sense of proportion in your thinking.   Take care, also, to prevent footnotes from becoming a hindrance to the smooth reading of the paper.

17. Put your ideas into correct English.   A paper should be free from mechanical errors of punctuation, spelling, grammar, diction, and so forth, and should measure up to the standards of good English usage in general.   The technique of these matters is treated in detail in composition courses and will therefore be omitted here, but one thing that should be noted at this time is the fact that the omission of words, the repetition of words, the failure to cross *t*'s and to include apostrophes, constitute a very large proportion of all the errors which appear in papers.   A single re-reading of the finished paper would catch these slips, and it would require very little time; yet scores of papers show positive evidence that such re-reading has not been done.

18. Provide for some kind of criticism and revision. The person who can prepare a perfect paper in the first draft is rare indeed. There is almost always some room for improvement. William James recommended writing at night and then revising the next morning after the enthusiasm of the night before has died down and the spell broken. The longer you can leave what you have written before you revise and rewrite it, the more intelligently you will be able to criticize your own product, because you can take a more detached and impersonal view of it. Reading the paper aloud to yourself will reveal many imperfections in it which silent reading would miss, and having another person read it aloud to you will make you aware of many imperfections which your own oral reading would fail to reveal. Naturally, also, another person's criticisms are greatly to be desired, since he can see the material from a viewpoint very different from your own.

19. Pave the way for future writing by saving and filing materials now. In many of the professions which students ultimately enter there is much assembling and organizing of material in the manner described in this chapter. Illustrations are teaching, the ministry, law, business, medicine, and politics, all of which professions require the preparation of comprehensive reports or addresses. By saving while at school the hundreds of excellent pieces of information that you acquire, you will have, by the end of your student career, a rather elaborate and diverse supply of material on practically any subject imaginable. If you save all your college notes and keep them well classified, you will be able to prepare an intelligent article or address on almost any topic that is likely to come up in ordinary business or professional life. It is said that the physicist Twiss attributed his rise to a university position to his purchase of a steel filing case; in this steel case he kept original ideas and problems which occurred to him, with the result that they were never entirely lost.[1] If you expect ever to be a scholar, or to depend for your success in life on your ability to handle knowledge on a large scale, start now by laying the foundation for a filing system; by so doing you will provide yourself with an abundance of material with which to work.

QUESTIONS AND EXERCISES

1. Outline the chapter.
2. Just what steps would you go through and in what order if you were asked to write a three-thousand word paper on the value of a college education?
3. Select a subject bearing on that phase of the technique of study in which you are most interested and write a three-thousand word paper on it, the paper to be completed by the end of the course.

---

[1] Mentioned in W. A. McCall's *How to Experiment in Education*, p. 8.

MATCHING TEST

Directions: Write beside each number the number of the paragraph in the chapter which discusses it.

.... 1. Plan of organization.
.... 2. Note-taking.
.... 3. Filing system.
.... 4. Headings.
.... 5. How people write books.
.... 6. Table of contents.
.... 7. Changing your mind.
.... 8. Scope.
.... 9. Limiting the field.
.... 10. Originality.
.... 11. Organizing last.
.... 12. Material.
.... 13. Writing from an outline.
.... 14. Fact versus opinion.
.... 15. Grammatical form.
.... 16. List of books on the subject.
.... 17. Second draft.
.... 18. Giving credit.
.... 19. Choosing a topic.

TRUE–FALSE TEST

Directions: Indicate which statement is true and which is false, using plus (+) for true and zero (o) for false.

.... 1. Reading a paper aloud helps to detect errors.
.... 2. Notes for term-paper purposes should be taken in short units.
.... 3. You should know what points you are to cover before you do the bulk of your reading.
.... 4. It is impossible to go too far in giving credit for borrowed material.
.... 5. A filing system is an aid to writing.
.... 6. A term paper should be based on reading and should have a minimum of your own opinion.
.... 7. If you have something to say, your command of English is a relatively small problem.
.... 8. Every term paper should have a table of contents.
.... 9. Writing term papers is not comparable to writing books.

.... 10. A paper should not be based on a single book, however good it be.

.... 11. You should never change your plan for a paper after you once begin it.

.... 12. A term-paper subject should be one on which you are already thoroughly informed.

.... 13. Most errors of English are due to carelessness rather than ignorance.

.... 14. The organization of a paper should be left until all the collecting is finished.

.... 15. A loose-leaf procedure is good for making your major outline.

.... 16. To outline a paper before writing it produces a highly artificial style of writing.

.... 17. Every term paper should have a bibliography.

.... 18. Nothing besides actual fact should go into a term paper.

.... 19. To present the skeleton or framework of your paper boldly in the body of the paper is bad taste.

SHORT–ANSWER TEST

Directions: Answer each question or complete each statement by inserting a word, phrase, or brief answer.

1. Where should you designate the source of quoted material?
....

2. Writing is largely based on .... rather than original thinking.

3. Before writing the paper out in full you should make ....

4. To what extent is original thinking important in a paper?
....

5. How can you best show that you have read widely for a paper?
....

6. The most striking thing about the methods of authors of books is ....

7. The big thing in the early part of work on a paper is to set up your ....

8. Should a bibliography be limited to works you have actually consulted? ....

9. How long an outline should the usual term paper have? ....

10. When should you do your own original thinking for a paper?
....

11. What should be your attitude towards the use of many heads and subheads in the paper? ....

12. At what time in the process should organization be done?
....
13. You should not settle upon a major outline until you have
....
14. How should debatable issues be dealt with?........
15. What is the most important essential of a good term-paper subject?........
16. What is the chief essential of a good paper?........
17. The best time to criticize what you have written is ....
18. The surest way to prevent errors of English is ....
19. At what place or places in the process should selection and evaluation be done?........

READINGS

1. Baker, Ray Palmer: *The Preparation of Reports.* The Ronald Press Co., New York, 1923.

    The book as a whole deals with the preparation of engineering, research, and scientific reports and papers.

2. Bogardus, E. S.: *The Technique of Preparing Social Science Papers.* University of Southern California Press, Los Angeles, 1918.

3. Book, W. F.: *Learning How to Study and Work Effectively.* Ginn & Co., Boston, 1926.

    Chapter XVIII, "How to Make an Investigation or Critical Study of a Particular Topic or Subject."

4. May, M. A.: *How to Study in College.* Syracuse University Press, Syracuse, N.Y., 1923.

    Chapter VIII, "Collecting and Organizing Information."

5. Reeder, Ward G.: *How to Write a Thesis.* Public School Publishing Co., Bloomington, Ill., 1925.

    Practically the whole book is directly pertinent to term papers as well as to master's theses.

6. Tryon, Rolla M.: *The Teaching of History in Junior and Senior High Schools.* Ginn & Co., Boston, 1921.

    Chapter VI, "Written Work in High-School History." Chapter VII, "The Term Paper and the Permanent Notebook."

CHAPTER XII

REVIEWING

"LEST we forget" expresses the almost universal feeling of students as they review. The very nature of the human mind makes knowledge only a temporary possession. The following paragraphs present a few suggestions on how to review in such a way as to make the material learned more permanent and serviceable.

1. Do not neglect reviewing because of the general disapproval of cramming. We have often heard cramming vigorously denounced as unworthy or even as dishonest, and sometimes the denouncers have failed to make a clear distinction between cramming and reviewing. To cram means to memorize a great deal of material at the last minute, and for temporary use only — getting the outer semblance of knowledge without assimilating its inner substance or reality. Such short-sighted and superficial work deserves all the condemnation it receives, and probably more, but genuine reviewing must not be confused with it. A well-conducted review is fully as educational as any portion of the course, and, in the opinion of the writer, ranks among the very best of the educational procedures ordinarily found in schools. The final organization, consolidation, perfecting, and checking-up of a course is very much to be encouraged, and it cannot be omitted without distinct loss.

2. Review for other purposes than getting good grades.   Grades do not always take into consideration everything of value that might be secured from a course.   Marks are likely to be based on the tangible and definite fruits of a course, such as information or skill, and to neglect the subjective results, such as better attitudes, improved tastes, or increased enjoyment.   If you review only for marks or grades, you are likely to miss some of the most worth-while aspects of the work.   It is well at times to go back over a course, after you have passed your examinations and are free from artificial restraints, and review it for its genuine personal contributions to you in the way of personal inspiration, increased enjoyment, or a broadened intellectual horizon.

3. Review in the way you are to be tested.   If you are to be tested for information, review for information; if for skill, review for skill; if for ability to think, review by solving problems, and so on. If your examination is to be of the essay type, it is well, in the interest of receiving good grades, to review your material by formulating possible answers for essay-type questions.   If, however, you are to face a true-false test, it may be more profitable to review by formulating your ideas with respect to the truth or falsity of as many points as possible. One major limitation to the principle being discussed here is that the examination is only one of the ways in which your knowledge is to be tested.   Even if you make a good grade on the examination, you may utterly fail on the test of life situations where also your knowledge is to function. It is well, therefore, not only to study for the examination, but also to be prepared for all the tests you are to face.

4. **Have the review involve new learning.** A review should be not only a viewing again, but also a viewing in a new light. It should include a certain amount of actual new learning. This does not mean so much the acquisition of new facts as the discovery of new significance of familiar facts or new relations between them. The new learning can easily be in the nature of evaluating or estimating the importance of ideas. Sometimes it will consist of your making up your mind and taking a stand after you have surveyed the facts on both sides of a question.

5. **Direct the review in some measure to the places where you are weakest.** If there are gaps in the foundation, the review should fill them before proceeding to the superstructure. The main attention should go to the things about which you know the least, provided they are of equal importance with the rest. This can be overdone, however, as when the reviewing is allowed to be mainly repairing and omits the actual process of building. If students would devote more time to repairing their knowledge at points where their examinations showed it to be weak, instead of stopping such repair activities at examination time, they would be better off.

6. Make the review original thinking, as well as assimilation of the thoughts of others. Form your own conclusions or estimates of the things reviewed. Make your own decisions with regard to issues or policies which are debatable or doubtful. Interpret the things studied, and try to get their actual significance. Think of applications of the facts or principles to new and different situations, or make up situations and apply them. Adapt general statements to particular cases or else to your own life situations, noting what they would mean to you personally. There is need for thinking and originality just as much in reviewing as in the original studying — possibly more, since in reviewing you deal with ideas which are on a larger scale and in more complex relations than those you deal with in the daily work.

7. Review to establish coherence and continuity between parts of the course. Connect the new lesson with the old one as a preparation for the new. Connect and unify the numerous elements in a subject by reviewing the background from which they spring. At the end of a series of lessons on parallel topics, the topics should be reviewed as one lesson and welded into a single unit of still larger rank. Similarly, at the end of the course all of these major divisions should be considered together and fused into a sort of over-view of the field. At intervals during your education it is well to take time to review your education as a unit, together with your everyday life experiences outside of school, and then to consolidate the whole into something of a general philosophy of life.

8. Review by organizing previous knowledge. If the work has been properly done day by day, the review may well be devoted to establishing the relations between the different parts and organizing them into a systematic whole. It should enable you to see the woods where you had previously been observing the trees. Only in cases where the day-by-day work has been imperfectly learned is it necessary to devote the review time to actual learning of the facts studied. If this daily work has been done properly, the facts will be at hand when review time comes, and then the whole, or at least the major part, of your energies can be spent on organization.

9. Make the review in part a process of checking and verification. If the course is compared to an airplane, the review might be compared to its final inspection before its first actual flight. Even with the best of care some errors and oversights will creep into anything you do, and inspection of the completed product for such errors and oversights will always be essential. The student's output is in fully as great need of final checking, verification, and general inspection as is the output of the factory. High ideals of craftsmanship as a student would require a genuine unwillingness to quit a given course or a year's work until all erroneous ideas had been corrected and all records had been checked and found accurate.

B 4 —   **10. Let review procedure and study procedure be
different.** Do not go over and over the material by
the same method. Reviewing or repeating your
study by the same procedure over and over again is
usually subject to the law of diminishing returns.
Each identical repetition yields less new knowledge
or power than the preceding one yielded. In order
then, to get the most from each repetition or review,
change the method of attack. For example, if you
studied the subject by reading it, review it by making an outline, or by solving problems on it, or by
asking and answering questions. If you review the
same material several times, let each review be by
a different method, in order that it may make its
maximum contribution to the sum of knowledge.
The exception to this rule is in the case of pure drill
work, where definite bonds are to be formed in
definite ways, and where uniformity of repetition is
necessary to fix those bonds in automatic form.

B - 5   **11. Review the subject, using a different classification from that by which it was originally studied.**
If you want two pictures of a person to supplement
each other, let one be a front view and the other a
side view. Likewise, if you want to obtain a fresh
or supplementary impression of a subject, view it
from a different standpoint. For example, if you
have studied history by periods, review it by tracing
different phenomena, such as transportation, manu-
facture, and democracy, one at a time, through all
the periods. Or if you have studied the history of
education or art by men, review it by movements,

etc. If you have studied physics by such topics as heat, light, sound, and mechanics, then review it by such topics as automobiles, doorbells, ventilating systems, etc., wherein the same field would be covered in new classifications.

12. **Review both as to pattern and as to the separate threads.** If the course is likened to a piece of beautiful silk embodying a design, your review of the course may be along either of two plans. You may study the design or pattern as a whole, or you may forget the pattern and follow single threads, noting how they are utilized to help in producing the design. If the major attention during the course was given to the individual threads, the reviewing should tend more to a study of the pattern as a whole, and *vice versa*. In reviewing, try to see as a whole what you have studied by pieces, and to see as pieces what you have studied as a whole.

13. **Review for main points rather than for details.** A common mistake in reviewing is to try to gather up all the little things that were overlooked in the original study. This is, of course, very common where the teacher's examination may be expected to stress details, but it is psychologically unsound. A better plan is to give attention to details as the course is studied the first time, working out each unit with a proper degree of analysis, and then in reviewing to try for the points of still greater importance and generality of application. What were the main points for a given daily lesson should become at review time merely supporting details for

still more important and general main points for the course as a whole.

14. Review by condensing what you know. The ability to put much thought into a few words is very useful, both for taking examinations and for permanent retention of material. It may be said that boiling your knowledge down to a few words is like putting it into a convenient receptacle from which it can be easily handled. When you have it tersely expressed, the brief, concise statement is a kind of handle by which you can manage what otherwise would be a bulky or awkward idea. In a sense, therefore, every review should be a process of summarizing and condensing your knowledge. Your grade on an examination is often determined largely by the number of ideas you can express in a given time or in a given amount of space. If you can give concentrated rather than dilute material, you can crowd more thought into the limited time and space. But it is too late to do this condensing after you reach the examination room. The process should be begun during the review and completed at the examination.

15. Review by making an outline of the course. After having learned the various parts, make an outline as a means of fitting them together into a unified and related whole. If you have outlines of the daily units, make a new outline including only the more general heads from the daily outlines. Not only is the preparation of such an outline a very thoughtful process, but the outline itself is a very definite aid to retention, since it can be readily visualized and remembered. It is, of course, important that you get more than a mere skeleton outline, since merely memorizing a skeleton outline that has no rich associations centered around its various headings gives you only the form of knowledge without the substance.

16. Review by solving problems which involve the material treated in the course. When you learn a fact by means of your memory, an excellent way to review it is to reason about it or use it as material in solving a problem. Well-selected problems for review should require for their solution many facts and specific items from the various parts of the course. Facts isolated from one another are often learned as the course proceeds, but when you solve problems the interrelationship of these facts is more clearly perceived and cross-connections are formed between them. Solving problems with your previous knowledge as material changes that knowledge from academic to practical knowledge, and thus constitutes an excellent form of review.

17. Use the chapter exercises in the textbook for reviewing. The questions and exercises at the end of textbook chapters are usually prepared with care by the author, and are intended for review and further study after the material in the chapter has been studied. If you can answer these questions or exercises, you are very likely to be able to do anything that may be asked by the teacher. They are by nature such as to apply a large number of the principles of efficient reviewing, and in using them for your guide you may be as certain, as a general rule, of employing a sound procedure for review as in using any other plan for review.

18. Use review questions as guides when they are available. It is much more economical to review on definite questions or topics than to review "in general," if the questions are well chosen. Some teachers employ the device of giving a list of questions for reviewing, and then choosing a sampling of questions from that list for the final examination. Whenever you can get such definite guidance for your reviewing, it is well to make the most of it. If the teacher does not provide such a list, you may sometimes secure one from the textbook, or from your own study of the subject. The main point is to find what some competent person considers the really crucial questions and to review for them, instead of working without aim or system.

19. Review for definite purposes. Having an aim is as important in the review as in the original studying. Aimless reviewing is likely to be worthless, or at least relatively so. Not every review, however, should have the same purpose. One review will be for drill purposes, another for evaluation, another for condensing, another for organizing, and so on. The aim in daily reviews should be different from that in semester reviews. It is conceivable that in some cases it would be well for you to review once with the aim primarily of passing an examination of a routine or factual kind, and then to review again in another way with the purpose of mastering the material so that it will be useful in life situations.

20. Test or measure yourself as you review. If you discover your shortcomings or deficiencies as you review, you have an opportunity to correct them before the teacher applies her measurements or before life situations confront you for which you are unprepared. If you ask yourself questions and try to answer them, not only do you find out whether you can or not, but also you get excellent drill or training in meeting the kind of situation which will confront you later. One of the standard rules for memorizing is to attempt recall as a method of learning, and the principle would seem to be the same when the learning is concerned with other outcomes than verbatim memory.

21. Facilitate review by means of the original method of studying. If the day-by-day studying is properly done the review can be on a much higher plane than it would be otherwise. This is not simply to urge the necessity of studying each day's lesson. It means that you should study each day's lesson with a view to leaving a record by which the work can be more readily reviewed. If important points are underlined or recorded in the notebook from day to day, the records are of great value in reviewing. It should not be necessary at review time to do over again what was done in the original study, but rather to start where the original study left off. This cannot be done, however, unless some cue has been left to indicate that point.

B—7   **22. Review by taking advanced courses in the same field.** Some subjects are by nature such that each advanced course uses all previous work as a foundation, and consequently each advanced course is a review of all previous courses. With these subjects it is important that you should learn well the foundational work and retain it for use in the advanced courses; also that before entering into an advanced assignment you review the work up to that point in order to be ready to begin. As you proceed with advanced work, it is often advisable to refer at intervals to the work of the elementary or foundational courses.

B—7   **23. Employ review methods which involve visualization.** Many a question has been answered in examinations by the aid of a visual image of the page in the book which treated it. Frequently you can recall the appearance of the page in your notebook, with its main divisions and subdivisions, and are thus enabled to remember ideas that would otherwise be lost. The device of underlining points in your notes to make them prominent is an aid to visualization. Making diagrams or sketches to show relations between things sometimes impresses the things on the mind in concrete images which are more permanent than words could possibly be. Associating events or facts with the place on a map where they have their setting is a plan that sometimes proves useful. In fact, it is well to employ whatever devices for visualization you can that will supplement verbal memory.

24. Review by means of previous notes. It is often more economical to review by your notes than to go back to the original sources from which the notes were taken, since the notes are in more condensed form than the other material. If you have outlined the work as you went along, you can well afford to review by studying the outlines, seeking for new meanings, noting relationships between points, and picking out from each unit those few points that are of the greatest importance. Revising or improving the original notes is a thoughtful and worthwhile method of reviewing. Going through them with a colored pencil and underlining the main points for special emphasis is recommended by some successful students. Combining your lecture notes and reading notes into a single composite outline is an admirable practice.

25. Employ group reviewing with discretion. Discussing a subject with another student is ordinarily an excellent study procedure, provided there is genuine thought on both sides of the discussion. When the members of a review or discussion group are evenly matched in interest, ability, and previous knowledge, they should be able to profit from the reviewing. When the group consists, however, of one or two capable students and several hangers-on, the work hardly deserves the name of review. Also if group work is reduced to a division of labor wherein each member looks up one topic and thereby tries to reduce the labor of the others, it has little to recommend it as a plan. It is seldom that one student can stimulate another student's mind so thoroughly and in a way so truly educative as a good book is capable of doing it. Short-cuts whereby one student tries to transfer his knowledge in predigested form to another are usually failures.

26. Some reviewing should be largely drill. When habit or skill is the aim of a course, the review should simply be a continuation of the drill work by which the desired habits are built up. Repetition is the central feature of habit-formation; the same nerve channels must be traversed over and over until the association is firmly fixed. This repetition tends to become uninteresting in many cases, but it is necessary to hold yourself to it until the bonds are formed, and to review the process by repetition at intervals in order to preserve them after they have been formed.

27. Review by consulting new sources. Read other books on the subject you are studying, and so obtain a fresh point of view. Get books that have another organization, or that treat a different list of topics so that you can find the same points in new combinations. Do not hesitate to give time even to new topics on the subject as they appear in these other books, even though you are not likely to be examined on them directly. Such fresh or supplementary knowledge will show up indirectly in the examination to your advantage. Comparing your textbook account with that in another book will very greatly enrich your knowledge of the subject.

28. Review both at short and at long intervals.

Since most of the forgetting that you are going to do occurred within twenty-four hours after you learned the material, a daily review would seem to be an inescapable necessity. Each day's work should be reviewed, however, before twenty-four hours have elapsed, else some things will be so completely forgotten that they can never be recalled. The fact that they will be seems to indicate the necessity of reviewing at night all that has been studied or learned during the day. At intervals of a week or so it is well to make a different sort of review, in which what has been learned during the week is consolidated or cumulated into one unified body. Similar reviews at intervals of a month or six weeks appear necessary for accomplishing this consolidation on a somewhat larger scale. Reviews for the course as a whole before final examinations are essential in order to accomplish the unification and organization of the course. For this reason the student who secures exemption from final examinations misses one of the most valuable parts of the entire course.

QUESTIONS AND EXERCISES

1. Outline the chapter.
2. Rate your own typical review procedure by the twenty-eight points in this chapter, giving 2 for excellent, 1 for fair, and zero for poor.
3. Review the entire course to this point preparatory to a test at the final meeting, applying the rules given in this chapter.

MATCHING TEST

Directions: Write beside each number the number of the paragraph in the chapter which discusses it.

.... 1. Self-measurement.
.... 2. New reading.
.... 3. Habit-formation.
.... 4. Grades versus knowledge.
.... 5. Finding answers to questions.
.... 6. Coöperative reviews.
.... 7. Purposes for reviews.
.... 8. Reclassifying.
.... 9. Visual methods.
.... 10. Time of reviews.
.... 11. Changing the procedure.
.... 12. Daily study technique.
.... 13. Fitting review to the test.
.... 14. Summarizing.
.... 15. Building on present foundation.
.... 16. Author's review exercises.
.... 17. Degree of detail.
.... 18. Part versus whole.
.... 19. Connecting up knowledge.
.... 20. Organization.
.... 21. Putting knowledge to use.
.... 22. Review versus new view.
.... 23. Written methods of review.
.... 24. Cramming.
.... 25. Final inspection.
.... 26. Originality.
.... 27. Notebooks.
.... 28. Filling the gaps.

TRUE–FALSE TEST

Directions: Indicate which statement is true and which false, using plus (+) for true and zero (o) for false.

.... 1. A good student will not turn in work without a final inspection to detect errors.
.... 2. The review should be in large measure repetition of the same bonds as were originally formed.
.... 3. It is practically impossible for a student to measure his own knowledge.

.... 4. The review should gather up all the little things omitted during the study.

.... 5. New learning should not be attempted during a review.

.... 6. The major reason for reviewing should be to get good grades.

.... 7. One should review in the same way as he studies.

.... 8. Reviewing should never be mere drill.

.... 9. Making a written outline of the course in a few pages is a good way to review.

.... 10. The exercises at the ends of chapters are good for study but poor for review.

.... 11. It is wise to have the examination questions to direct review.

.... 12. The point of view in reviewing should be different from that in the original studying.

.... 13. Originality is less important in reviewing than in the previous study.

.... 14. To read a second textbook on the same subject is a good way to review.

.... 15. The kind of examination given should be the major factor in determining the kind of review.

.... 16. Reviewing in groups should generally be discouraged.

.... 17. Reviewing should involve reducing much to a few words.

.... 18. Problems are poor bases for review because they are usually too indefinite.

.... 19. Visual images are of little permanent value.

.... 20. If daily work is done well there is little left to do in reviewing.

.... 21. Review should be in part a kind of repair work.

.... 22. When you get ready to review you had better forget about your old notes.

.... 23. Reviewing should be in general rather than for specific results.

.... 24. Most forgetting takes place in the first twenty-four hours.

.... 25. Second year mathematics is a review of first year mathematics.

.... 26. A review is as educational as any other part of a course.

.... 27. In reviewing you should try to see as a whole what you have studied by parts.

.... 28. A course cannot become a unified body of knowledge without reviews.

SHORT–ANSWER TEST

Directions: Answer each question or complete each statement by inserting a word, phrase, or brief answer.

1. How does the use of review questions affect reviewing?........
2. How is a course like an airplane?........
3. What use should be made of daily notes in reviewing?........
4. When the object of a course is habit-formation, what kind of review is best?........
5. To make an outline of the whole course aids memory because it can be ....
6. What is the result of reviewing only for good grades?........
7. How should review and original study procedure be related? ....
8. To summarize a point in a few words is to provide a .... for a bulky idea.
9. What is to be gained by reviewing a whole year's work in all subjects at once?........
10. How much original thinking is desirable in reviewing?........
11. How should review periods be spaced?........
12. What kind of tests besides the ordinary examinations should you prepare for in reviewing?........
13. What is the best way to take up the reviewing where the daily studying leaves off?........
14. What is a good way to force yourself to review a course after you have passed it?........
15. To what extent should reviews be encouraged?........
16. What is the main value of a diagram in reviewing?........
17. Reviewing should not be merely viewing again but also ....
18. When, especially, should the repairing of weak places in your knowledge be done?........
19. If history is studied by periods it should be reviewed by ....
20. Main points during the daily work become .... in reviewing.
21. What is the main result of reviewing by solving problems? ....
22. If you have studied a topic as a unit it may be well to review it by ....
23. What is the result of reviewing by using different books? ....
24. An advantage of self-measurement is that you discover your faults before ....
25. What is the value of group reviewing?........
26. Of what value are the exercises at the ends of chapters for reviewing?........

27. If daily work has been done well the review should consist mainly of ....

28. To what extent is it desirable to review for one particular outcome? ....

READINGS

1. May, M. A.: *How to Study in College.* Syracuse University Press, Syracuse, N.Y., 1923.

   Chapter XI, "How to Prepare for Examinations."

2. Strayer, G. D.: *Brief Course in the Teaching Process.* The Macmillan Co., New York, 1911.

   Chapter IX, "Review or Examination Lesson."

3. Waples, Douglas: *Procedures in High School Teaching.* The Macmillan Co., New York, 1924.

   Chapter XIX, "The Review."

CHAPTER XIII

TAKING TESTS

MUCH has been written in recent years about improved methods of measuring educational results. Not so much thought has been given, however, to the student's side of the measurement problem. Since tests and examinations have apparently come to stay, in spite of opposition to them from certain quarters, the following points on how to make the best of them may be of some service.

1. **Find out what kind of test to expect.** Find out what ground is to be covered and the kind of mastery of the subject that will be expected of you. Find out whether the test will be in the essay form or of the objective type; whether it will emphasize memory or problem-solving; whether it will require merely acquaintance with tools or the ability to use them. The general principle of studying for a specific purpose is as applicable to preparing for tests as to any other kind of work. It is hardly fair to have to prepare for a test when you have no idea what its nature is to be, to say nothing of the wastefulness of such aimless preparation.

2. **Prepare for different kinds of tests.** One kind of test measures one thing and another kind another. For example, a true-false test measures ability to recognize, while a completion test meas-

ures ability to recall. The essay test emphasizes ability to organize your ideas and express them well in English, while the problem test requires you to reason with the aid of that which you have learned. For the immediate purpose of passing a test it is advantageous to get ready for the particular kind that is to be given, if you can find out what it is, but for the more remote purpose of mastering the subject it is necessary to acquire all these different kinds of ability by studying and reviewing for each kind of test instead of for only a single kind.

3. Be patient with the shortcomings of our present imperfect marking system. Few well-informed persons would claim that our marking and examination system is perfect. It is seldom possible to sample with entire accuracy the knowledge that is to be measured. Usually you are over-measured on some things and under-measured, or not measured at all, on others. Habit and memory are likely to be measured at the expense of thought and attitude. What you write in the test is often very imperfectly judged by the teacher, and you get more or less than you deserve because the teacher has to guess what your answer is worth. Two papers identical in content and form may receive different grades, or the same paper graded at different times may receive different grades. An "A" from one teacher may mean the equivalent of a "C" from another, and so on. Teachers are aware of these imperfections in the system and are remedying them as fast as possible. It is your part to be patient and not to expect the impossible. An imperfect measuring program is far better than none at all.

4. **Do not resist or oppose tests and examinations.** The customary response to a teacher's announcement of a test is a groan. Too often tests are looked upon as things to be endured rather than as things to be used for profit or educational growth. The reason you ordinarily dislike an examination is that both reviewing for it and taking it involve the traversing of certain new nerve circuits. Exercising new nerve cells is not so pleasant as exercising old and familiar ones, but it involves more learning and mental growth. The dislike for taking an examination is, therefore, based purely on mental laziness, and when you get excused from an examination you are simply dodging an educative experience in order to avoid the work that it involves.

5. **Use your tests as instruments for new learning.** Tests are ordinarily thought of as means of measuring a student's present knowledge, but they may also be very useful in teaching him new things. There are several ways in which to learn by means of tests. You can improve your ability to use English by practicing it in a test where effective expression is important. You can improve your ability to organize your ideas and to think rapidly and effectively. You can clarify your ideas on the subjects covered in the test by thinking them through while the test is in progress. You can get a new viewpoint from the questions and follow the subject up afterwards in this new light. You can learn from the

examination what the teacher considers the most important matters in the course. You can study your errors after the papers are graded, and thus learn the correct answers. You can ask questions after the test is completed and enter into educative class discussions on topics that it brings up.

6. Follow directions to the letter. Directions are given for a better reason than to occupy time or space; they are given to be followed. If you are asked to write only on certain parts of the paper, to sign your name in a particular place, or to fold the paper in a specific way, do so. Any paper that is not prepared according to directions is in the "awkward squad," and should be given a lower grade for that reason if for no other. In certain kinds of tests, particularly the new-type or in the standardized tests, failure to follow directions is likely to result in complete failure. The writer has observed, however, that in spite of the importance of following directions, and in spite of all that has been said and written on the subject, out of any typical group of thirty students there is generally at least one person who gets a low grade because he disregarded directions.

7. Take standardized tests according to standardized procedure. Occasionally you are asked to take a test that has already been given to several thousand students, and for which norms or average scores have been established. The greatest value of such tests is that the established norms offer a basis of comparison that is more stable and reliable than the scores of the few students in your own class or school. In order to utilize this value, your procedure during the tests must be comparable with that of the students who established the norms. If you fail to observe the time limits scrupulously, or disregard or overlook directions, or interrupt the test to ask questions, or get nervous or excited — in short, if you do any kind of freakish or exceptional thing, you may spoil the value of the test as a measurement of your knowledge and ability. For example, bright but thoughtless students have received low ratings in such tests because they did not sharpen their pencils beforehand and consequently had to waste valuable time during the test.

8. Learn how to take new-type objective tests. Teachers are turning in ever-increasing numbers to the use of true-false, completion, best answer, matching, and similar objective tests which can be given and scored quickly and which require a minimum of writing on the part of the student. In these devices many questions are asked and each question is answered briefly and is less important than the average question in the essay type of test. It is well to be on your guard against certain common mistakes which students frequently make in this type of test. One of these is the mistake of trying to guess your way through. Since any single question is relatively unimportant, it is easy to take the whole test lightly — with a low score as the result. When you recall that a difference of one point in the score may decide your fate between a "B" and a "C," you see the importance of taking each question seriously. Another error is that of taking too much time on a difficult question. Frequently these tests are given with a time limit, and if you dwell on one item very long you may have to leave ten others unanswered. A better plan is to leave a troublesome question until all the others have been dealt with, and then, if there is time, return to it. A third error is that of trusting first impressions in answering these tests. Some students and teachers stoutly maintain that, in a true-false test, if you stop to think you are more likely than not to make the wrong answer; that your first reaction is more reliable than second thought. Some unpublished data collected under the writer's direction reveal, however, that, when persons have second thoughts on true-false tests and change their answers accordingly, they raise their grades about twice as often as they lower them. The writer's recommendation would be to take the test at a reasonably vigorous and rapid rate and then go back and revise the previous answers, instead of dwelling a long time in the first instance on each item.

9. Make your test paper as objective as possible. A test paper is objective if two or more persons can rate it independently and each give it the same score or rating. One of the great weaknesses of the old style of examination is its lack of objectivity; in that kind of examination the teacher who scores a paper has to guess what it is worth. If you can write your paper in such a straightforward, concise style that the things you say stand out clearly, each with its own special significance, the teacher will be able to grade the paper objectively, or with a minimum of guessing. Every teacher appreciates a paper that leaves no doubt as to what the writer meant.

10. **Simplify your answers.** When a tired teacher who is laboriously grading papers finds one in which the answers are concise and directly to the point, with each point clearly set off from the others, he is usually disposed to add a few points to the grade for simplicity. If you can think the question through and then write your conclusion instead of doing the thinking as you write, your paper will be likely to have this very desirable quality. If you answer in outline form or in a list of points, or if you underline the key words so that they will strike the teacher's eye without his reading the body of the paragraph, you thereby improve the quality of your paper. The test of whether you have really thought a question through is whether or not you can discuss it simply.

11. **List and number the points you want to express.** If in answering a question you want to say three things, number those things 1, 2, 3 in your paper, so there will be no danger of the reader's missing any of them. The mere fact that you are able to list and number these points shows that you have them clearly separated in your mind, and is evidence of well-defined knowledge. If you are to discuss each point at some length, enumerate all the

C. *Special hints*

points briefly before treating the first one, in order to give the reader a bird's-eye view of your plan before going into details. For your own use as a means of arranging your ideas preparatory to writing them in final form, it is well to list or outline the points that you are going to include in your answer.

C-1 12. **Do not assume that the teacher knows what you mean.** Write your ideas down distinctly instead of expecting the teacher to read between the lines. Papers are graded, as a general rule, rather impersonally, and with little consideration of the writers. Some teachers try to eliminate the personal element entirely by covering up the names on the papers until after they have done their grading. It is seldom safe to assume that because you discussed a question orally in class the teacher will recall what you said when he grades your paper. When you consider the further fact that large numbers of papers are graded by student assistants who know nothing of your reactions in class, you see the great importance of putting on record everything that you expect to be considered in the making of your grade.

C-2 13. **Use good English in your test papers.** Whether you are taking an English test or not, you are almost sure to be judged in it, to a certain extent, by your English usage. A few misspelled words or errors of grammar mark you as illiterate and reduce your grade. If a paper is written in poor English, it is difficult for the teacher to avoid being influenced by that fact, even though the ideas ex-

pressed are good.   Some schools have a regular rule
that no paper in any subject should be given a passing grade unless the English will pass.   The writer
has collected data on this point from members of
a university faculty.   The seventy-nine professors
who replied to his inquiries reported that an average
of fifteen per cent of the test grade was to be based
on English.   Many of them added, however, that as
a matter of fact they based more than that on English, since judgment of content was prejudiced by
poor English beyond the discount consciously made
on account of it.

14. **Be sure you understand the meaning of the
questions.**   Low grades on tests are often due to
the fact that the students do not stop long enough
before writing to ponder the real meaning of the
questions, with the result that their answers are
directed into the wrong channels.   If there is any
ambiguity or uncertainty about the questions, ask
the teacher what is meant.   A very good plan is to
read all questions over before answering any of them,
in order to give the meaning and significance of each
question a few minutes to mature in your mind.
In taking true-false or new-type tests, however, the
situation is somewhat different from that in the
essay test.   Frequently in this type the purpose
of a question is to determine whether you understand the meaning of one of its leading terms, and
in that case to ask the teacher what the question
means would be entirely out of order.   New-type
tests should ordinarily be taken without asking any

questions, except in regard to the directions about the test procedure as a whole.

15. **Make some kind of answer to each question.** Whether you know the answer to a question or not, write something on it. The grading of the essay or discussion type of examinations is not very exact or definite, and if you try a question you are likely to get a few points for your effort, but if you leave it blank you can only get zero for it. You have everything to gain and nothing to lose by attempting an answer to each question. Furthermore, you fail to do yourself justice if you refuse to write unless you are sure of yourself, since other students in the class are certain to resort to bluffing, and if you are over-modest you simply let them take the higher grades without knowing the work any better than you do. There is another and still better reason for writing something on each question. That is that in the act of doing it you are likely to recall or reason out something that is really an answer to the question, whereas, if you refuse to write, your mind simply remains blank. Your best ideas are usually developed in connection with your efforts to express them.

16. **Answer questions in the order of difficulty.** If a question is very difficult, it is well to delay answering it until you have worked on other questions, in order to acquire a kind of momentum or get warmed up mentally. Frequently a question that seems impossible when first read is easily answered after you have been thinking and writing

for an hour on similar or related questions. During the interval there takes place a kind of unconscious learning or forming of mental associations which results in a richer fund of ideas than you had at the beginning of the examination. In long examinations, however, there is one limitation to the policy of answering questions in the order of difficulty; it is the fact that the most difficult questions should not be left for answering after extreme fatigue has set in. If the test period is very long, it might be well to cover some of the easy questions first, then take the difficult ones, and finally finish the period by answering the other easy ones.

17. Remember that tests are usually based on the principle of sampling. It is impossible for the teacher to test you on everything you know, and consequently most tests are devised to sample your knowledge more or less thoroughly. The assumption is that, if you answer well the questions that are asked, you could answer those that were not asked equally well. This implies or suggests two points regarding student procedure, as follows: (1) Be ready for the sampling by being prepared on all points, instead of trying to guess where the test will fall. (2) Do intensive work on the topics that are asked for. If you get ten questions, do not try to answer them in such a way as to include all you know about the course, dragging in material from other topics, but rather stick to those ten questions and give the richest and fullest answers to them that you can, leaving the teacher to imagine what you could do on the points not included in the test.

18. Give due attention, during a test, to the factor of time. Some tests are given with a definite time limit so short that it is impossible for any one to complete them, and success is measured by the amount completed in the time allowed. Other tests allow time enough for all the students to finish provided they use reasonable discretion in the distribution of time among the different questions. In such a case keep your watch handy and budget the time so that each question gets a proportionate share, since surplus time devoted to one question raises your grade on it less than it lowers your grade on the one which was neglected. The writer has compared the time spent on examinations with the grades received, and has found no noticeable relationship. Some bright students finish quickly and get good grades, while other very poor students quit early for lack of anything to write. Similarly, both extremes of grades were found to be earned by the students who were last in turning in their papers. Probably the solution of the speed question lies in the direction of mental hygiene. Find the speed at which your mind works best and at which you are least nervous, and then stick to it.

19. Do honest work. Calling your attention to the question of honesty may be unnecessary because you already have highly developed moral standards. In that case this paragraph is intended to enlist your coöperation in raising the standards of

honor among those few students who are in need of
it.   There are two facts about honor that should
help to improve the moral standards in an examination.   The first is that honesty is a social matter.
If you get a higher grade because of dishonest
methods, you take that high grade away from some
one else.   It is exactly comparable to walking past
several persons in a waiting line, as every person
whom you pass dishonestly has been injured by
your act.   The other point is particularly applicable
to the new-type tests.   It is easy to copy another's
paper in these tests because of the short and objective answers, but it is equally easy to detect
such copying.   If you have more identical errors
than can be explained on the basis of chance, it
is conclusively established that you have copied;
persons have been dismissed from colleges on the
basis of such internal evidence in the examination
papers.

20. **Start off in a course with a high grade.**
"Well begun is half done," according to the proverb.   In courses which involve subjective grading,
or the exercise of the teacher's judgment, it is advantageous to get a high grade on the first test or
written work, because this first impression of ability
which you establish in the teacher's mind is likely
to be somewhat permanent.   It is easier to keep up
a good first impression than it is to overcome a bad
first impression.   Furthermore, the effect upon
yourself and your own attitude of a good start is
such that it is easier to maintain your interest and

pride in your work if you do well on the first test
of the course.

21. Save the test questions. If you keep a record
of the questions of a test, you can continue to study
after the test by looking up the answers to the
questions you missed. Much of the potential value
of a test is lost if the matter is dismissed from the
mind as soon as the paper is passed in. It is a good
plan to save the questions and use them as guides
in later reviewing for future tests in the course.
The questions for the weekly tests should prove
helpful as guides in reviewing for final examinations.
So helpful have old examination questions proved
as instruments for reviewing that published lists of
questions that have been used for civil service examinations or for teachers' examinations are widely
sold for the use of candidates preparing for these
kinds of examinations. A question of honor arises
in this connection. It is well known that some
teachers use the same tests over and over for succeeding classes. Some far-sighted students save
their tests and coach later generations of students on
them. It is useless to tell them not to do it, since it
is impossible to enforce the command. The solution
lies in a more extensive practice of saving the questions by students; this will make it necessary for
professors to prepare new tests for each class.

**22. Find out what you missed in a test or wherein
you failed.** Improvement is much more rapid
when you know the outcome of your efforts than
when you are striving blindly, because with a know-

ledge of where you failed, it is possible to correct your errors. After a test you should try to find out specifically what you missed and why you missed it. The mere knowledge that you are ill is worth little in getting well unless you discover the nature and cause of the trouble, and this is as true of educational as of physical kinds of illness. Some special tests for diagnostic purposes have been made for certain school subjects; they are designed to reveal the exact nature of students' difficulties. Where these tests are not available, you must rely on the less refined but nevertheless quite useful diagnosis that your teacher is able to make of you and your work. If you will devote a little effort to looking up the answers to the questions after the test, it will be very helpful, as a rule.

23. Insist on a class discussion after each test. A test should be useful for diagnosis as well as for measurement. That is, it should reveal wherein you are deficient. If the results are not discussed, this service is lost. One of the most profitable forms of class discussion is the "post mortem" after an examination, in which the various answers are explained. If you answered wrong, insist on being shown your error, and ask further questions until you are entirely satisfied. In such a discussion you not only have your own errors cleared up, but also get some light on the errors that other students have fallen into and so can avoid them in future.

24. After the tests are scored, find out your relative standing in the class group. A mark or grade means little until you know what your fellow students got on the same test. On one test the grades may run high, on another low, but if you are in the upper fifth of the class each time, you know that you are relatively successful. It is not to be expected that you should know the grades received by different individuals in the class, but there is seldom any good reason why you should not know the average score for the class as a whole, and possibly something about the range over which the scores of the class are distributed. It is of interest and value also to know whether your score is high or low in comparison with the scores of classes that took the same test in previous years, or in other schools, provided it is a test that can be given and scored uniformly.

25. Try not only for a high score, but also for a relatively high score. The normal distribution is followed to some extent by all teachers, consciously or unconsciously, and a student's grade is based more or less on how well he stands in comparison with other students in the class. Since this is the case, you must not only get a good score, but a better score than the others in order to receive an "A" grade. The race is won, not by the swift, but by the swiftest. It is well, therefore, to compare yourself with others and to try to surpass them. The number of high grades is consciously limited, as a rule, and if you are to get one you must beat others to it. Similarly there are usually about a certain number of students to get low or failing grades, and if you avoid falling into this category, you must accomplish it by being sure that you not only do good work but *better* work than some one else, because the failing grades are given to the lowest students in the class. The situation is similar to that of the race for the swimming-hole when the cry is raised, "The last one in is *it*."

26. Give yourself tests of your own. Tests are given in large measure to determine how well you have succeeded in the work, but you do not always have to have a teacher's test in order to find that out. You can measure with a fair degree of accuracy the success with which your work has been done. Some of the tests which you can give yourself to measure your own success are as follows:

(1) Compare your work with that of your fellow students.

(2) Give yourself a grade of "A," "B," or "C," etc., after completing a lesson, to indicate how well you think you have learned it.

(3) Compare your work with your past record to discover whether you are improving, and as a stimulus to beating your past record.

(4) Rate yourself on such personality traits as character, initiative, originality, punctuality, dependability, etc.

(5) Rate yourself as to the portion of your ability that you have used, or as to whether you have worked up to the limit of your capacity.

27. Submit your personality, character, and interest for measurement, as well as your informa-

tion. After all, it is what you are that counts most, not what you know. The recommendation that you get when you graduate depends on many things other than academic or scholastic achievements, important as these are. A student who ranks "A" in information, but "F" in coöperation or dependability, has failed utterly. One of the things you are trying to learn in school is how to live in the world, and the world's tests and examinations are often based on personal qualities or character traits. These things may not register on the paper, but they register daily on the memory of your teachers and fellow students, and your worth as an individual is determined by them.

28. React to each day's class exercise as if it were a test or examination. Your final grade in a course is based on a composite of many measurements, and one of the most important of these is your daily conduct and reaction in the course. Some teachers use tests as an objective or tangible screen to stand behind while they give the grades they think you deserve, and what they think you deserve is largely the result of their personal estimate of you. It costs you little to be courteous, polite, coöperative, and positive in your attitude in a class — in fact you yourself are happier when you react that way; and that kind of behavior is usually appreciated and rewarded by being given better grades. The writer can recall giving "A's," because of such personal factors, to students who seldom earned "A's" on their tests, and he has also given grades of "C" to students who had few test scores that low, marking them down because of their uncoöperative attitude toward the work of the course.

29. **Treat each piece of written work to be done outside of class as a test or examination.** Papers assigned for preparation at home ordinarily receive scores or grades and are used to measure your work in the course. Because of their definiteness and concreteness, as compared with daily recitations and unrecorded reactions, they usually have a relatively large and important part in determining your grade in the course. The safe thing to do is to consider each of these assignments as a test, and to carry it out with as great care as if it were a regular examination.

30. **Take every opportunity to assist in grading or correcting the papers of other students.** Grading papers for your first time is comparable to your first opportunity to witness a theatrical performance from the back stage. There are several mysteries about it that clear up. If you could only see your paper as your teacher sees it, in comparison with twenty or thirty other papers, you would learn many things about how to present your ideas. Furthermore, grading or reading a whole set of papers will give a great variety of viewpoints and reveal relationships that are entirely new to you. If you show ability in your subjects, you are likely to be selected as a student assistant during the later years of your course and to receive payment for the

very educative work of reading all papers for one or more courses. Such honors are well worth striving for and well worth accepting when offered. Even if you are not offered a job as paid assistant, you always have the privilege of offering your services free. Such an offer is usually appreciated by the instructor, whether or not he is able to accept it.

QUESTIONS AND EXERCISES

1. Outline the chapter.
2. Rank the thirty points into three groups as to their worth or helpfulness, as follows: Very helpful, fairly helpful, of little practical value.
3. Apply the principles given in this chapter to the taking of a test on the book at the final meeting.

MATCHING TEST

Directions: Write beside each number the number of the paragraph in the chapter which discusses it.

.... 1. Leaving the teacher in doubt.
.... 2. Grading on attitude.
.... 3. Advance information.
.... 4. Home work.
.... 5. Talking the test over.
.... 6. Instructions.
.... 7. Misunderstanding the question.
.... 8. Student assistants.
.... 9. Bluffing.
.... 10. Self rating.
.... 11. Tests as teaching devices.
.... 12. Normal curve.
.... 13. Speed.
.... 14. Diversified ability.
.... 15. Easiest questions first.
.... 16. Studying the questions afterward.
.... 17. Objective tests.
.... 18. What the others made.
.... 19. Simplicity.
.... 20. Hating tests.

.... 21. Keeping the questions.
.... 22. Language.
.... 23. Good grades on first test.
.... 24. Sampling.
.... 25. Numbered points.
.... 26. Test norms.
.... 27. "Reading between the lines."
.... 28. Weaknesses of measuring devices.
.... 29. Daily grades.
.... 30. Cheating.

TRUE–FALSE TEST

Directions: Indicate which statement is true and which false, using plus (+) for true and zero (o) for false.

.... 1. Preparing for a particular type of test yields a narrow type of knowledge.
.... 2. It is unfair to ask what kind of a test you are going to have.
.... 3. Every recitation is an examination.
.... 4. The grade you get on the first test is relatively unimportant.
.... 5. Objectivity in a paper means avoiding the use of the pronoun "I."
.... 6. Numbering points improves your grade.
.... 7. When a test is over you should forget about it.
.... 8. There is little good to come from a class discussion of answers after a test.
.... 9. You should start with the easiest questions first.
.... 10. A test attempts to judge all your knowledge by a few samples.
.... 11. Those who finish first make the best grades.
.... 12. Students can grade each other's papers quite effectively.
.... 13. Copies of test questions are usually worth keeping.
.... 14. A standardized test is one that is made by a committee rather than an individual.
.... 15. If you do not know a question you should bluff.
.... 16. In practically every class there is at least one person who will not follow the directions.
.... 17. Cheating on an examination is primarily an offense against the other students.
.... 18. A test is graded for content and not for form.

.... 19. Dislike of examinations is due simply to mental laziness.
.... 20. You learn very little through tests.
.... 21. Grades should never be based on other things besides actual knowledge.
.... 22. The marking system should be abolished.
.... 23. Your grade should be based on your rank in the class.
.... 24. First impression is better than second thought in taking a true-false test.
.... 25. Written work is a more important determiner of grades than oral work because more easily graded.
.... 26. If you get an idea down at all, the teacher will usually know what you mean.
.... 27. It is out of order to ask questions about a new-type test.
.... 28. You can measure your own work with considerable accuracy.
.... 29. Grades for all students should be posted in a public place.
.... 30. The test of real knowledge is ability to discuss a thing simply.

SHORT–ANSWER TEST

Directions: Answer each question or complete each statement by inserting a word, phrase, or brief answer.

1. What is the significance of the first grade under a teacher?
....
2. What is the special evidence of dishonesty on a new-type test?........
3. What is the correlation between time spent and grades earned on tests?........
4. Why are the directions for a standardized test so important?
....
5. To what extent can you expect the teacher to read between the lines in grading your paper?........
6. What should you learn about the scores of other students?
....
7. How many methods of self-measurement are mentioned?
....
8. What effect does an attitude of coöperation have on your grades?........
9. What should be done about a puzzling question in a new-type test?........

10. What type of ability does the true-false test measure?........
11. What should you do if you do not know the answer?........
12. How many suggestions are given growing out of the fact of sampling?........
13. What value is there in saving the test questions?........
14. What should be the meaning of an "A" grade?........
15. What principle of study is illustrated by finding out the kind of test to expect?........
16. Why is taking a test unpleasant?........
17. Of what value is it to grade other students' papers?........
18. What is the value of numbering the points in your answer? ....
19. How can you achieve simplicity in your answers?........
20. How much of a grade is usually based on English?........
21. What is a good way to be sure to understand the questions? ....
22. What is meant by an objective answer?........
23. To what extent is your grade based on personal qualities?......
24. What is meant by an examination "post mortem"?........
25. Of what value are tests for teaching?........
26. What is a sure way to get into the "awkward squad"?........
27. In what order should questions be answered?........
28. What is the proper attitude toward the marking system? ....
29. What is meant by the statement that a test is diagnostic? ....
30. Why are papers of unusual importance in determining grades? ....

READINGS

1. Adams, John: *Making the Most of One's Mind.* Geo. H. Doran Co., New York, 1915.
   Chapter X, "Examinations."

2. Clippinger, Walter G.: *Student Relationships.* Thomas Nelson & Sons, New York, 1926.
   Chapter VIII, "Examinations."

3. Dearborn, G. V. N.: *How to Learn Easily.* Little, Brown & Co., Boston, 1918.
   Chapter VI, "Examination-Preparedness."

4. Headley, Leal A.: *How to Study in College.* Henry Holt & Co., New York, 1926.
   Chapter XIII, "How to Meet an Examination."

5. Kitson, H. D.: *How to Use your Mind.* J. B. Lippincott Co., Philadelphia, 1916.

Chapter XI, "Examinations."

6. May, M. A.: *How to Study in College.* Syracuse University Press, Syracuse, N.Y., 1923.

Chapter XI, "How to Prepare for Examinations."

7. Touton, F. C., and Struthers, A. B.: *Junior-High-School Procedures.* Ginn & Co., Boston, 1926.

Chapter VII, "Measuring and Recording Progress."

8. Waples, Douglas: *Procedures in High School Teaching.* The Macmillan Co., New York, 1924.

Chapter XVIII, "The Informal Test."

CHAPTER XIV

WORKING IN THE LABORATORY

THE introduction of laboratory work into the schools is an innovation of quite recent date. The work has now reached a point, however, where it is generally recognized as an essential part of the work in the natural sciences and the practical arts, and in many of the more academic subjects as well. Two serious problems, though, are involved in this method of doing school work. They are the problem of time and the problem of expense. If schools are to continue the use of a method which consumes so much time and money, they are justified in insisting upon results which are worth the price paid. The following paragraphs undertake to help bring about these results.

1. **Turn the work of all courses into laboratory form.** The laboratory method need not be limited to the sciences; it is equally applicable to English, social sciences, and other studies. Going on an excursion to some point of interest, or making a relief map of South America, or helping to get out an issue of the school paper — all these are laboratory exercises. The meaning of the laboratory method is different in the minds of different educators, but the three most common implications of the term are: (1) muscular activity or movement; (2) con-

crete observation and sensory contact with objects; (3) investigation or discovery of things for yourself, instead of mere assimilation of information in the exact form presented by others. These three elements might well be introduced into any and all school subjects.

2. **Adapt laboratory procedure to the purpose for which you are studying the subject.** Laboratory students fall roughly into two classes, those who should learn principles and those who should acquire technical skills. The ordinary student in a chemistry class in high school or college falls in the first group while the student who expects to follow a career as a chemist falls in the second, as does also the ordinary student in a cooking laboratory. At the outset you should decide whether your purpose is to learn the principles and theories of a subject, or to become a technician in that field. The prospective specialist in chemistry should give considerably more attention than the non-specialist to acquiring good form, establishing high standards of workmanship, developing skill in handling apparatus or instruments, and mastering all the details of practical procedure. It is doubtful whether these skills are worth the cost of their acquisition to the student who is not going to use them in any definite way. In fact, schools might well separate students into two classes so far as that is possible, laymen and specialists, giving lecture-demonstrations to the laymen and individual laboratory work to the specialists, since it has been found possible to teach

the principles of a subject as well by demonstration as by individual experiments.

3. Subordinate quantitative work to qualitative. Exact and precise measurement has considerable value, especially in the laboratory work of the specialist, but it is not so much an end in itself as a means to the understanding and appreciation of the qualitative nature of the things that are measured. Too often the real purpose or meaning of an experiment is lost because of too much attention to the manipulation of measuring instruments. Do not let yourself become so engrossed in the small details of measurement as to overlook the interpretation of the major problem before you.

4. Avoid obscuring the underlying principles by placing too much emphasis on the more concrete elements. One of the most serious weaknesses of laboratory work is the failure to learn what the experiment proves. It is entirely possible to perform every step of an experiment with accuracy and secure a perfect outcome, and yet not really know what it is all about. You should always ask yourself "why" in addition to "what," and classify each specific result under a more general principle. If you do not know the meaning of what you have found, ask the instructor, or look it up in the text or reference books. A good rule is to compare your results with those of other students, or with those reported by other scientists, and to judge their general reasonableness in the light of these comparisons, pointing out the possible explanations of dif-

ferences which you may find. It is a common report that the weakest part of the usual laboratory write-up is the section on interpretation of results. If the experiment is performed thoughtfully as a problem instead of mechanically as a routine exercise, with a clear understanding of the reason for each step, it should go far toward producing a clear understanding of the major principles or laws studied.

5. **Strike a compromise between discovery and verification of facts.** To attempt to rediscover all scientific facts would not be economical even if it were possible. The process of discovering a single scientific law, if carried out completely, might require an entire lifetime; but the major steps that were originally employed in the discovery of that law may be repeated in a few hours in the laboratory, under competent guidance, and will result in a greatly enriched understanding and appreciation of that law. Having repeated these steps, you will remember and understand them better than if you had only read about them. Occasionally a situation will arise when some law of science is seemingly contradicted by facts from your own personal experience, in which case you can resort to the laboratory to establish the truth. In other cases the experiment will reveal particular application of a law which is new to you. Beyond such "discoveries" as these the laboratory work of the average science course will probably not attempt to go.

6. **Perform some laboratory exercises as practice**

or drill. Certain laboratory activities are for the development of skill rather than for the understanding of principles or the acquisition of information. The typewriting laboratory, so called, is an example; this involves almost no content except the drill type. The activities in home economics and manual training vary considerably in this respect, but frequently they are largely for manual skill. Where drill is the major purpose, the procedure should be that described in the chapter on skill.

7. **Look for practical applications of what you learn through the laboratory.** You can make a laboratory exercise as abstract or as practical as you like, according to the way in which you go about it. As the experiment is usually planned it is somewhat artificial and remote from life situations, but there are plenty of parallels or resemblances between laboratory situations and life situations if you will only look for them. One way to give the work this practical significance is to think how you would do the experiment in your own home, without the special instruments and apparatus of the laboratory. Another way is to find out how the industrial world performs the operation, where factors of economy and financial profit have to be considered more than in the laboratory. Another method is to bring your own practical problems to the laboratory and solve them there with the help of the special instruments and apparatus. In fact, if you insist on a practical outcome there will usually be one, but if you are

content to deal with mere generalizations and abstractions you may never see their applications. One of the common complaints against scientists is that they have been content to work in their laboratories and unwilling to experiment in practical life situations.

8. Correlate laboratory work with class work. Connect experiments in the laboratory with the material studied in the text and discussed in the class. Make them an outgrowth and final testing out of problems raised in class. Make lecture and text help the laboratory, and make the laboratory help out the lecture and textbook work. Follow each experiment by further reading to discover its deeper meanings, and precede each laboratory exercise by readings so that you will be able to see all there is in it for you to see. Different instructors have different policies in regard to whether a topic should be studied first in the laboratory or in the text, but as a matter of fact it should be studied in neither first, to the total exclusion of the other. Alternation of the two types of study is the wisest method.

9. Prepare for the experiment before you come to the laboratory. You can see more if you know what to look for, and you can get more ideas from an experiment if you bring a few of your own with you. Certainly there is as good reason for preparing for a laboratory lesson as for preparing for a recitation or a lecture. Read the directions for the experiment before you begin; read preferably, in some reliable source outside of the laboratory manual, material in regard to the factors, elements, or principles involved and continue such study until you know, before you perform the experiment, what is going to happen. A good student should be able to predict the outcome of his experiment before he begins it, provided he has given it sufficient previous study. He should be able to plan his steps in such a way as to avoid useless operations, and should know exactly what data he expects to secure and how to secure them. He should know at least what questions could be answered by the experiment, and probably the answers to most of them. If you go to the laboratory prepared in this way your whole effort can be devoted to problems of a higher sort involving more advanced considerations and the discovery of more subtle implications. Each step in an experiment should be performed with a definite and conscious purpose, and careful preparation is the best way to insure the achievement of this purpose.

10. **Proceed according to the principles of scientific method.** Each laboratory experiment should be a lesson or exercise in application of the scientific method of thinking. A very clear statement of the essential elements of this procedure is given in a leaflet entitled *The Scientific Method*, published by The Character Education Institution, of Washington, D.C., from which we quote, with permission:

The scientific method necessitates intensive, systematic, and persistent brain work under control against misunderstandings, superficiality, and bias, and in complete loyalty to reality and the truth.

None but those having aptitude, instruction, and training can be successful in the use of the scientific method of thinking.

DESCRIPTION OF THE METHOD

(1) *Gather data* on the problem or within a selected field according to some adequate, sound plan by means of numerous and accurate observations made with the human senses, assisted and corrected by instruments of precision. The observations are usually with a well-defined purpose, but sometimes for information according to opportunity. Observations must be recorded in definite terms and measurements and in specific statements. Many observers may collaborate in gathering data.

(2) *Classify and organize data* on the basis of similarities, variations, activities, processes, causes, results. Distinguish between essential and superficial characters.

(3) *Generalize* to get principles and theories into tentative form. Use constructive imagination, discernment, known principles to formulate reasonable generalizations that solve the problem or explain the known facts in the selected field. Many researches accept a mass of classified data and verified generalizations and then proceed to solve some problem by formulating hypotheses thereon and verifying these, without including general gathering of data and classification work.

(4) *Verify* generalizations by controlled experiments, by tested predictions of results, by repetition of experiments, and the gathering of additional data. Appraise data by coefficients of variations and of correlations, and by probable error. Determine sources of error in method and apparatus, and evaluate by auxiliary investigation. State all assumptions and include them in the conclusions.

(5) *Report* the research in full, and subject results to criticism and verification by others competent to collaborate.

(6) *Announce* the results of the research to the general public for practical use.

THE CHARACTERISTICS OF THE SCIENTIST

(1) Sincere and open-minded; not diverted by personal interests.

(2) Alert and alive to the truth, vital; not complacent.

(3) Poised; not excitable, hysterical or melancholy.

(4) Discerning and thorough; not superficial.

(5) Accurate; not indefinite.

(6) Inventive and constructive; not lacking initiative.

(7) Independent; not suggestible.

(8) Thoughtful and persistent; not merely impulsive.

(9) Industrious and energetic; not lazy and dilatory.

(10) Executive; not haphazard.

(11) Purposeful; not led merely by likes and dislikes.

(12) Self-confident; not timid.

11. Follow directions. The laboratory manual ordinarily gives more or less explicit instructions as to the order of procedure. Failure to follow them not only may result in failure to achieve the end in view, or failure to discover some of the elements that should have been noted, but is likely to result in a waste of materials or in injury to the specimens with which you are working. Such little mistakes as using hot water instead of cold, or concentrated instead of dilute acid, or pouring water into concentrated sulphuric acid instead of pouring the acid into the water, have been responsible for serious injury to others working near by. Laboratory work should consist of more than simply following routine directions, but usually that is taken care of by the writer of the manual, who leaves something to the initiative of the student. When he puts directions into the manual he does so for a reason, and they should be followed.

12. **Secure the necessary equipment, and learn how to use it effectively.** When getting ready for an experiment list the apparatus and supplies needed, and before you begin provide everything that you need. In courses which require individual ownership of instruments, such as dissecting sets in biology, feel free to buy a standard grade of materials and an adequate amount. Not only secure necessary instruments but take a pride in them, for the real workman loves his tools. Learn the specialized functions of each instrument or piece of apparatus, and the special technique of using it. For example, note the following suggestions for the use of the microscope, which might be equalled by similar special directions for other laboratory equipment: Do not close one eye when observing through the microscope, but rather learn to ignore what you see with the other eye. When drawing what you are observing, observe with one eye and direct the drawing with the other. Do not employ an unnecessary amount of magnification since by shutting out all but a very small area, you deprive yourself of the opportunity to see the relation between the parts studied.

13. **Make up informal experiments of your own.**

It would be extraordinary indeed if the manual included all the exercises that are of value to you, and yet numbers of students fail to realize that it does not contain *all the experiments there are*. Laboratory exercises are like textbook subject-matter in that they are selected from a large number of possible exercises with a view to choosing the few which will have the greatest value to the largest number of students. Individual students, however, have special interests and special problems of their own which suggest the value of doing certain exercises as self-initiated individual projects — exercises comparable to individual readings and reports in the more academic subjects. You might do well even to sacrifice certain experiments in the book in order to make room for home-made experiments of your own, or else to do the latter during the time that remains after the completion of those in the regular list. A capable student should be able to complete his project in less than the time allowed, in which case he can fill up the remainder of the period with experimental work of his own.

14. **Make a compromise between independent and coöperative work.** Common practice in laboratories has settled upon the plan of the students working in pairs with each member of the pair held individually responsible for the whole experiment. Much of the benefit that you get from the work depends on the extent to which you do, see, and think for yourself, but there is also much to be gained by comparing your results with those of

another and thus carrying the whole process of interpretation a step further than you could go alone.   If you can secure a partner of ability equal to your own, and if each then does his best and supplements that by the stimulation received from the other, you both have a most promising outlook. The great danger, of course, is that in any coöperative plan one person is likely to lean on the other for the majority of the work, with loss to both.   The group project, in which a large number of persons coöperate, is particularly subject to this danger.

15. Ask for criticism of your work.   Criticism is an important factor in promoting the learning process, and is particularly important in the laboratory, where the outcome of the work assumes a tangible and definite form.   An instructor or assistant is usually in the room to serve you in this respect, and it is a good idea to call on him for his approval or suggestions as you proceed with the work.   If it is not being done in the right manner, he can help you to correct the error and start you in the right course. Care should be taken, however, to ask for criticism after making an effort of your own, instead of asking for help before you start.   It is not the function of the instructor to do your work for you.

16. Employ special devices to improve observation.   What you learn from observing any ordinary object is limited only by your ability and resourcefulness as an observer.   There are enough matters of interest in even a commonplace thing to engage the energies of a scientist for his whole lifetime.   The

following are a few suggestions on how to observe:

(1) Study beforehand about the thing to be observed.

(2) Make a list of points to look for so that you can look for something definite.

(3) Follow up any unusual details, since they will probably lead you to discover elements of greater importance connected with them.

(4) Divide the object observed into parts or aspects, and observe one part at a time rather than look at the thing as a whole or in a general way.

(5) Observe from different points of view or at different times, coming back each time to see the material in a new light.

(6) Seek the inner significance of what you see, instead of being content merely to receive visual impressions.

(7) Compare the object observed with others in its general class.   For example, you see more when you compare two crawfish, or two school buildings, or two specimens of prize poultry, than when you observe only one.

(8) Compare your observations with those of other persons in order to raise them to a higher stage of consciousness and in order to interpret them better.

(9) Make use of drawing as an aid to observation, both to direct your analysis and to provide a record of what you observe.

(10) Record some written notes about such phases of the object as do not lend themselves readily to drawing.

17. Use drawing as an aid in your laboratory work. Drawing is not only an aid to observation, but also an excellent check on the completeness or thoroughness of your analysis of the thing drawn. It directs your attention, at the time, to the important features of the object, and it leaves a record for later use. The following suggestions relate to drawing as a part of laboratory work:

(1) Draw on a large scale, so that you have room enough to work out the parts without crowding.

(2) Draw first with pencil lightly, and when the drawing is satisfactory make the lines darker.

(3) Do not attempt complete representation of the details, but rather make a sketch of the outstanding features.

(4) Let your drawings be practical devices for expressing your ideas rather than artistic attempts at doing so.

(5) Label the parts clearly, so that the labels can be read without turning the sheet around.

(6) Label the drawing as a whole in a prominent manner to show what it is to portray.

(7) Give drawings to represent each major stage in the progress of the experiment.

(8) Use colored lines whenever they will contribute to the clearness of the representation.

(9) Have your drawings criticized, and secure constructive suggestions for improvement.

(10) Make up diagrams to represent your own ideas or to illustrate numerical data in addition to representing actual objects.

(11) Secure necessary specialized tools and drawing instruments.

18. Write up the report on the experiment as you go. The written laboratory report is more than a form of evidence to satisfy your instructor that you have done your work; it is a distinct element in the learning process. That a student learns more from the exercise when he writes up his own report than when he does not, has been revealed by actual investigations. Writing down what happens requires more accurate observation of what takes place, and also requires him to clarify his thinking as to why it takes place. There may be times when it is necessary to defer writing until a reaction or an operation has been completed, but as a general rule the notations should be recorded as the work progresses, and then the whole written up in full before you leave the laboratory.

19. Write up the report on the experiment in good form. Write a true account of what happened instead of writing what should have happened. Write it, as a rule, in the first person, saying, "I heated the solution" instead of "The solution was heated." Use complete sentences, and have them correct as regards English usage. List clearly the various steps in the procedure, so that a person who has not seen the experiment could tell exactly what was done. Employ well-constructed tables, properly labeled, to present numerical data systematically. Include your graphs or drawings in the report in such a form that they both supplement and are supplemented by the other parts of the report. Write up not only the reactions but also their meaning or significance.

For a general plan some such outline as the following should be used to report experiments: (1) Problem, (2) Materials, (3) Procedure, (4) Results, (5) Conclusions. Special mention should be made of the importance of graphical presentation of these elements. It is usually possible and desirable to include drawings of your apparatus, successive stages in the procedure, and also sketches or graphs setting forth the results obtained.

20. Economize time. Keep busy and purposefully active while in the laboratory. Avoid loitering, dawdling, or playing with things. Rapid work in the laboratory is as important as it is elsewhere. Work out economical plans or methods of managing your time so that you will have adequate time for each part of the task, instead of letting the assembling of materials and the setting up of apparatus take up time that is needed for the actual performance of the experiment and the interpretation of results. Probably one of the best ways to economize laboratory time is to know what you are going to do before you come. Another is to ask for assistance when you need it instead of repeatedly going over the experiment and making the same error each time.

21. Get acquainted with the laboratory. Early in the course take a survey of the laboratory and the storeroom, and find out what is there, where each thing is located, what each is for, and what condition it is in. It frequently happens that you use a crude or improvised set-up of apparatus to perform a certain function when a special instrument is available, simply because you do not know what facilities are to be had.

22. **Be a good housekeeper in the laboratory.** Put things in their proper places when through with them. Arrange supplies, vessels, apparatus, and so on in even rows or in some other systematic order, instead of just piling them up promiscuously. Keep things classified, with all objects of a kind together. Mark or label articles so there will be no confusion — such as would be caused, for example, by forgetting what a given bottle or vessel contains. Clean up thoroughly before you leave the laboratory, not only with respect to floor, desk, and apparatus or instruments, but also with respect to your person. There are so many objects to be handled in a laboratory, and so many persons who have to use them in common, that a high standard of housekeeping and a considerable amount of coöperation in preserving order and system are absolutely essential.

23. **Help reduce the financial cost of laboratory work.** The laboratory subjects are among the most costly in the whole curriculum, even when the utmost effort is made to reduce the waste. When you, realize that one lens in a microscope may have cost $75, that a chemical you are using cost $10 per ounce, or that a thermometer you are handling is worth $15, it becomes evident that you are under a distinct social obligation to be economical. A few

specific ways in which greater economy may be secured are as follows:

(1) Use small samplings of supplies instead of large ones. A chemical reaction that involves two grams of an element is usually just as effective as if it had involved twenty grams.

(2) Plan the work before you spoil the materials. The "cut-and-try" method in carpentry is less wasteful than the "put-and-fry" method in chemistry, because in carpentry you can usually utilize the wasted parts for other things, but when two chemicals have once been mixed it is practically impossible to salvage them.

(3) Reduce the cost due to breakage. This is one of the large items in laboratory expense, and it is largely preventable.

24. Help to preserve order and reduce routine distractions. The activity and stir that naturally grow out of laboratory work normally produce a considerable amount of confusion and noise, and the necessity for securing supplies from specified sources sometimes causes congestion around the tables. Naturally certain codes of ethics or rules of conduct have to be evolved, else the group cannot function to the best advantage. As a general rule, such a group after a short time either naturally evolves more or less unconsciously a student self-government system, or develops into a socialized community which preserves real working conditions. The example of a few students can go far toward helping either of these processes along.

25. Respect the rights of others in the laboratory. The very nature of a laboratory makes it something of a social institution, involving a give and take on the part of the workers. Courtesy and politeness, willingness to give way to others who are waiting to use instruments or apparatus, thoughtfulness with respect to releasing unnecessary amounts of obnoxious gases in the room, and carefulness to refrain from borrowing your neighbor's apparatus when he needs it, are all illustrations of important ways of respecting others' rights. Certainly the general state of happiness of students in laboratory classes would be greatly improved if better standards along these lines could be established.

26. Help to promote safety and to prevent accidents. The writer bears a scar to-day that is a gentle reminder of the importance of safety first in the laboratory. Also he has just received a report to the effect that a former acquaintance was killed in an explosion in a chemical laboratory. In the laboratory you are frequently working with materials or forces which have the power to destroy the whole building or to snuff out dozens of lives unless properly controlled. Frequently, also, the accident involves the suffering of others in the laboratory who are in no way responsible. Nor should this warning be thought of solely with regard to major accidents. Probably the sum total of the lesser accidents is really more serious than that of the larger ones. When the whole cost of injured clothing, medical attention, broken instruments, wasted

supplies, and disfigured furniture is computed, the
price of carelessness is found to be very high.

QUESTIONS AND EXERCISES

1. Outline the chapter.
2. Giving yourself a score of 2 for excellent, 1 for fair, and zero for
   poor, rate your own laboratory procedures on each of the
   twenty-six points in the chapter.   Total up your score.
3. Take one of your "non-laboratory" subjects and point out as
   many ways as you can in which it can be made into a "laboratory" subject.

MATCHING TEST

Directions: Write beside each number the number of the paragraph
in the chapter which discusses it.

.... 1. How to draw.
.... 2. Relation of text to laboratory.
.... 3. Discipline.
.... 4. Selfishness.
.... 5. Accidents.
.... 6. Home-made exercises.
.... 7. Expense.
.... 8. Cleanliness.
.... 9. Form of write-up.
.... 10. Locating materials and apparatus.
.... 11. Time for writing report.
.... 12. Rediscovering facts.
.... 13. Obeying instructions.
.... 14. Meaning of laboratory method.
.... 15. Instruments and apparatus.
.... 16. Specialist versus layman.
.... 17. Having your work checked.
.... 18. Measurement.
.... 19. How to observe.
.... 20. Working in pairs.
.... 21. Speed.
.... 22. Pure versus applied science.
.... 23. Acquiring skill.
.... 24. Previous preparation.
.... 25. Scientific method.
.... 26. Interpretation.

TRUE–FALSE TEST

Directions: Indicate which statement is true and which false, using plus (+) for true and zero (o) for false.

.... 1. The experiment should be studied before you enter the laboratory.

.... 2. Laboratory work should be more than following directions.

.... 3. A survey of the laboratory and storeroom improves your laboratory work.

.... 4. Laboratory work should be done according to scientific method.

.... 5. The laboratory method is adaptable only to the sciences.

.... 6. The little accidents in a laboratory cost more than the big ones.

.... 7. Talking in the laboratory should be forbidden.

.... 8. The laboratory manual contains only a few selected experiments.

.... 9. Laboratory work should be strictly a discovery of facts rather than a verification of facts.

.... 10. All apparatus of a kind should be kept together.

.... 11. In using a microscope you should shut one eye.

.... 12. The laboratory report should be written in the first person.

.... 13. The ordinary student in the laboratory does not need great skill in handling apparatus.

.... 14. It is almost never desirable to do laboratory work rapidly.

.... 15. Laboratory work should not attempt to be practical.

.... 16. Laboratory exercises should never be drill work.

.... 17. It is possible to do an experiment without understanding it.

.... 18. A laboratory is very much of a coöperative workshop.

.... 19. Observation is an art that is easy to improve.

.... 20. Each student should work absolutely alone.

.... 21. Drawing aids observation.

.... 22. The text study should always precede the laboratory

.... 23. Laboratory work should be largely quantitative.

.... 24. There is much need of criticism of laboratory work.

.... 25. Laboratory courses cost more than the other subjects in the curriculum.

.... 26. A laboratory drawing should be on a rather large scale.

SHORT–ANSWER TEST

Directions: Answer each question or complete each statement by inserting a word, phrase, or brief answer.

1. How many divisions should a laboratory report ordinarily contain?........
2. How many rules are given for improving observation?........
3. How can safety in laboratory work be increased?........
4. What is the best way to speed up laboratory work?........
5. How can you be sure to select the most suitable apparatus? ....
6. What is the chief element in laboratory housekeeping?........
7. In addition to securing needed instruments you should ....
8. What is the chief aim of the scientific method?........
9. To what extent is it desirable to study an experiment beforehand?........
10. What is the most commonly accepted solution of the problem of coöperative laboratory work?........
11. How many rules are given for improving drawing?........
12. What should you do when you finish an exercise before the close of the period?........
13. Excessive emphasis on measurement causes neglect of ....
14. What is the chief danger or weakness in laboratory work? ....
15. In what order should textbook study and laboratory work be arranged?........
16. You should not ask for help or criticism until ....
17. How many methods are given for reducing laboratory costs? ....
18. When should a laboratory report be written up?........
19. What is the disadvantage of too detailed directions?........
20. Why is science so far ahead of practice?........
21. To what extent is it desirable to *discover* scientific principles in the laboratory?........
22. Who should bear major responsibility for discipline in the laboratory?........
23. How can the social atmosphere of the laboratory be improved? ....
24. What is the chief feature in a typewriting laboratory?........
25. What type of student particularly needs individual laboratory work in chemistry?........
26. How many definitions of the laboratory method are given? ....

READINGS

1. Dearborn, G. V. N.: *How to Learn Easily.*   Little, Brown & Co., Boston, 1918.
   Chapter II, "Observation and the Taking of Notes."
2. Parker, Samuel Chester: *Methods of Teaching in High Schools.* Ginn & Co., Boston, 1915.
   Chapter XIX, "Laboratory Methods."
3. Sanford, Fernando: *How to Study Illustrated Through Physics.* The Macmillan Co., New York, 1922.
   An excellent treatment of laboratory procedure and scientific method.

CHAPTER XV
TEACHING STUDY HABITS

THE previous chapters have been addressed to students. The present one is intended primarily for teachers or for students who are preparing to enter the teaching profession. It has seemed appropriate, in view of the fact that the students of to-day will be the teachers of to-morrow, to include in a book written for students certain suggestions looking to the future as well as the present. The suggestions which follow cover most of the major lines along which experts have been working in their efforts to improve study habits, and may be useful as guides to further reading, thinking, and experimenting on the subject.

1. **Give a definite course on methods of study.** To a considerable extent incidental or informal methods of teaching how to study are likely to be accidental and haphazard methods. In former years teachers were trained for their profession by the incidental method, just "picking up" the art as they practiced it, but as we learned more about methods of teaching, we began to offer definite courses. It would seem that we have reached somewhat the same stage now with regard to methods of study. The publication of recent books on studying makes it possible, these days, to secure an abundance of good material that is suitable for use as textbooks

and reference works in courses on the subject. Some of the books available for such courses have been listed at the ends of chapters throughout this book.

2. **Teach study habits by giving training in addition to advice.** Merely telling a student how to study is not enough. He must be given actual practice in studying. The best kind of instruction in studying is in the form of directions for doing actual tasks. When teaching a regular course on methods of study, it is essential that you provide actual exercises which apply the principles and advice included in the course. For example, have practice in note-taking, using the library, preparing term papers, and the like, as you take up those topics for direct treatment in the course. Teaching study habits is like teaching character, in that it is entirely possible to teach *how* to study or *how* to be honest without teaching *to* study or *to be* honest. The actual habits must be formed. Ability to study does not come from being vaguely urged so much as from slow growth and habit-formation.

3. **Encourage different students to compare their methods of doing particular tasks.** Wherever there is diversity of practice, some one is certain to have a better way of doing the thing than the others, and comparison of methods will reveal this superior method to all. Encourage student discussions of the ways of doing lessons in order to distribute good ideas among the entire group. Even the plan of having a student grade the papers for the class may

be used at times to special advantage, since it gives
the student who does the work a notion of the variety that actually exists within a small class group.
If the students take turns at the task, each can have
this valuable training, which is usually more educative than any regular lesson. Every high-school
teacher can testify to the value of being behind the
desk the first year, and it is a fact that much of that
first year's contribution to his or her mental growth
is the opportunity offered to compare the reactions
of many minds in the same lesson or situation.

4. Provide subject-matter that is worth studying.
Eliminate material that has little or no bearing on
life. Put in what is useful and clearly worth while
and it will stimulate a better grade of mental effort.
It is not strange that study is crude and inefficient
when the material that is studied has no apparent
utility.

5. Provide motivation for the students' study.
Learning does not take place without the will to
learn. An important essential, therefore, is to
establish in the mind of the student a strong convic-
tion that study is important and worth while, and
that the particular pieces of work that are being
done are worth doing. Strive to develop a craving
for knowledge in general and for certain knowledge
in particular. Employ all known methods and
devices for arousing interest. Provide the student
with a stimulus. Get his whole-hearted support
and coöperation in the work instead of driving him
to his tasks against his will.

6. Show the student the reason why the material should be studied.   Many things that are worth while are not obviously worth while; their value has to be shown.   School subjects are like merchandise in that they must be handled by a salesman if they are to impress the customer.   As a general rule, however, the best goods least need the service of a salesman, for they sell themselves.   Likewise the teacher who has great difficulty in "selling" her school subject had better examine her wares.   If a critical examination of the material justifies the price, then the next step is to make clear to the customer-student just what the hidden values are, what the subject will do for him, and how he can profit by studying it.

7. Provide an aim in life and also an aim in the particular unit of subject-matter to be studied.   It is impossible to conceive of efficient study without an aim or objective.   Any mental effort without an aim must be classed as mere mental exercise or gymnastics.   If a student expects to be a physician or an engineer he has a goal to study for which at least makes purposeful study possible.   A life objective, however, is not enough; a prospective engineer might take a course which had no apparent connection with his life objective and, lacking that connection, drop back into the old groove of purposeless exercise in that particular course.   Each student must be encouraged to set up his major life objective for his education as a whole, and also his more immediate objectives for particular courses and assignments.

8. Induce study by requiring students to get results. After making an assignment, follow it up to see that it has been carried out. When poor work is done be sure to discover it. Be equally sure to discover good work and reward it. Give examinations and tests to make certain that progress is being measured and also to let students know that "sloppy" or superficial work will not be tolerated.

9. Direct study by means of the kinds of tests that are to be employed to measure results. Students will naturally study in such a way as to make the best grades they can on the kind of tests they have to take. If they are tested for details they study for details, and if tested for important points they study for important points. If they are tested superficially they study superficially. In order to cultivate many different kinds of study techniques, give a variety of different kinds of tests. If you want to encourage the thoughtful use of books in place of the mere memorizing of books, substitute open-book examinations for the usual memory type of examination, and ask questions which really tax ability to use the book in the solution of problems. When written work, such as a term paper, is handed in by a student, grade it not only in terms of final results, but also for its process or technique, even requiring that the scratch notes be submitted with the paper. This plan makes students feel responsible for having good methods of study. Have the students report their methods of solving problems as well as their solutions of the problems.

Measure by standardized tests and scales in addition to home-made tests, in order to measure actual abilities as well as relative abilities. Use home-made objective tests, such as true-false, completion, and best-answer tests, since each of these calls for its own particular type of ability and encourages its own particular type of study. Give tests that have been announced and tests that are entirely unexpected. As the student is measured, so will he study.

10. **Teach in the way you expect your students to study.** If you want the students to stress main points, stress them yourself as you teach. If you want them to study for specific purposes, plan your lessons for specific purposes. If you want them to organize their ideas, organize your own before you present them. If you want them to learn how to take good notes, let them see that you yourself take notes and use them in teaching. If you want them to study lessons with a view to mastering them thoroughly, do not teach the lessons in a superficial manner. As the teacher teaches, so will the student study.

11. **Show samples in class of good study technique.** Study the lesson with the class group occasionally to show them how to do it. In assigning a new lesson, take time to study one unit of it with the students so that they can continue the other units in the same way. Discuss in class the possible ways of attacking a given lesson or task, and then decide which is the best. Devote occasional class

periods to group study, when all students work coöperatively on the task. Bring to class for exhibition pieces of work done by individual students, so that the other students can see how the work was done. A model or pattern for imitation often brings about greater improvement than do the most careful directions.

12. **Improve study by means of the assignment.** Give such definite and well-planned assignments that the student will know exactly what is to be accomplished. Have an aim in each assignment yourself, and be sure that the students know what that aim is. Take plenty of time in making the assignment, so that you can give the students clear objectives to work for and clear directions for achieving those objectives. Include in the assignment suggestions as to methods of work to employ on it. Clear up the difficult points in order to prevent errors which can be foreseen. Get the students interested so that they will attack the lesson in the right mental attitude. The major purpose of the assignment is to get the study process properly started and to make possible its effective continuation when the student is working alone.

13. **Give more assignments which require original investigation.** Give topical or problem assignments for which complete answers or solutions cannot be found ready-made in any single book, and which will therefore require a search for materials and organization of the materials after they have been found. As students increase in age, in maturity,

and in command of the study arts, give more and more assignments of the term-paper type, such as are commonly employed in college courses. Bright and capable students may even be encouraged to collect really original data and do simple pieces of research, after the style of masters' theses in college, though on a less ambitious scale. Many potentially good students have never been discovered or developed because the assignments given have not been sufficiently original to challenge them.

14. **Make use of mimeographed study-guides and self-teaching textbooks.** Prepare a syllabus for the course, listing the materials to be used, the problems to be solved, the tasks to be done, and the objectives to be achieved. Mimeograph the instructions, so that each student will have definite and accurate guidance in his work. Schools of the Dalton and Winnetka types have their work so completely outlined in this way that their students are able to proceed with all the work without class meetings. They are not obliged to stop at frequent intervals to wait for further directions, because their textbooks are practically self-teaching.

15. **Reveal the course as a whole to the students, instead of presenting it in daily "spoonfuls."** Give the students, at the beginning of the semester, an outline of the whole course. Prepare a program of the term's work, and mimeograph it or post it on the bulletin board where it can be seen by all. This will involve your planning your course rather completely before you begin, instead of feeling your way

blindly as you go. It demands that you have a major objective for the whole course as well as an objective for each daily assignment. When the student is given a bird's-eye view of the territory he is to cover and what he is to do, he is given an opportunity to plan his work and to arrange some system of his own; but if he has to take the course by daily "spoonfuls" there is no incentive and little opportunity for him to exercise initiative or to do any large-scale work. One of the most valuable study-abilities that students can acquire is the ability to plan and do a large unit of work that must be distributed over a long period of time.

16. **Allow individual freedom of choice in the matter of some study techniques.** It is possible, by prescribing student technique down to the smallest details, to overdo the policy of directing study. In our present state of limited knowledge as to study methods, it is frequently unsafe to require all students to study a given lesson in a specified way, because we cannot be sure that all minds operate in the same manner. In those cases where we know we have discovered the best methods, and where we know that these methods are best for all the pupils, we may be justified in prescribing for all the students the technique to be used. Where such scientific knowledge does not exist it is wise to be content with suggesting methods, thus allowing the students freedom for individual choice and experimentation. In such cases hold the student definitely responsible for good results, and he

will work out his own techniques for achieving them.

17. Improve study by concentrating on the students' difficulties. Christ said, "They that are whole have no need of a physician, but they that are sick." Frequently, however, people are sick without knowing it, and are having difficulties without being able to discover their nature or source. To discover the weakness in the study of the average student it is often best to observe a student who is failing; in a case of that kind the difficulties take on an exaggerated form and so are more easily discerned. Locate the most common difficulties or mistakes, and by giving warnings or assistance beforehand keep other students from falling into them. Diagnose individual students who have difficulties of a kind peculiar to themselves alone, and try to correct their specific shortcomings. Prevent errors wherever it is possible, but when they do occur, apply remedies that go directly to the source of the trouble.

18. Give assistance wisely to individuals who need it. Frequently only a few suggestions will be sufficient to help a student out of the pit into which he has fallen, and for economy's sake, if for no other reason, he ought to be helped. If he has tried and failed several times there is no sense in letting him give up in despair for lack of a helping hand. Sometimes a persistent student will finally get out of his difficulties unaided, but he may do so by adopting a crude or wasteful method instead of the best. Individual help is often more worth while before a failure than after, on the old principle that prevention is better than cure. The great problem is to know when to give help, how much to give, and in what form to give it. Too much help is as dangerous as too little, since it makes the student lose confidence in his own ability and rely on the teacher as on a crutch or a burden-bearer. Conducting a study clinic for failing students is similar in a way to conducting a health clinic. You must get systematic and scientific facts about the individual case, diagnose it, and treat it according to its actual needs. The results of tests should help.

19. **Adjust the work to the capacity of the student.** A bright student will not learn to study effectively unless he has tasks to do that tax his maximum ability. Unless his course is enriched he will become confirmed in mental laziness and slouchy work since he can get by with that. If it is true that necessity is the mother of invention, then the dull student is more likely than the bright one to work out his most effective study techniques, because he is hard pressed and the bright one is not. There is another side to the question, however, since overloading a student may put him into such a state of discouragement that he does not do even what he is capable of. If tasks are too long or too difficult the temptation to use short cuts and superficial methods of study is greatly increased, and the result may be the permanent fixing of habits of hasty and superficial study. In the light of these two opposite

dangers, then, we see plainly that it is obviously impossible to develop the maximum ability to study in all students without varying the assignments a good deal in order to adapt them to individual capacities.

20. **Direct study by regulating the amount of time allowed for tasks.** In cultivating in students habits of working rapidly make use of time-limit exercises, such, for example, as giving only ten minutes to prepare for a test on a body of new material. In cultivating in them habits of mature and critical thinking, allow them sufficient time to think instead of demanding an immediate answer. It is often wise actually to require the student to wait a while before responding; in some instances, when he wants to discuss a question to-day, it is well to require him to wait until to-morrow. Science teachers frequently have laboratory students remain in the laboratory for the full period instead of letting them go when their experiments are done, because they want to encourage them in more mature consideration of the work in hand.

21. **Improve study by regulating the study schedule.** Provide a period for study after each class period, so that study on a given lesson may be begun while the assignment and the study directions are fresh in mind. Put into the daily schedule periods in which study can be done under teacher supervision. In making long-term assignments, as for individual projects or term papers that are to be spread over a period of days or weeks, help the

student to budget his time so that he will be able to emerge at the end without a last-minute rush that forces him to lower his standards of work and sacrifice his ideals of study. Encourage and assist students in making their own personal schedules or time budgets in such a way as to provide a proper amount and distribution of time for their different tasks.

22. Provide an environment that is favorable to study. Arrange for proper heat, ventilation, light, quietness, seating comfort, and accessibility of materials and supplies. While such things do not guarantee effective study, the lack of them may readily prevent the development and practice of high-grade study habits. One of the main reasons why study at school has been replacing, in recent years, study at home is the general lack of suitable environment for study at home.

23. Cultivate friendly student-teacher relations. Students will study better for a teacher whom they respect than for one whom they dislike. Strained or unpleasant relations between student and teacher encourage the "getting-by" or "putting-one-over" attitude, and it may set back pupil progress in the art of a study more definitely than many months of peaceful conditions can advance it. Try to get the pupil's point of view and seek his coöperation in the work rather than have him work merely from compulsion or for fear of getting low marks if he does not.

24. Teach study habits by providing appropriate

sources of information. How to study is closely related to what is studied. The style of organization of a textbook has much to do with the mental process of the student who studies it. If the textbook is not logically arranged and is carelessly thrown together, the student is likely to follow the example that it sets. Moreover, if all studying is done in connection with textbooks, only those study habits which are required for the assimilation of textbook material will be developed. In order to train a student in all-round ability it is necessary to make use of many kinds of materials, such as textbooks, encyclopædias, dictionaries, yearbooks, almanacs, newspapers, laboratories, personal interviews, lectures — in fact every source of information which is important in the daily out-of-school life of the world for which the students are being trained.

25. Assume the responsibility for drill instead of putting it all on the student. Efficient study is in considerable degree a question of finishing up the job of learning instead of leaving it at the halfway stage. Drilling is likely to become uninteresting and to be abandoned by the pupil before bonds are perfectly established unless the teacher intervenes and keeps the process going until it is completed. The teacher must, therefore, provide the proper conditions and inducements for keeping up the drill process until the material has been thoroughly learned. He must provide also for reviews in order to guarantee the retention of what has once been learned. The lack of inherent interest in drills and reviews makes it impossible to expect students to provide for them on their own responsibility.

26. Teach study habits by means of written exercises. Slouchy work is much more noticeable when it is recorded on paper than when it is in the form of oral or silent thought. Similarly the steps in study processes are much more clearly formulated on paper than otherwise. When you require a task to be done in writing you compel the student to become more definitely conscious of his technique. The mere fact that writing is a slower process than speaking or thinking makes possible a maturity and a perfection in written study that are not achieved in the more rapid forms of work. Written work also gives the student something to check himself by, since what he has done remains on record before him for later criticism. Likewise it gives the teacher something objective and tangible as a basis for diagnosis of the pupil's difficulties and for suggestions for improvement. Written study makes possible large-scale mental operations involving organization of many ideas, since one thing will wait while the attention is turned to other things. In order to take advantage of these benefits from written work the teacher should give assignments that call for summarizing, note-taking, outlining, tabulating, listing, condensing, expanding, contrasting, comparing, drawing, computing, organizing, and other processes. It has been the writer's personal experience that study habits and

techniques can be taught much more effectively in connection with such written exercises than otherwise. For example, instruction on how to read for main points does not strike home to a student nearly so strongly as instruction on how to take notes or to outline what he reads.

27. Use questions to stimulate and direct study. It is said that all thinking begins with a doubt, perplexity, or problem. Questioning is the teacher's easiest method of arousing such a mental state in the student. A few well-selected questions might well replace the usual assignment, "take the next ten pages," and would afford the necessary stimulus to real study which page assignments usually fail to provide. Asking a student a few questions will often start him on his problem much more effectively than telling him the answers or teaching him how to solve them; moreover, it discourages mental laziness in him. The kind of questions which the teacher employs has a great deal to do with the kind of studying which the student adopts. If they are trivial questions, the student will study for trivial things; if they are factual, he will study to memorize facts; if they are thought questions, he will think and reason in trying to answer them.

28. Teach both special and general study habits. Each subject or task has its own peculiar problems, and for each there is a best method of study. No one method will really serve for studying all kinds of subject-matter. When you teach a rule or method of study that is sufficiently general to apply in a way to all subjects there is great danger that its actual application to any one subject or task will be lost.   Before the major generalizations about study technique are serviceable as guides to the student they must be analyzed into smaller units to correspond to the mental stride of the learner, and when they are so particularized they have to be stated in terms of particular subjects or lessons. After you have taught how to study mathematics, foreign languages, history, science, use of library, laboratory, note-taking, and so forth, it is possible to arrive at certain major generalizations which are true for all study, but these are of value chiefly as a final summary of specific methods and procedures.

29. **Understand the psychology of the subject your students are studying.** To direct the learning process of the students you must know the general psychology of learning and the particular applications of it to your particular subject.   Do not rely on intuition as your guide, but study a few professional books on the subject.   Put the center of attention on the learner rather than on the subject-matter which you are teaching.

30. **Observe the actual studying that your students do.** To know where a student is *now* is one essential in the business of getting him where you want him to be.   The survey of present study habits is a useful device for securing ideal study habits. The final result of a student's effort frequently looks quite different from the various intermediate forms through which it passed as he blundered around

with it, and if you observe only the finished product you never know how crude and wasteful were the methods by which it was produced. Move around the room while he is working and see how he is going about his tasks. In special cases it is well to have a student write out his work as he does it, so you will be able to observe it more accurately. Even having him study or think aloud instead of silently may frequently be advisable, since that method will reveal steps in his work which would never be known otherwise.

31. Supervise the work of your students as they study their lessons. Set aside a time in the day when you will have nothing to do except to direct the study of your students. Plan your work for the supervised study hour with as much thought as for a teaching hour, instead of leaving it to take care of itself. Formulate your own ideas as to how the particular lesson should be attacked and have some definite things in mind that you are going to accomplish during the period. Let some supervised study periods be group coöperative-work periods in which all students study together and wherein you tell all of them at once what you want them to know about directions and methods of attack. At other times conduct the period as individual study, wherein you give special guidance to individuals or small groups whose needs are different from the needs of the others. Vary the work from day to day, having a definite aim and a definite method of achieving it.

32. Cultivate study habits by having more study and less teaching. Put more responsibility on the student, and let the teacher do less of his work for him. Lengthen the study period and shorten the recitation period. Give your major attention and effort as a teacher to teaching the students how to study instead of to teaching them subject-matter directly. There is much to be said in favor of letting the teacher be a guide and an efficiency expert on methods of study and letting the students learn their subject-matter by their own efforts. Such schools as Winnetka and Dalton get along very nicely with no class recitations at all, allowing all learning to take place as individual work, with such individual supervision by the teacher as the student may need.

33. Provide a proper balance between home and school study. For mature students a certain amount of home study is essential, since the daily schedule at school consists of short periods in which there is seldom an opportunity to take up a piece of connected work for more than an hour at a time. Some school study, however, is also highly necessary, since home study does not permit the proper amount and kind of guidance and supervision. New kinds of work should ordinarily be studied under supervision at school, at least until the method has been learned and a good start made, after which the task may be continued economically at home. The desirability of studying a lesson immediately after it is assigned suggests the need of school study as a part of the regular schedule.

Ordinarily the issue between home and school study hinges on the question of the total amount of study time desired, and when the school day is not long enough to allow the accomplishment of the desired amount of work, tasks are completed at home. Two alternatives are before us, then: (1) Increasing the length of the school day; and (2) Providing better guidance and direction for the student when he is obliged to study at home.

QUESTIONS AND EXERCISES

1. Outline the chapter.
2. Which of the methods presented are direct and which indirect methods of teaching study habits?
3. Draw up a plan or program for teaching study habits which could be adopted by the school with which you are connected.
4. Work out a program for improving study technique in the particular school subject in which you are most interested.

MATCHING TEST

Directions: Write beside each number the number of the paragraph in the chapter which discusses it.

....   1. Help.
....   2. Liking the teacher.
....   3. Special methods of study.
....   4. Teacher in the background.
....   5. Directing drill work.
....   6. Definite formulation.
....   7. Research.
....   8. Setting an example.
....   9. Long-unit assignments.
....   10. Room.
....   11. Prescribed methods.
....   12. Asking questions.
....   13. Practice versus precept.
....   14. Diagnosis.
....   15. Direct instruction.
....   16. Open-book examinations.

.... 17. Demonstration.
.... 18. Observation.
.... 19. Time limits.
.... 20. Dalton and Winnetka.
.... 21. Supervised study.
.... 22. Curriculum.
.... 23. Books used.
.... 24. Responsibility for results.
.... 25. Home versus school study.
.... 26. Mental processes.
.... 27. Assigning lessons.
.... 28. Vocational choice.
.... 29. Comparative studies.
.... 30. Salesmanship in study.
.... 31. Interest.
.... 32. Order of tasks.
.... 33. Individual differences.

TRUE–FALSE TEST

Directions: Indicate which statement is true and which is false, using plus (+) for true and zero (o) for false.

.... 1. The mental processes in all school subjects are about the same.
.... 2. Students could train themselves in study technique if they would simply compare their methods.
.... 3. A bright boy will be a poor student if the work is easy.
.... 4. There is a close relation between the schedule and the kind of study employed.
.... 5. Written study is superior to silent or oral study.
.... 6. Without a purpose a lesson is simply a piece of mental gymnastics.
.... 7. The better the goods the more the need of salesmanship.
.... 8. Good study requires a good motive.
.... 9. Students will adopt the kind of study habits that prepare for the kind of tests used.
.... 10. A regular period for supervised study is of little value.
.... 11. The only real essential for teaching efficient study is to require students to get results.
.... 12. The kind of study you do depends very little upon the study room.
.... 13. To develop a good student without other materials than textbooks is impossible.

.... 14. Students should be given an outline of the whole course at the beginning.
.... 15. The Dalton schools have the assignments mimeographed so that they are practically self-teaching.
.... 16. All thinking begins with a question.
.... 17. The student should be held solely responsible for his own practice work.
.... 18. How you study depends on what you study.
.... 19. The assignment should clear up difficulties.
.... 20. Showing how to study beats telling how.
.... 21. An assignment should not be given which is not clearly answered in the book.
.... 22. A student who likes his teacher will acquire better study habits.
.... 23. A student should never be given help.
.... 24. The Dalton plan involves no regular class work.
.... 25. There is never any advantage in forcing a person to study slowly.
.... 26. The main need in teaching study methods is for telling students how to study.
.... 27. New kinds of work should be taken up at school rather than at home.
.... 28. The teacher's technique is of little importance in determining the student's technique.
.... 29. There is little you can learn about a student's study by watching him.
.... 30. Study training should cover all processes alike.
.... 31. Not only should the teacher say what to study but also exactly how to study each part.
.... 32. Study is the same, whatever the subject.
.... 33. How-to-study training should all be given incidentally.

SHORT–ANSWER TEST

Directions: Answer each question or complete each statement by inserting a word, phrase, or brief answer.

1. What is the good of comparing methods?........
2. You should teach in the way you want your students to ....
3. A teacher who has difficulty in selling her subject to the students should ....
4. How can models or patterns for student work be made available?........
5. As a student is measured, so does he ....

6. What is the main issue between home and school study?
....
7. What kind of psychology study is needed for the teacher of study habits?........
8. What is the main problem about giving individual help?.......
9. How does the result of a student's work relate to his process?
....
10. What is the advantage of a research assignment?........
11. What is the effect of dislike for the teacher on study habits?
....
12. Why is "take the next ten pages" a poor assignment?........
13. What effect on study technique is produced by setting a rigid standard for work?........
14. How does study technique for mathematics relate to that for foreign languages?........
15. How does the "daily spoonful" assignment affect study?
....
16. The teacher should teach more about how to study and less
....
17. What effect on study habits is produced by teaching useless subjects?........
18. A course on study should contain .... in addition to study directions.
19. When should the study period come with respect to the recitation period?........
20. How should the increase in the number of publications on study affect methods of giving how-to-study training?........
21. Why do students neglect drill work?........
22. What is the effect of too difficult work on study?........
23. What is the effect of having a student use many kinds of books and materials?........
24. What is the advantage of a self-teaching textbook?........
25. Of what value are written exercises in teaching study habits?
....
26. What study habit is encouraged by a short-time limit?........
27. Why is school study replacing home study?........
28. When is the teacher justified in prescribing a student's study technique?........
29. What effect does a choice of a vocation have on study?........
30. What is the major purpose of the assignment?........
31. How should the teacher's work resemble that of the physician?
....
32. Learning does not take place without a ....
33. What is the chief factor in conducting a successful supervised study period?........

READINGS

1. Book, W. F.: *Learning How to Study and Work Effectively*
   Ginn & Co., Boston, 1926.

   Chapter XXIII, "True Basis for Supervised Study."

2. Butterweck, Joseph S.: *The Problem of Teaching High School
   Students How to Study.*   Teachers' College Bureau of Publications, New York, 1926.

   A report of a scientific experiment in directing study.

3. Doermann, Henry J.: *The Orientation of College Freshmen.*   The
   Williams & Wilkins Co., Baltimore, 1926.

   The entire book is an excellent scientific study of methods of helping
   freshmen students.

4. Douglass, Harl R.: *Modern Methods of High School Teaching.*
   Houghton Mifflin Co., Boston, 1926.

   Chapter IV, "Supervising Pupil Study."   Chapter V, "Teaching Young
   People How to Study."

5. Earhart, Lida B.: *Teaching Children to Study.*   Houghton
   Mifflin Co., Boston, 1909.

6. Edwards, A. S.: *The Fundamental Principles of Learning and
   Study.*   Warwick & York, Baltimore, 1920.

   Chapter XVI, "The Directing of Learning and Study."   Chapter XVII,
   "Supervised Study and the School Curriculum."

7. Hall-Quest, A. L.: *Supervised Study.*   The Macmillan Co.,
   New York.

8. Hall-Quest, A. L.: *Supervised Study in the Elementary School.*
   The Macmillan Co., New York, 1924.

9. Judd, C. H.: *Psychology of High School Subjects.*   Ginn & Co.,
   Boston, 1915.

   Chapter XVIII, "Teaching Students to Study."

10. McMurry, F. M.: *How to Study and Teaching How to Study.*
    Houghton Mifflin Co., Boston, 1909.

11. Miller, Harry L.: *Directing Study.*   Charles Scribner's Sons,
    New York, 1922.

12. Parker, Samuel Chester: *Methods of Teaching in High Schools.*
    Ginn & Co., Boston, 1915.

13. Thomas, F. W.: *Principles and Technique of Teaching.*   Hough-
    ton Mifflin Co., Boston, 1927.

    Chapter XIV, "Planning and Directing Study."

14. Thomas, Frank W.: *Training for Effective Study.* Houghton Mifflin Co., Boston, 1922.

    The entire book is a teacher's guide for improving study.

15. Touton, F. C., and Struthers, A. B.: *Junior High School Procedures.* Ginn & Co., Boston, 1926.

    Chapter VIII, "The Management of Study Helps."

16. Tryon, Rolla M.: *The Teaching of History in Junior and Senior High Schools.* Ginn & Co., Boston, 1921.

    Chapter II, "Teaching Pupils How to Study History."

17. Wilson, H. B.: *Training Pupils to Study.* Warwick & York, Baltimore, 1917.

INDEX

Accuracy, and speed, 98, 99.

Advisers, difficulty of securing unprejudiced, 3, 4.

Agricultural Index, 210.

Analogy, dangers to straight thinking, 151, 152.

Analysis, of problem into parts, 137, 138.

Annual Magazine Index, 210.

Appendix, study of, 76.

Apprenticeship method, dangers in vocational training by, 10.

Assignments, aids to study in, 325, 326.

Association, in memorizing, 114–16.

Bacon, F., on reading, 214.

Bennett, H. E., *Psychology and Self-Development*, 81.

Bibliographies, prepared, 204, 205; in textbooks, 205, 206; making, 206–11; complete and working, 210, 211; making working, 215, 216; in term papers, 246, 247.

Biology, value of courses in, 15, 16.

Book Review Digest, 210.

Books, marking and underlining, 31, 32; note-taking on, 40; care of, 227.

Call numbers, schemes of library, 202.

Capacity, choice of courses according to student's, 5; adjustment of work to, 329, 330.

Catalogue, study of college, 3.

Character, choice of courses to promote, 18.

Character Education Institute, *The Scientific Method*, 302.

Charters, J. A., on outlining, 81; on reciting lesson to self, 83.

Charters, W. W., technique of assembling material, vi.

Charts, study of, 77.

Chemistry, value of courses in, 15.

Citizenship, choice of courses to contribute to, 17, 18.

Class work, as test, 289, 290; correlation with laboratory work, 301.

Classification, from different viewpoints, as aid to thinking, 140, 141; in review, 258, 259.

Comparison, and contrast in thinking, 141.

Competition, to develop interest, 176.

Condensation, technique of, 34.

Contents, study of table of, 76.

Coöperation, in reviewing, 265, 266; in laboratory work, 306.

Courses, development of interest and choice of, 163, 164; laboratory work in different, 296, 297 on methods of study, 319, 320

Courses, selection of, 1–24; for educational career as whole, 1, 2; specific objectives, 2, 3; study of catalogue, 3; disinterested advice, 3, 4; according to individuality, 4, 5; according to capacity, 5; according to time continuing in school, 5, 6; relative values, 6; for probable value, 7; emphasizing current problems, 7, 8; specialization, 8, 9; in many fields, 9, 10; variety, 10, 11; survey courses before specialization, 11, 12; on spiral plan, 12, 13; fundamental subjects, 13; according to school facilities, 14; by best teachers, 14, 15; to promote health, 15; to contribute to home membership, 15, 16; vocational studies, 16, 17; to contribute to citizenship, 17, 18; to promote character, 18; to contribute to enjoyment of leisure, 18, 19; in study arts, 19, 20; questions, exercises, and tests, 20–23; reading references, 23–24.

Cramming, 253.

Crawford, C. C., on value of lecture notes, 54 *n.*; on intelligence and the voice, 61 *n.*

Cumulative Book Index, 208.

Current problems, value of courses in, 7, 8.

Dalton type schools, 326, 337.

Data, completeness of, 146, 147.

Diagrams, to illustrate lecture, 58.

Dictionary, use to enlarge vocabulary, 190, 191.

Dramatic Index, 210.

Drawing, as aid to laboratory work, 309, 310.

Drill, use of textbook for, 84; in review, 266; in laboratory work, 299, 300; teacher's responsibility for, 332, 333.

Education, to be viewed as a whole, 1, 2; emphasis on forward-looking, 7, 8; spiral plan of, 12, 13.

Encyclopædias, use of, 212.

Engineering Index, 210.

English, term papers and correct, 247, 248; test papers and correct, 279, 280.

Environment, as aid to study, 331.

Equipment, use of laboratory, 305.

Ethics, value of courses in, 18.

Exercises, teaching study habits by written, 333, 334.

Experts, this an age of, 8, 9.

"Fallow period," in memorizing, 124.

Filing, of materials used for papers, 248, 249.

Filing system, for notes, 27, 28.

Fine arts, value of courses in, 19; as aid to development of interest, 172, 173.

Footnotes, study of, 76; in term paper, 247.

Franklin, B., method of thinking, 136.

Geometry, possible value of, 7.

Glossary, study of, 76.

Grading. *See* Marking.

Graphic presentation, as aid to thinking, 142.

Greenough, N. C., *Manual of Instructions and Exercises for English A*, 35.

Habit, in acquiring skill, 107; as aid in development of interest, 172.

Habits, teaching study, 319–43; course on methods of study, 319, 320; training as well as advice, 320; comparison of methods, 320, 321; worth of subject-matter, 321; motivation, 321; showing reason for study, 322; providing aim, 322; requiring results, 323; choice of tests, 323, 324; teaching as example, 324; showing examples of study technique, 324, 325; assignments, 325, 326; study-guides, 326; outlining whole course in advance, 326, 327; individual choice of technique, 327, 328; concentration on difficulties, 328; individual help, 328, 329; adjustment to capacity of student, 329, 330; regulation of time allowed, 330; arrangement of study schedule, 330, 331; environment, 331; student-teacher relations, 331; providing sources

INDEX

of information, 331, 332; teacher's responsibility for drill, 332, 333; value of written exercises, 333, 334; use of habits, 334; both special and general, 334, 335; psychology of subject, 335; observation and supervision of actual studying, 335, 336; emphasis on study rather than on teaching, 337; balance between home and school study, 337, 338; questions, exercises, and tests, 338–41; reading references, 342, 343.

Headings, in term papers, 245, 246.

Health, choice of courses to promote, 15.

Home, choice of courses to improve life in, 15, 16; study in school and in, 337, 338.

Honesty, in taking tests, 283, 284.

Imitation, to develop interest, 176, 177.

Incentives, in development of interest, 162, 163.

Index, study of, 76.

Individuality, choice of courses according to student's, 4, 5.

Industrial Arts Index, 210.

Instincts, as aid to development of interest, 173–76.

Interest, development of, 161–84; importance of definite objective, 161; reason for work, 162; remote and immediate incentives, 162, 163; purpose in life, 163; choice of studies, 163, 164; sense of duty, 164; encouraging stimuli, 164, 165; positive rather than negative interests, 165; application of studies to everyday life, 165, 166; purely intellectual, 166; originality and individuality, 166, 167; new experiences, 167, 168; specialization, 168; sense of success,

168, 169; challenge of difficult tasks, 169; assuming interest, 169, 170; self-measurement, 170; effect of physical condition, 170; critical points, 171, 172; use of habit, 172; emotions as aid, 172; fine arts as aid, 172, 173; new interests from present ones, 173; instincts as aids, 173, 174; collecting instinct, 174, 175; manipulation or construction, 175, 176; pride, 176; competition, 176; imitation, 176; association with others, 177; social factors, 177, 178; oral speech, 178; concreteness, 178, 179; variety, 179; work instead of play, 179; questions, exercises, and tests, 180–83; reading references, 184.

International Index, to periodical material, 209.

Interruptions, of lecture, 63, 64.

Introduction, to lecture, 55, 56; to textbook, 76.

James, W., on learning, 103; on revision, 248.

Key words, value of, 56, 57.

Laboratory work, 296–318; in all courses, 296, 297; meaning of method, 296, 297; adaptation of procedure to purpose of course, 297, 298; quantitative and qualitative, 298; emphasis on underlying principles, 298, 299; discovery and verification, 299; for practice or drill, 299, 300; observation of practical applications, 300, 301; correlation with class work, 301; preparation, 301, 302; principles of scientific method, 302–04; following directions, 304, 305; equipment and its use, 305; individual experiments, 305, 306; independent and coöperative, 306, 307; criticism, 307; devices to